LINGUISTIC FOSSILS

JOHN D. BENGTSON

CHIEF EDITOR
CINDY DROVER-DAVIDSON

JOHN D. BENGTSON

LINGUISTIC FOSSILS:

STUDIES IN
HISTORICAL LINGUISTICS
AND PALEOLINGUISTICS

© John D. Bengtson, 2008
Published by Theophania Publishing
All rights reserved. This publication is protected by copyright, and permission should be obtained from the publisher prior to any prohibited reproduction, storage in a retrieval system, or transmission in any form or by any means, electronic, mechanical, photocopying, recording, or likewise.
Editing and formatting by Cindy Drover-Davidson.

Table of Contents

On Fossil Dinosaurs and Fossil Words	9
Global Etymologies Involving Six Macro-families	15
The "Greater Austric" Hypothesis	17
The Problem of "Isolates" I: Basque	25
A Genetic Comparison of Basque and Caucasian Vocabulary	45
The Problem of "Isolates" II: Burushaski	55
Basque and Caucasian Words for 'Blue ~ Iron'	71
Genetic and Cultural Links between Burushaski, Caucasian, and Basque	73
Basque Phonology in the Light of the Dene-Caucasian Hypothesis	93
On the Position of Haida	211
Lateral Affricates in Na-Dene	215
References	220

FOREWORD

My career in historical linguistics began as a teenager, when my father[1] told me about Grimm's Law. As a young "scientist" with a lab in the basement, I was astounded to learn that language development could be governed by scientific "laws." From that moment on, I devoured all the reading I could about languages and historical linguistics. While still in high school, I corresponded with a great linguist and dialectologist, Frederic G. Cassidy[2] of the University of Wisconsin. Another eminent linguist, Eric P. Hamp, was kind enough to write to me and send his bibliography of Indo-European studies. With the earnings from my part-time job as a "printer's devil," I purchased linguistic classics by Brugmann and Meillet that I still own. When I went to college, I took several languages (Greek, German, Old Norse, and Swahili),[3] classes in Scandinavian[4] and Indo-European historical linguistics, and anthropology. Though I loved Indo-European, I was never satisfied with stopping at its time depth of seven or eight millennia, and longed to probe deeper into linguistic prehistory.

At some time during the 1980s, I became aware of the work of Alfredo Trombetti. Intrigued with his wide and deep vision of human language, I resolved in 1984 to research the question of the monogenesis of language for myself. I remember watching the Olympic Games on TV, taking care of my young daughter, Samantha, and making notes about languages from all around the world. I soon concluded that Trombetti was right – at least in principle, if not in every detail – and that there was abundant evidence for the monogenesis of all human languages.

The next stage for me was correspondence with Roger Williams Wescott, who would later be a vice-president of the Association for the Study of Language in Prehistory. Roger shared my interest in linguistic prehistory, and he told me about the Nostratic School that was gaining notice in America, thanks to the efforts of Vitaly Shevoroshkin.

---

[1] H. Bernhard Bengtson (1913-1967) was a Lutheran pastor, missionary, theological teacher, and "linguist" (in the popular sense: he knew at least seven languages, including Swahili and Chasu, a local language of Tanzania). At an early age, I became acquainted with his books about several languages.

[2] Cassidy was author of *Jamaica Talk* (1961) and later became Editor of the *Dictionary of American Regional English*.

[3] Swahili class was a refresher of the 'pidgin' Swahili I knew from my early childhood in Tanzania (1948-1957).

[4] At the University of Minnesota, I had the privilege of studying under Professor Nils Hasselmo, an excellent historical linguist and later President of the University of Minnesota (1988-1997), then President of the Association of American Universities (AAU). He retired in 2006.

Early in 1986, I went to the Symposium on the Genetic Classification of Languages at Rice University in Houston (organized by Sydney Lamb), where I met several people who would become influential in the linguistic prehistory "movement" that was burgeoning at the time. Among them were two in particular who would work closely with me from that day through the present: Vitaly Shevoroshkin and Merritt Ruhlen.[5] Vitaly, Merritt and I found that all three of us were compiling what we called "global etymologies," lists of words with similar sound and meaning that recur in many different language families and, we think, are traces of the original Proto-World vocabulary.[6] Merritt and I had independently compiled a collection of words that sounded something like TIK and had the meaning 'finger' or 'one' in languages around the world (see below).

1986 was a banner year for the language in prehistory movement, for in the fall of that year an anthropologist named Harold C. ("Hal") Fleming would go to Moscow and meet the members of what was known as the "Moscow School" of historical linguistics. Hal became so enthusiastic about the long-range linguistic work of the Moscow scholars, who were trying to extend genetic taxonomy of human languages beyond the time-depths accepted at the time, that he started a circular letter which evolved into the newsletter *Mother Tongue*. As soon as I heard of this newsletter, I wrote to Hal, beginning another association that continues to the present day. The Association for the Study of Language in Prehistory (ASLIP) was incorporated in 1989, and I have since served as President (1995-2000), Vice-President (2000-present), and Editor of its journal, *Mother Tongue* (1994-2005; 2007-present).

In November 1988, Vitaly Shevoroshkin and Benjamin Stolz organized the First International Interdisciplinary Symposium on Language in Prehistory at the University of Michigan in Ann Arbor. Taking advantage of the recent loosening of the Soviet system, they managed to bring a large contingent of scholars from Russia,[7] promoting an unprecedented dialogue between the Moscow School and western scholars. Besides the Moscow scholars, I had the pleasure of meeting Hal Fleming and another scholar with whom I would work closely in the years to come: Václav Blažek, from what was then Czechoslovakia.

Merritt Ruhlen and I worked for several years on an article we called "Global Etymologies." After being rejected by the journal *Language* (for

---

[5] Joseph Greenberg was present at the Symposium, but he left before I arrived, and I was not to meet him until a decade later.

[6] See the first two chapters of this book.

[7] These were: Vladimir Dybo, Anna Dybo, Eugene Helimsky, Vyacheslav Ivanov, Andrei Korolev, Alexander Militarev, Oleg Mudrak, Sergei Nikolayev, Vladimir Orel, Ilia Peiros, Viktor Shnirel'man, and Sergei Starostin.

what we consider spurious reasons), it was finally published in Merritt's book *On the Origin of Languages* (Ruhlen 1994a).[8] This article has since become an object of renown (among those who agree with our thesis) and of derision and scorn (among many "mainstream" linguists, who think global etymologies are an artifact of the authors).

Around 1994, I began my debates with the linguist R.L. (Larry) Trask about the external relationships of the Basque language (see Trask 1994-95, 1995, 1997; Bengtson 1995a, 1995b). Although Trask was correct in pointing out a large number of errors and mistranslations in my work and that of others, I still maintain that he was misguided in his assertion that there was "zero evidence" of external relations of Basque. (Extensive evidence is cited in this volume.) In the first two volumes of *Mother Tongue* (Journal), several colleagues contributed articles supporting my position.[9]

In December 1996 I had an extraordinary opportunity when I learned Sergei Starostin would be teaching, temporarily, at the University of Michigan, thanks again to Vitaly Shevoroshkin. I stayed several days with him in Ann Arbor, enjoying discussions of all manner of things, not limited to the Dene-Caucasian macro-family the principal intellectual interest we held in common. (See Bengtson 1997e.)

From the mid-1990s through 2003, I had the honor of acting as the Editor of *Mother Tongue* (Journal), volumes II through VIII. It was a pleasure and privilege to work with so many excellent scholars and to cover a number of fascinating topics: paleolinguistics, Proto-World hypotheses, the problems of linguistic "isolates," and deeper linguistic taxa. It has also been a great honor to work with ASLIP President Michael Witzel and former President and current Vice-President Hal Fleming.

In 2001, I was invited to join the Evolution of Human Language (EHL) Project, sponsored by Murray Gell-Mann and the Santa Fe Institute. My main project has been to investigate the Dene-Caucasian hypothesis, and in particular the relationship of Basque within this macro-family. As of the present (2007), the Basque portion of the EHL databases consists of 510 etymologies. The latest version of my paper on Basque comparative phonology, written for an EHL workshop in 2003, is a large part of this volume.

---

[8] All references are listed near the end of the book.

[9] See Blažek (1995), Ruhlen (1995), Shevoroshkin (1995), Starostin (1996), Wescott (1995).

ACKNOWLEDGEMENTS

This book would not have been possible without the friendship, encouragement and valuable assistance of my mentors and colleagues throughout the past twenty-three years. To list them all would make far too long a roster for this space. But I should at least specify those with whom I have worked closely, as co-authors, editors, and ASLIP officers: Václav Blažek, Allan Bomhard, Hal Fleming, Peter Norquest, Ilia Peiros, Merritt Ruhlen, Vitaly Shevoroshkin, Georgiy Starostin, and Michael Witzel.

For valuable technical assistance with this book and other projects, I thank Brita Maia Bengtson, Petr Hrubiš, and David Marjanović. And I thank my wife, April Rankin, for her support of, and supreme patience with, my avocation.

Of my teachers and mentors who are now departed from this earthly life I would like to mention: my Father and Mother,[10] Paul Benedict, Hermann Berger, Frederic Cassidy, Joseph Greenberg, Mary Ritchie Key, Rev. Herbert G. Loddigs, Karl Menges, and Roger Wescott.

I am deeply thankful to Murray Gell-Mann and the EHL Project for its support, and especially to the late Sergei A. Starostin for many fruitful discussions we had about methodology, Dene-Caucasian, and Basque.

For the preparation of this volume, I am greatly beholden to Vitaly Shevoroshkin, the late Vladimir Orel, and Cindy Drover-Davidson for their inspiration, guidance, and logistic support.

John D. Bengtson
Savage, Minnesota
Spring 2007

---

[10] Before she met my father Doris Mae Furrer (1921-2002) was a Second Lieutenant in the U.S. Army Nurse Corps, serving fourteen months in France and Luxembourg during WWII. Mother was my teacher at home until I went off to boarding school at the age of seven.

PREFACE

The articles in this book represent a large part of my work in historical linguistics and paleolinguistics over the past few years. Other published articles are cited in the bibliography at the end of the book.

The first two articles or chapters concern the worldwide picture of a human language family: global etymologies. (See also Bengtson (1989, 1992b), Bengtson & Ruhlen (1994).)

The third is a brief summary of my current view of the Austric macrofamily. (See also Bengtson (1992a, 1996b, 1997a, 1998a, 2006), Bengtson & Blažek (2000).)

The next six articles are concerned with the so-called "isolates," Basque and Burushaski, and my view that they are just members of a larger macrofamily, Dene-Caucasian. The two essays with titles beginning "The Problem of 'Isolates'..." approach the issues in a narrative, minimally technical style, while the other four papers are more detail-oriented and technical.

The last two articles concentrate on the Na-Dene family, which I consider an integral part of Dene-Caucasian. (See also Bengtson (1994a, 1998b, 2002a, 2002b, etc.), Blažek & Bengtson (1995).)

It hardly needs saying that much of the content of this book is out of the mainstream of historical linguistic work. This might be a good place to mention some of the guiding principles in my work that have led to the hypotheses developed here.

- The standard comparative method, developed by historical linguists over the past two centuries, is a powerful tool that can help to shed abundant light on the prehistory of the human race.

- The method called "mass comparison," or - much better - multilateral comparison, is not a substitute for the standard comparative method, as some linguists have alleged, but the first inductive step in it. New knowledge and new hypotheses can only come about by inductive reasoning.

- Subsequent deductive operations of the comparative method, such as formulating phonological correspondences and reconstructing proto-languages are essential and important steps, but they are only possible after at least a rough hypothesis of classification has been established by multilateral comparison.[11]

- The supposed "temporal ceiling," self-imposed by some historical linguists, limiting (in their view) the effectiveness of comparative method to language families or relationships no more than 6,000 to 8,000 years, has no foundation in actual fact and practice. For one thing, it is apparent that some of the universally accepted language families of Africa must be much older than 8,000 years. Khoisan may be 20,000 years old.

- Another way to "break the ceiling" is to compare reconstructed proto-languages. The Nostraticists have compared several proto-languages and arrived at a proto-proto-language that may be as much as 15,000 years old (Bomhard). S.A. Starostin compared another set of proto-languages to reconstruct Sino-Caucasian, which seems to date to a comparable age. When we then compare Proto-Nostratic with Proto-Dene-Caucasian, as Starostin (1989) has done, we are implicitly probing back far beyond fifteen millennia. There is theoretically no limit to this process, though inevitably, as we compare hypotheticals, there is a progressive loss of resolution that affects individual details but probably not wider conclusions.

- Other factors that allow us to defy the "temporal ceiling" are localized phonetic conservatism, random phonetic retention, and multilateral lexical recovery.[12]

- The application of multilateral comparison has allowed us to classify most of the languages of the world into a few – perhaps eight to twelve – macro-families. The further reduction of these macro-families to even deeper macro-macro-families, and determining their branching structure, will provide valuable insights into the deepest relationships and oldest migrations of the human family. These macro-family hypotheses should always be regarded as provisional – the best explanation currently available – rather than any final and permanent formulation.

- The comparison of macro-families has led to the discovery of many common lexical elements. When we exclude

---

[11] I am indebted to Joseph Greenberg and Merritt Ruhlen for making this principle clear.
[12] For details and examples, see the article "On Fossil Dinosaurs and Fossil Words."

chance resemblances, onomatopoeia, and borrowings between languages, what is left – global etymologies – is most parsimoniously explained as archaic residue from the original Proto-Sapiens language.

- Our task as scientists is not to restrict ourselves to theories that are so highly probable that they can be regarded as virtually "proven" – for example, language families such as Indo-European, Austronesian, and Algic. To do so leaves us with the absurd result that the world is home to hundreds of unrelated language families. Our task is to use the powerful methods described above to hypothesize a minimum of linguistic taxa and thus provide results that are comparable with the bold hypotheses being proposed by geneticists and archeologists. It is only in this way that historical linguistics can take its rightful place in the study of human prehistory.

I harbor no illusions that the hypotheses proposed or developed in this book are the final answers to the problems of human prehistory. They are my attempts to provide the best explanatory models available to me and my colleagues. We fully expect that all of our hypotheses will be corrected, amended, and amplified in the years to come.

ON FOSSIL DINOSAURS AND FOSSIL WORDS

A startling recent development in paleontology has interested me because of its implications for paleolinguistics and for the history of science in general. Researchers, headed by Mary Higby Schweitzer, of North Carolina State University, have claimed to have found soft tissues in dinosaur fossils 68 million years old (Schweitzer, *et al.* 2005). This finding has caused a sensation and aroused tremendous controversy, since it is "a matter of faith among scientists that soft tissue can survive, at most, for a few tens of thousands of years, not the 65 million since T. rex walked what's now the Hell Creek Formation in Montana" (Yeoman 2006: 37). Nevertheless, Schweitzer has gained the support of some paleontologists, including the eminent dinosaur expert John R. "Jack" Horner of the Museum of the Rockies, and Jan Toporski of the Carnegie Institution (both co-authors of the *Science* article).

On the other hand, some scientists have insisted that the soft-tissue discoveries cannot be possible, and that they can be explained as outside contamination, or improper or incomplete testing of the samples (Yeoman 2006: 40).

Apart from the data and their analysis, it has been interesting to see the behavior of scientists when confronted with information that may overturn a scientific "dogma" (an oxymoron) that they have been taught to believe is immutable. Schweitzer reports that "I had one reviewer tell me that he didn't care what the data said, he knew that what I was finding wasn't possible. I wrote back and said, 'Well, what data would convince you?' And he said, 'None'" (*Ibid*, p. 37). Horner adds, "Frequently in our field people come up with new ideas, and opponents say, 'I just don't believe it.' [Schweitzer] was having a hard time publishing in journals (*Ibid*, p. 38)." This type of attitude is, in fact, very common in the scientific world, and it is well known that every new scientific paradigm has been met with the opposition of experts who insist that the new idea is impossible.

It is also well known that some of the greatest new hypotheses and paradigm shifts have been instigated by scholars who, in some way, are outsiders to the scientific establishment – the most famous example being a patent clerk named Einstein. It is of interest here that Schweitzer, a mother of three and a substitute teacher, came into paleontology in a rather unorthodox manner. Horner recalls that "she really wasn't much of a scientist – which is good... Scientists all get to thinking alike, and it's good to bring people in from different disciplines. They ask questions very differently (*Ibid*, p. 38)."

I have been struck by the parallels this story holds with recent developments in paleolinguistics. Maverick linguists have published evidence claiming that taxonomically deep and temporally old language families, encompassing many of the universally accepted language families, can be demonstrated, and even that comparisons of these deep families show that all known human languages share a common origin, and that remnants of specific words of that Proto-Sapiens language can still be found.[13] The rationale of these studies is well summarized by the mission statement of the Evolution of Human Languages Project, under the auspices of the Santa Fe Institute:[14]

> Nevertheless, despite widespread scepticism and reluctance to tackle the problem [of remote linguistic relationships], there are a number of scholars who believe that these obstacles are not insurmountable. Research has been going on over the past several decades that appears to indicate that larger genetic groupings are not only possible, but indeed quite plausible. It can be shown that most of the world's language families can be classified into roughly a dozen large groupings, or macrofamilies. Two sorts of evidence can be used for this purpose:
> 1) Even a superficial analysis of the vocabulary of a large number of linguistic families reveals numerous lexical similarities extending far beyond the borders of the smaller genetic units. They are frequently restricted to individual macrofamilies (such as Eurasiatic, Afroasiatic etc.), but a significant number of such matches have already been found between the macrofamilies themselves, pointing to the probability of common origin.
> 2) Classical historical linguistics has developed a very powerful tool - the comparative method - that allows the reconstruction of unattested language stages, so-called proto-languages. It turns out that whereas modern languages may vary significantly, protolanguages in various cases tend to be much more similar to one other. This is the case, e.g., with Indo-European, Uralic and Altaic: modern English, Finnish, and Turkish may have almost nothing in common, but their respective ancestors - Proto-Indo-European, Proto-Uralic and Proto-Altaic - appear to have many more common traits and common vocabulary. This means that the possibility exists of extending the time perspective and reconstructing even earlier stages of human language and much of this research has already been conducted.

---
[13] For a recent and sympathetic summary of this work, see Ruhlen (2005).
[14] See http://ehl.santafe.edu.

The ultimate goal is to arrive at a stage when an absolute majority of the world's languages can be reduced to a minimum number of huge language macrofamilies, which in turn can be traced back to a Proto-Sapiens stage, should the databases provide sufficient evidence to support the hypothesis of monogenesis.

To many orthodox historical linguists, these claims are anathema and some have vigorously opposed them. Terrence Kaufman declares that "a temporal ceiling of 7,000 to 8,000 years is inherent in the methods of comparative linguistic reconstruction," and Paul Hopper dismisses long-range linguistic comparison as "broad-based guesses."[15] R.L. Trask (1999) said "Like many linguists, I am deeply skeptical of the very possibility of identifying genetic links at the kind of time-depth [15,000-20,000 BP] envisaged here: my prejudice, based upon decades of experience, is that language change is just too rapid and too remorseless." James Matisoff (1990) derides the work of Joseph Greenberg and other paleolinguists by coining the words "megalocomparison" (cf. megalomania) and "columbicubiculomania,"[16] implying that this research is the result of mental pathologies!

It is clear from the above that developments in paleontology and paleolinguistics have many parallels. In both sciences, we have scholars who have found evidence of what they think are very old phenomena (in the first case soft tissues in dinosaur fossils, in the other case linguistic "fossils" – the actual words spoken by early humans), and we have the old guard, who "know" – *a priori* – that such things are impossible, and "defend" the "received truth" against the upstarts. Let me elaborate on "fossil words":

Some years ago, Merritt Ruhlen and I published an article that claimed to document twenty-seven Proto-Sapiens words and their descendants in languages all over the world (Bengtson & Ruhlen 1994). Some of the evidence we offered is shown (in greatly simplified form) in Table 1.

---

[15] For a discussion of these remarks see Ruhlen (1994: 9-38).
[16] "A compulsion to stick things into pigeonholes" (Matisoff 1990: 108).

Three Global Etymologies[17]

Proto-Sapiens	Africa	Western Eurasia	Eastern Eurasia	Ocenia[18]	Amercas
BUR[19] 1 ashes, 2 dust, 3 smoke	Bongo *buru*-ku 1 Shilluk *bur* 1	Finnish *poro*[20] Malayalam *puṛu* -ti[21]	Altai *pur* 1 Manchu *bur*-aki[22]	Common Australian **burin* 3 Tasmanian *būrana* 3	Uncasica *bura* 1 Lupaca *pur*-ka 1 Goajiro *purpura* 2
K'OLO[23] 1 hole, 2 anus, 3 buttock	!Kung *!kảro* 1 Teda *kulo* 2	Latin *cūlu*-s 2,3 English *hole* (< **kulo*-) Finnish *kolo*[24] Akhwakh *q'ːoro*[25]	Gondi *kula* 3 West Tibetan *kor*[26]	[27]	North Yokuts *k'ol*-woṣ 1 Hopi *qölö*[28] Tonkawa *ko-l*-was 3 Botocudo *kro* 1
MI(N) 1 what?, 2 who?	Kxoe *ma*[29] Hausa *mèè*, *mìì* 1 Ancient Egyptian <*m*> 1 <*m(j)*> 2	Hebrew *mī* 2 Middle Breton *ma* 1 Georgian *ma* 1 Hungarian *mi*[30] Finnish *mi*, *mi*-kä[31] Batsbi *me* 2	Burushaski *men* 2 Ryukyuan *mī* 1 Mon *mu* 1	Arapesh *mane* 1 Common Australian **minha*, **minya* 1	Mandan *mana* 2 Wappo *may* 2 Guambiana *mu* 2

How, the critics ask, is it possible for the words in Table 1 to exist, in recognizable form, after what must be at least 50,000 years of linguistic evolution? (Recall the statements by Kaufman and Trask, above.) Because they "know" there is a "temporal ceiling of 7,000 to 8,000 years," they dismiss the evidence above, and everything else that purports to represent a state of affairs earlier than the "temporal ceiling." Just as it is "a matter of

---

[17] Based on Bengtson & Ruhlen (1994), with some additions and modifications.
[18] Including all the islands south and east of Asia and the Pacific; Papua-New Guinea, Australia.
[19] Some have claimed that Ruhlen and I have attempted to "reconstruct" Proto-Human words. We have never made that claim, in the strict sense of phonological reconstruction, but the "phonetic glosses" such as **BUR** roughly represent what the original word may have sounded like.
[20] 'hot ashes, coarse dust'.
[21] 'dust, earth'.
[22] 'dust, sand'.
[23] /k'/ represents a glottalized sound: /k/ accompanied by glottal closure.
[24] 'hole, crack'.
[25] 'burrow'.
[26] 'hollow in the ground, pit'.
[27] There are several possible explanations for the gap here, for example: (1) The word **K'OLO** was lost by the ancestral language(s) of this area; (2) cognates may exist, but have not been recognized, due to phonetic or semantic changes; (3) cognates may exist, but have not been found due to lack of documentation.
[28] 'hole (in the ground)'.
[29] 'who, which.'
[30] 'what, which.'
[31] 'what, which.'

faith" among paleontologists that soft tissue cannot remain after millions of years, it is just as much a matter of faith among historical linguists that words cannot remain recognizable beyond 8,000 years.

Ruhlen and I, along with other paleolinguists, have argued that there is no evidence that a "temporal ceiling" exists in historical linguistics. In fact, there are several factors which, we think, make it possible for us to detect the traces of Proto-Sapiens words that persist to modern times. These factors may be denoted as (a) localized phonetic conservatism, (b) random phonetic retention, (c) multilateral lexical recovery, and (d) reconstruction.

(a) **Localized phonetic conservatism**: Some languages tend to exhibit less phonetic change than others. Within Europe, this can be demonstrated by French and its close taxonomic relative, Italian. Many French words have changed drastically from the original Latin form; for example, Latin *aqua* 'water' has been reduced in French to a single vowel *eau* /o/. Likewise, Lat. *cattus* (5 phonemes) 'cat' has become *chat* /ša/ (2 phonemes), *collum* 'neck' is now *cou* /ku/, etc. In Italian, on the other hand, the same words have undergone much less change: *acqua, gatto, collo,* respectively. In simple terms, French words have a more "worn down" appearance than their Italian cognates. The modern Italian word for 'water', *acqua*, is little changed from Proto-Sapiens **ʔAQ'WA** 'water' (Bengtson & Ruhlen 1994: pp. 327-328).

Lithuanian is often cited as a phonetically archaic language, thus Lithuanian words such as *naũjas* 'new,' *sãpnas* 'dream,' *ketvir̃tas* 'fourth,' differ but little from their Vedic Sanskrit cognates dated some 3,500 years ago: *návyas, svápnas* 'sleep,' and *caturthás,* respectively.[32] Indeed, Lithuanian is, in some respects, more archaic than Vedic. Finnish also seems to be archaic in this way, with many words remaining virtually the same since the Proto-Uralic stage of some thousands of years ago, so Proto-Uralic **śilmä-* 'eye,' **korwa-* 'ear,' **jalka-* 'foot,' are still *silmä, korva, jalka,* respectively, in modern Finnish. (Note that Finnish happens to figure in all three of the global etymologies cited in Table 1).

(b) **Random phonetic retention**: Another factor is the phenomenon of random phonetic retention, so that even in languages not particularly archaic phonetically, some words, by chance, escape radical phonetic changes. For example, English *water, new,* and *yoke* retain much the same form as was recorded in ancient Hittite some 3,100 – 3,600 years ago: <watar>, <newa-> and <yuga->, respectively. Rumanian *nepot* 'grandson, nephew' is still essentially the same (after ca. 8,000 years) as its reconstructed Indo-European ancestor **nepo-t-* 'grandchild, sister's son'.[33]

---

[32] Though written down much later, it is thought that the Vedic texts were preserved by oral tradition from about 1500 B.C.

[33] This and other examples are cited by Bengtson & Ruhlen (1994: p. 287).

(c) **Multilateral lexical recovery**: When languages of the same family are compared, the chance of recovering the original vocabulary of their proto-language increases with the number of languages compared (Greenberg 1987b). Thus, for example, if one is working with a large language family, such as Sino-Tibetan (with more than 250 languages), there is a much better chance of recovering the original vocabulary of the proto-language than there is with a smaller family, such as Uralic (some 24 languages). The same principle works on the global level, if we are testing the hypothesis that all human languages are genetically related (*i.e.,* descend from one original proto-language). For example, there is a widespread and ancient word for 'tail' found throughout Eurasia; for example, Georgian *k'ud-,* Turkish *kuyruk* (from **kud-ruk*), Orok (Tungusic) *xudu,* Korean *k:ori.*[34] However, it seems to have been lost from the Indo-European family, except for one language: Latin *cauda.*[35] Out of ten branches of the Indo-European family,[36] the word happened to be kept by only one.

(d) **Reconstruction**: The techniques of historical linguistic reconstruction – the reconstitution of older linguistic forms – allow us to recognize cognations that otherwise would escape us. Thus, for example, one might not suspect a common origin of Russian имя [ímya] 'name' and Hungarian *név* with the same meaning, but if we compare their respective ancestral forms, Proto-Indo-European **(e)nomen-* and Proto-Uralic **nimi-,* the similarity is easily seen.

Paleolinguists think that these four factors, and possibly others, make it possible for us to recover at least a fraction of the original Proto-Sapiens lexicon. Historical linguists need to look at this evidence objectively and not dismiss it out of hand on the basis of what we have shown to be erroneous preconceptions.

---

[34] Cf. also (with semantic shift) Uralic **kuttV* > Hungarian *hát* 'back, backside', etc.

[35] Lat. *cauda* gave rise to It. *coda,* Rum. *coadă,* Port. *cauda,* Span. *cola* (with an unexpected shift of *d* > *l*), Fr. *queue,* etc. The long-range comparison (with Georgian, Turkish, etc.) was cited by the Russian paleolinguist Vladimir Illich-Svitych, and before that by the Italian Alfredo Trombetti.

[36] Ruhlen (1987) cites Anatolian, Armenian, Tocharian, Indo-Iranian, Albanian, Greek, Italic, Celtic, Germanic, and Balto-Slavic.

Global Etymologies Involving Six Macro-Families

	Kongo-Saharan	Afro-Asiatic	Eurasiatic / Nostratic	Dene-Caucasian	Austric	Amerind
'not' (negative or prohibit-ive morpheme)	NS *mV (verbal negative) > Songay mana, Murle, Ik maa, Kunama mme, Kanuri ba, etc. NK: Mande maa ~ mee, Vai, Sango maa, Susu mu, etc. 'not'	PAA *ma(ʔ) negative / prohibitive: Arabic mā 'not' Old Egyptian m (prohibitive) Xamir -m (neg. affix); Saho mā- (neg./prohib.) Angas man (prohib.), etc.	PIE *meʔ > *mē prohibitive > Greek μη, Armenian mi, Sanskrit mā K: Svan mād 'no, not', māma 'no' Alt: Old Turkish -ma-/-mä- (negative infix); Korean mōt 'no, not', Japanese -ma- (dubitative)	MC: PNC *ma (prohibitive): Chechen, Lak ma, Abkhaz m-, etc. Burushaski be 'no, not' PST *mā(H) 'not': Old Chinese *ma, Tibetan, Kanauri ma, etc. PYen *wə-: Ket bań 'no, not', Kott mon ~ mōn 'not'	Nihali béʔ, béthe 'not' Santali ba 'not,' baŋ 'no,' Khmer bū(pūm) 'ne pas, ne, non'	Panoan: Chacobo, Cashibo ma 'not' Andean: Inga Quechua mána 'not' Chibchan-Paezan: Awa man 'not', Paez –mee
'joint' 'knee,' 'elbow,' 'shoul-der'	NS *kon- 'elbow'> Gao kɔŋ-kor Berta k'on-, Kunama ukun-, etc., Anej kukūn 'knee', Masai kúṇú 'knee', etc. NK: Yoruba ekun, Grebo kona, Pam gooni 'knee'	Chad: Banana gwonɛ 'elbow' Cush: Saho gina' 'hand'	PIE *genu- 'knee' > Latin genū, Greek γον υ, Sanskrit jānu, etc. PUr *küjñä-(rä) > Finnish kyynär-pää, Hungarian könyök 'elbow,' etc. Alt: Turkish kanat 'wing, fin', Even kō:nčen 'shin'	MC: Lezgi q·ün 'shoulder,' etc. ST: Old Chinese *kēn 'shoulder' Yen: *ke(')n- > Kott hēnar, hinar 'shoulder,' etc.	MK: Bahnaric *kɛ:ŋ 'elbow,' Katuic *-gɛ:ŋ 'elbow' Ainu *komta 'elbow'	Penutian: Yuki kan, kank 'kneel,' Coast Yuki kʼenk 'knee' Andean: Inga Quechua kungúr 'knee,' kuníxa 'elbow' Macro-Carib: Witoto Nɨpode káiɲɯ 'knee'
'skin, bark'	NS: Songay kob-ta, Naadh gwɔb, Mangbetu – képi 'skin' NK: PBantu *-kóba, *-gùbò, *-gòbj 'skin', Ndem-li hōbi 'bark'	Om: Wolaytta guobba 'bark' Cush: Burungi qafa, Bilin ḵäf 'bark,' etc. Chad: Zar kàbù 'bark,' etc.	PUr *kopa 'bark' > Estonian kōba 'fir bark,' Kamassian k'uba 'skin, hide,' etc. Nivkh xip 'birchbark' PAlt *kʼäp·V > Turkish kabuk 'bark,' Turkmen gapak 'eyelid,' Japanese kawá 'skin, bark' IE: ? Arm. kopʼ 'eyelid'	Burushaski gap 'hide' PST *qruap 'scale, shell': > Jingpo kop² 'crust, rind, shell,' etc.	Ainu kap (*kʌp) 'skin, fur,' sik-kap 'eyelid' Nihali jiki-kapri 'eyebrow' Stieng kup 'skin, bark'; Semai cko:p 'bark' AN: Kanakanabu káva 'skin'	Almosan-Keresiouan: Ojibwe -kopy 'bark' Penutian: Mixe kɨp-ak 'bark' Equatorial-Tucanoan: Itene kapi-ye 'skin,' etc.
'night, dark'		Arabic gamm ā 'darkness,' Soqotri ʕmd '(sun) to set'	PK *γam-(e) 'night' > Georgian γame- 'night,' sa-γam-o 'evening'	MC: Basque gau, gab- 'night,' Tsakhur χam 'night' PST *γVm(H) 'dark, shade' > Old Chinese *ʔamʔ 'dark', etc.	PAN *γabi = *Rabi 'night' > Tagalog gabi	PAmerind *xama 'night, dark, black' > Lake Miwok ʔúme 'night', Chimariko hime 'night', Tucano yami 'night', etc.

	Kongo-Saharan	Afro-Asiatic	Eurasiatic / Nostratic	Dene-Caucasian	Austric	Amerind
'tail, back'	NS: Bari kɔt-, Nandi katut 'tail'	Chad: Warji kwatarę, Tangale kodọr, Musgu gider, Gidar kútra	PK *k'ud-/k'wad- 'tail' > Georgian k'ud- IE: Latin cauda ~ coda 'tail' PAlt *k'udurgi 'tail' > Turkish kujruk, Orok xudu, Korean kori 'tail,' etc.	MC: Burushaski git 'anus' ND: Haida Gut 'buttocks'	PAN *likud 'back' PMK *(Cə)kVt 'back, hind part'; Car Nicobar likụn 'neck, nape' Ainu *dekut 'neck'	Penutian: Yokots k'ut' 'tail' Chibchan-Paezan: Tsafiqui Pila kudan 'neck,' Chapalaachi kutu 'neck'
'person / family'	NS: Songay har 'man,' Teda, Daza aŋ kar 'male', etc. NK: Wolof gur 'man,' Serer o-kor-oxa 'person', Fula gor-ko 'person', Sango koli 'man', etc.	Sem: Arabic kull-at 'tribe' Chad: Lamang kol 'to marry'	Proto-Eurasiatic *k'Ul'V 'person' > Russian čelo-vék 'person, human,' Sanskrit kúla- 'family, herd,' Mongolian qulu-nča 'ancestor,' etc.	PNC *χōlʔV 'male' > Khwarshi χol 'husband', etc. Yen: Ket qíliŋ 'adulterous'	Ainu *kur 'man, person' Nihali Kol-ta 'Nihals', kol 'woman, wife' Korku koro 'man, person' PAN *hulun 'man (human being)'	Penutian: Chinook i-kala 'man,' Yakonan qaalt 'man,' Maidu kyle 'woman' Macro-Panoan: Sanapana kilaua 'woman'
'blood'	NS: Masai -sárgé, Kuliak *seh 'blood'	Om: Gimojan *sugu-c 'blood' Cush: Mbugu saxo 'blood,' etc. Egyptian zχn 'flesh'	PIE *HesH-r /*HsH-n 'blood' > Hitt. esḫar, Ltv. asins, Latin aser, etc. PK *zisxL- 'blood' > Georgian sisxl- Alt: Evenki sēkse 'blood,' Turkish sağ 'healthy,' etc.	MC: Basque izerdi, izardi 'sweat, sap,' Batsbi c'ig 'blood,' Hurrian zurgi 'blood,' etc. PYen *sur 'blood' > Ket śūʎ, etc.		AK: Bella Coola six 'blood,' Squamish caqʷ 'bleed' Penutian: Yuki es, Choctaw issiš 'blood' Hokan: Jicaque ʔas, Washo ašang 'blood', etc.
'year, old'	NS: PNubian *šen 'year'	Egyptian sn-f 'next year' Sem: Arabic mu-sinn 'old,' Hebrew šānā 'year,' etc. Chad: Tera soni 'year'	PIE *sen- 'old' > Old Irish sen, Welsh hen, Latin sen-ex, Sanskrit sana-, etc.	MC: Burushaski šiní 'summer'; PNC *śwǎnɨ 'year' > Avar son, Lak šin, Tsakhur sen, etc. Yen: Ket śi:ñ, Yug sin 'old, withered' Sumerian sun ~ sumun '(be) old' ND: Tlingit šaan, Navajo sā, Mescalero sáán-é 'old age'		Penutian: Mayan Chontal šnioš 'old,' Kekchi šaʔan 'old woman' CAm: Tewa sēŋ do 'old man' MPanoan: PPanoan *šɨni- 'old,' Chacobo šɨni-pa 'year' Eq: Zamora a-ssan-d 'old,' Kandoshi sin-ap-či 'old'

Abbreviations: AA Afroasiatic; AK Almosan-Keresioua; Alt Altaic, AN Austronesian; CAm Central Amerind; Chad Chadic; Cush Cushitic; Eq Equatorial; IE Indo-European; K Kartvelian; MC Macro-Caucasian; MK Mon-Khmer; NC North Caucasian; ND Na-Dene; NK Niger-Kordofanian; NS Nilo-Saharan; Om Omotic; P Proto-; Sem Semitic; ST Sino-Tibetan; Ur Uralic; Yen Yeniseian.

THE "GREATER AUSTRIC" HYPOTHESIS

"Austric" is a hypothetical language family proposed by Wilhelm Schmidt, a Lutheran clergyman from Germany who worked as a missionary in Southeast Asia. He hypothesized (1906) that the Austroasiatic language family and the Austronesian language family (see below) came from a common origin and should be be grouped together into a new phylum named Austric (from Latin *auster* 'south').

[Schmidt] presented phonological, morphological, and lexical evidence in support of this hypothesis. The consensus of the linguists who have looked into the matter has been that the phonological and morphological evidence is convincing, but not the lexical, and for that reason, Austric has never been generally accepted as a valid taxonomic unit (La Vaughn Hayes). [37]

In the ensuing century, various scholars have sought to "expand" the Austric family, to include other languages that seem to have the same grammatical and lexical features as Schmidt's Austric. Beginning around 1996, I proposed a "Greater Austric" macro-phylum of macro-family that includes the following languages:

Nihali: a tribal language of central India, thought to be the last remnant of an ancient language family.

Austroasiatic (Munda - Mon-Khmer): about 155 languages spoken in India, Nicobar Islands, and Southeast Asia: includes *Santali, Mundari, Sora* (India), *Nancowry, Mon, Khmer* (Cambodia), *Vietnamese, Pear, Katu*, etc.

Hmong-Mien (Miao-Yao): a small number of languages (4-7?) scattered through southern China, Hainan, Vietnam, Laos, and Thailand: includes *Hmong, Ke-cheng, Kao-p'o, Kao-t'ung, Yao-lu*.

Daic (Tai-Kadai): about 55 languages spoken in Southeast Asia: includes *Thai, Lao, Kam, Sui, Lakkia*, etc.

Austronesian: a vast family of nearly 1000 languages, ranging from Madagascar through Indonesia, Philippines, Taiwan (aboriginals, not Chinese), to the Pacific islands: includes *Malagasy, Malay, Bahasa Indonesia, Javanese, Paiwan, Bontok, Tagalog, Fijian, Maori, Tahitian, Samoan, Hawai'ian*, etc.

---

[37] See http://home.att.net/~lvhayes/Langling/langpg3.htm.

Ainu: an almost extinct minority language of Japan. Formerly more extensive, Ainu was also spoken on the Kuril Islands, Sakhalin Island, and the Kamchatka peninsula. It is thought to have been the language of the ancient Jomon culture (about 10,000 BC to 300 BC).

GRAMMATICAL EVIDENCE FOR GREATER AUSTRIC

For many linguists, the existence of a common grammatical system is the best evidence of original kinship. One of the most convincing pieces of grammatical evidence for Austric is the basic first-person singular pronoun, widely of the type that can be reconstructed as *ku* 'I, me':[38]

Nihali *jó* 'I'
Austroasiatic: Proto-Viet-Muong **kwa* 'we, I', Central Nicobar *chuu-ö* 'I'
Hmong-Mien: Biao *kəu*, Hmong *ko* 'I'
Austronesian: **aku* 'I' > Pazeh *yako*, Javanese *aku,* Tagalog *akó*, Tahitian *au, vau*, etc.
Daic: Proto-Tai **ku* 'I'
Ainu **ku* 'I'

Other grammatical evidence includes prefixes or infixes of the type **pa-* / **-ap-* "causative," both in Austroasiatic [AA] and Austronesian [AN]:[39]

AA: Katu (Vietnam, Laos) *sooq* 'to flee': *pa-sooq* 'to cause to flee'; Sora (India) *jUm* 'to eat': *ab-jUm* 'to cause to eat = to feed'
AN: Bontok (Philippines) *kán* 'to eat' : *pa-kán* 'to cause to eat = to feed', *téy* 'die': *pa-téy* 'to cause to die = to kill'

And an "agentive marker":[40] **ma-* / **-am-* in Austroasiatic = **mu-* / **-um-* in Austronesian:

AA: Nancowry (Nicobar) *'itkéch* 'to pluck': *m-itkéch* 'one who plucks, plucker'; Pear (Cambodia) *snik* 'light': *am-snik* 'to lighten';

---

[38] Asterisk * is used by historical linguists to denote reconstructed words or morphemes (grammatical elements) that are not directly attested but can be inferred from descendant forms.
[39] For a summary of grammatical evidence for Austric, see Reid (1994); cf. also Itabashi (1998).
[40] Agentive marker: like *-er, -or* in English *bak-er, sail-or*, etc.

Khmer (Cambodia) *rut* 'to run away': *r-m-ut* 'one who runs away, fugitive'

AN: Bontok *'ákew* 'to steal': *'-um-a'ákew* 'one who steals = thief'; *'inum* 'to drink': *'-um-inum* 'one who drinks = drinker'

Unfortunately for the comparative linguist, some Austric languages (*e.g.*, Vietnamese, Hmong, Thai) have become monosyllabic and the old prefixes have dropped off. However there are still some clues about their earlier presence. For example, the Hmong-Mien languages have the contrast of initial consonants in **day* 'die' *vs.* **tay* 'kill,' a contrast that seems to go back to Proto-Austric stative **ma-t(r)ay* 'to die' *vs.* causative **pa-t(r)ay* 'to make die, to kill' (see the etymology **die**, below).

LEXICAL EVIDENCE FOR GREATER AUSTRIC

The most convincing word comparisons are those that involve the most basic (non-cultural) meanings, such as parts of the body (blood, head), basic natural phenomena (root, fire, sky), simple social terms (man), and basic verbs (die). Studies have shown that basic words of these types are far more likely to remain in a given language over hundreds and even thousands of years than words with non-basic meanings (such as 'chair, table, tea, card,' items that are likely to be traded between cultures along with their names).[41] Only a few of the many Austric word comparisons are cited below.[42] Some phonetic transcriptions have been simplified.

man: prototype **qulo*
Nihali *Kol- sa, Kal- so* 'men, Nihals' (self-name), *kol* 'wife, woman'
Austroasiatic: Korku *koro* 'man'; Khmer *kur* 'Bahnar or Sro'

---

[41] While most basic words in English are still of Anglo-Saxon (Germanic) origin, the four words cited in the parentheses are of non-Anglo-Saxon origin: *chair* < French < Latin < Greek; *table* < French < Latin; *tea* < Dutch < Malay < Chinese, *card* < French < Latin < Greek < Egyptian (originally 'a sheet of papyrus').

[42] See, e.g., Benedict (1966, 1975), Bengtson (1992, 1996, 1997a), Bengtson & Blažek (2000), Diffloth (1994), Gjerdman (1926), Hayes (1992, 1996, 1997, 1999, 2000, 2001), Kosaka (2002), Kuiper (1948), Norquest (1998), Schmidt (1906), Shorto (1976), Sidwell (1998), Vovin (1992).

Austronesian: Proto-Malayo-Polynesian *qulun 'outsiders, alien people' > Bintulu, Katingan *ulun* 'person,' Merina *ólona,* Punan Kelai *lun,* etc.

Ainu *kur* 'man, person'

blood: prototype *(m-)kyemu*
Austroasiatic:Mundari *mayam,* Khmer *jha:m,* Mon *chim*
Hmong-Mien: Yao **dzhyaam,* Hmong **ntšheng*
Austronesian: Formosan[43] **dzamu(')* 'blood' > Paiwan *djamuq,* etc.

Ainu *kem*

head: prototype **Pengu*
Nihali *peng, pyeng* 'head'
Austroasiatic: Khmer *tpu:ng* 'above'
Austronesian: **bunguh* 'head' > Formosan: Kanakanabu *nabúngu,* Siraya *bungu,* Central Amis *fungoh,* Tsou *fngúu* 'head', etc.

Ainu **pa* 'head' (if from earlier **pang*)

root: prototype **riat(s)*
Austroasiatic: Santali *rɛhɛ'd,* Mundari *re:'d* 'root'
Khmer *ris*; Mon *ruih*; Sre *rias,* Vietnamese *rẽ* 'root'
Austronesian **'uRat* 'blood vessel, vein, sinew, tendon' > Formosan: Kanakanabu *urátsə* 'blood vessel,' etc.; Iban, Maloh *urat* 'root', Dayak Ngaju *uhat,* Tagalog *ugát,* etc.

Ainu **rit* 'root, blood vessel, tendon'

fire: prototype **-apoy*
Nihali *a:po* 'fire'
Austroasiatic: Brao *pa:y,* Tampuon *pae,* Katu *mpoih* 'fire'
Hmong-Mien: Ke-cheng *fwi* 'ash', Yao-lu *fui,* Thailand Yao *whi* 'ash'
Austronesian: **Sapuy* > Paiwan *sapuy,* Pazeh *hapúy,* Malay *api,* Tonga *afi,* Maori, Hawaiian *ahi,* etc. 'fire'
Daic: Thai *fay,* Kam-Sui **pwai* 'fire'
Ainu **apOy* 'fire, hearth' > *ape, abe, ambe, aboi* (in various dialects)

---

[43] "Formosan" denotes aboriginal languages of Taiwan, a.k.a. Formosa (Portuguese for 'beautiful').

sky: prototype **langit(s)*
Nihali *lēgē* 'up'
Austroasiatic: Sora *leng.leng* 'very high, inaccessible,' *bəleng* 'roof,' Juang *aling* 'top'; Khmer *lîng* 'to climb, ascend,' Bahnaric **le:ng* 'sky'
Austronesian: **langiC*[44] 'sky' > Saaroa *langica*, Puyuma *ranget*, Merina *lánitra*, Tagalog *lángit*, Malay *langit*, Maori *rangi*, Hawaiian *lani* 'day, heaven, sky,' etc.
Ainu **nis* 'sky, cloud' > *nish* 'clouds, heavens, air, sky' (if from **langit[s]*)

die: prototype *(ma-)t(r)ay / *(pa-)t(r)ay
Nihali *páDa:* 'to kill' (if *pa-* corresponds to the Proto-Austric causative prefix **pa-*)
Hmong-Mien: **day* 'die' vs. **tay* 'kill'> Hmong *dua* 'to die'
Austronesian: Saisiat *masay* 'die', Paiwan *matsay* 'die' / *pa-patsay* 'kill', Malay *mati* 'die', Maori *mate*, Hawaiian *make* id.
Daic: Proto-Tai **trai* 'to die' > Thai *taay*, Lakkia *plei* id.
Ainu **day* 'die' > Yakumo, Saru *ray*, Nairo *tay*, etc.

HISTORICAL IMPLICATIONS OF THE GREATER AUSTRIC HYPOTHESIS

If the Greater Austric hypothesis is correct, people speaking a "Proto-Austric" language spread out over a large part of Asia, an area probably stretching from India in the west, continuing through Southeast Asia (the old "Indo-China") and southern China, and to the northeast, possibly as far as Korea and Manchuria. There is much evidence that Austric-speaking peoples were formerly more numerous and widespread in all of these areas, and that the subsequent expansions of other language families (mainly Indo-European, Dravidian, and Sino-Tibetan) have pushed Austric languages to the south. Austric languages have left traces (loanwords)[45] in non-Austric languages ranging from Pakistan in the northwest (Burushaski, Indo-Aryan and Dravidian languages) through the Himalayan regions (Tibeto-Burman

---

[44] **C* denotes "hypothetical consonant of unknown quality."
[45] Historical linguists use the term "loanword" to denote words that are not part of a language's native lexicon, but were "borrowed" from other languages. See the discussion of English *chair, table, tea, card*, above, and footnote 4.

languages), in Tibetan and Chinese, and in the northeast, in languages such as Korean and Japanese.

The Austric proto-language has been identified by some with the Hoabinhian archaeological industry dating from the late Pleistocene to mid-Holocene (roughly 6,000 to 12,000 years ago). Primary Hoabinhian sites have been identified in Sumatra, Thailand, Laos, Myanmar, and Cambodia, while isolated inventories of stone artefacts displaying Hoabinhian elements have been found in Nepal, South China, Taiwan, and Australia.[46] Except for Nepal and Australia,[47] all of these areas are home to Austric languages, and, as mentioned in the preceding paragraph, there is evidence that Austric may formerly have been spoken in the Himalayan foothills.

The time-depth of the Hoabinhian industry is consistent with the diversification of Proto-Austric into about 1000 languages, and the lexical diversity among them. In this light, Austric seems comparable in age to the Afro-Asiatic language family (consisting of the Semitic, Egyptian, Berber, Chadic, Cushitic, Omotic families). There is tremendous lexical diversity among the Afro-Asiatic languages, yet some grammatical features are widely found among them.

Secondary to the original dispersal of Austric, one Austric sub-family, Austronesian, has made a tremendous expansion to the south, southwest, and east. Austronesian speakers are thought to have migrated from southern China about 8,000 years ago, first to Taiwan (where aborigines speaking Austronesian languages still live, though the languages are now endangered or extinct), then (about 6,000 years ago) to other islands, ranging from Madagascar through Indonesia, Philippines, and throughout the Pacific islands as far as Hawai'i and Easter Island. During these 8,000 years, Austronesian has diversified into a huge number of languages (959 according to Merritt Ruhlen, 1268 according to Ethnologue), making up about one fifth of the world's languages. Of these, some are official (national) languages, especially Malay (Indonesia and Malaysia), Tagalog (Philippines), Malagasy (Madagascar), and several Pacific languages (Samoan, Tahitian, Maori, etc.).

Of the remaining Austric languages, only very few are offical or national languages, namely Vietnamese, Khmer (Cambodia), Thai, and Lao. Apart from these four, the Mon language (Myanmar, Thailand)

---

[46] Thanks to Wikipedia article on Hoabinhian.
[47] No Austric languages are native to Australia, but Austronesian languages are spoken close to Australia, in parts of New Guinea and Indonesian islands.

has a long literary tradition dating back to the 7th Century A.D. The vast majority of Austric languages are minority or "tribal" languages that have only recently acquired a written form (if at all). Nevertheless, the Austric language macro-family is of tremendous importance in understanding the history and prehistory of Asia and Oceania.

THE PROBLEM OF "ISOLATES" I: BASQUE

The Basque language spoken in parts of Spain and France (and secondarily in parts of the Americas, such as Argentina and Nevada) is generally regarded as an **isolated language**, a language with no demonstrable family affiliation.[48] If the Basque language is *only* compared with western European languages, this appears to be true, since there is little or no resemblance between Basque words and words in other European languages, or between their respective grammatical systems. However, we know from past experience that it is sometimes necessary to search for linguistic relatives in distant locations, as William Jones found when he compared the classical Sanskrit of India with the classical languages of Europe. When this approach is tried with Basque, I believe we may have some hope of finding its closest relatives. (See Table 2.)[49]

Some observations on this table: (1) Where there is a space (-) in the table, it simply means that the language in question has a word that is not deemed a cognate with the Basque word. Thus the table is "Basque-centric." (2) All the words cited are basic, as defined above. Only the last one, 'thread,' can perhaps be considered a cultural word, though it obviously belongs to a very old stage of culture, since bone needles are known to have been used in the Paleolithic. (Cf. the meaning 'sinew' in Tsezian languages: Bezhta *7ila,* Tsez *7ero,* etc.) (3) The languages cited to the right of Basque are all spoken in the Caucasus mountain region. In fact, they all belong to the East Caucasian family, a family that is universally accepted by historical linguists. (4) The fact that there are more Avar-Andi-Tsez words in the table than, for example, Chechen (Nakh), is simply fortuitous.

---

[48] So, for example, Trask (1997), an opinion that is, naturally, widely accepted as from an expert.

[49] In Table 2: the meaning in the far left column is assumed for all the words in the horizontal line, unless indicated otherwise by a footnote. The phonetics of Caucasian languages are generally very complex and some of the consonants are difficult for western Europeans. I have tried to simplify the Caucasian words wherever possible; special symbols are as follows: *t', q', ts', č'* are **glottalized** consonants; *kk, χχ, ts' ts', čč* are intensive (or tense) consonants; *š, ž* as in Eng. *sure, azure*; *č* as in *chop, č'* is the same with a glottal catch; *χ* and *G* are deep throaty **fricatives**, as in German *Bach, Wagen,* only farther back in the throat (**uvular**); *G* is similar to the Parisian or Danish *r*; ʕ is a "voiced emphatic laryngeal fricative," similar to the ʕ (*'ayn*) of Arabic. Caucasian words are taken from the *North Caucasian Etymological Dictionary* by Nikolayev & Starostin (1994).

BASQUE AND CAUCASIAN

(gloss)	Basque	Nakh[50]	Avar-Andi Tsez	Lak/Dargwa	Lezgian
'tears'	nigar[51]	not'q'a[52]	máʕu	nerG[53]	naGʷ
'tongue'	mihi[54]	mott	mits'ts'i[55]	maz	mez
'tooth'	hortz	-	gožó[56]	kkarčči	gʷarž[57]
'beard'	bizar	-	bizal-ba[58]	-	mužur[59]
'milk'	ezne	šin[60]	šširu	-	-
'mouse'	sagu	šat'q'a[61]	tsatl'tl'ú[62]	-	sok[63]
'bird'	txori [čori]	-	č'orólo[64]	č'ịlmu[65]	-
'water'	(h)ur[66]	-	ʕor[67]	-	hül[68]
'fire'	su	ts'e	ts'a	ts'u	ts'ay
'soot'	kedar	-	q'q'et'an[69]	q'it	-
'star'	izar	t'ʕeyri[70]	ts'ts'ʷa	zure[71]	-
'hunger'	gose	-	-	kkaši	kkaš
'old'	zahar[72]	šira	asrá-ya-b	-	sur
'thread'	hari /, hal[73]	χal	χila[74]		Gal

[50] Unless indicated otherwise by footnote, the words in the third column are from Chechen, fourth column: Avar; fifth column: Lak, sixth column: Lezgi.

[51] Generally *negar* in western Basque dialects, *nigar* in eastern. The word means 'weeping, tears.'

[52] 'pus,' a common semantic shift involving body fluids.

[53] Dargwa

[54] Basque *h* is sounded only in northeastern (French) dialects; elsewhere it is silent, so 'tongue' is *mii* or *mi*. Basque *mihi* appears to have developed from something like **missi* or **misši* (cf. Andi *mits'ts'i* 'tongue'), a change similar to that in Greek *heptá*, Persian *haft* 'seven' < PIE **sept-*.

[55] This is from a close relative of Avar, Andi. The Avar word is *mats'*: 'tongue.'

[56] 'fang, canine tooth'

[57] Agul 'prong (tooth) of a rake'

[58] Bezhta 'mustache'

[59] Agul 'beard'

[60] 'udder'

[61] 'weasel' (a normal semantic shift from 'mouse'); other Caucasian languages (Adyge, Kabardian) have cognate words with the meaning 'mouse'.

[62] 'weasel'

[63] Tsakhur 'weasel'

[64] 'quail'; cf. Chamalal *č'or* 'bird'

[65] '(small) bird'

[66] *hur* only in the Zuberoan dialect; elsewhere *ur* 'water.'

[67] 'river'

[68] 'sea, liquid'

[69] Karata

[70] Batsbi

[71] Dargwa (Chirag dialect)

[72] See the note to *mihi* 'tongue.'

A table using other Basque words could well show more Chechen (or Lak, etc.) cognates. I see no evidence that Basque is closer to any one sub-group of the Caucasian family than it is to the others. (5) Though not shown in this table, several of the Basque words (*mihi* 'tongue,' *sagu* 'mouse,' *su* 'fire,' *izar* 'star,' *gose* 'hunger,' *zahar* 'old') also have likely cognates in West Caucasian languages. In addition, some Basque words (*handi* 'big,' *toki* 'place,' *bizkar* 'back,' *gizon* 'man,' *asto* 'donkey') have likely cognates in West Caucasian but not in East Caucasian.

On the basis of the above comparisons (and many others), I have proposed the following provisional hypotheses: (1) Basque is not totally isolated from all other languages, but is probably most closely related to the East Caucasian and West Caucasian which all these languages belong to (**Vasco-Caucasian** or **Macro-Caucasian**),[75] and is at least as old as Indo-Hittite, probably even centuries older. This is shown, for example, by the many gaps in the table, and by the semantic shifts (indicated in footnotes). Another indicator may be that Basque shares few numeral words with Caucasian (possibly just *bi* 'two,' *lau(r)* 'four,'[76] and *hogei* '20'), while most IE languages have the same numeral words from 1-10.

One could well ask here whether the above lexical resemblances might just be **chance resemblances** and not evidence of a family relationship. In fact, a critic of my work, R.L. Trask, has claimed just that – that these proposed "cognates" (and others) are simply chance resemblances, and thus there is "not the slightest shred of evidence" that Basque is related to the Caucasian languages – or any other![77] There are two scientific methods to test whether my claim or Trask's is correct, and they are (1) phonological evidence (**sound correspondences**), and (2) **morphological evidence.** That is to say, if the lexical resemblances listed above are true cognates, then there should be recurrent correspondences between the sound systems of Basque and the Caucasian languages, and there should also be

---

[73] *hari* 'thread'; *hal-* appears in compound words such as *hal-gai* 'textile material, thread-stuff.' Most of the Caucasian languages have -*l*- in this word, but cf. also Tsez χ*ero* 'sinew.'
[74] Bezhta 'sinew'
[75] Since this family is not yet generally accepted by historical linguists, a standard term has not been agreed upon.
[76] The word that appears to be cognate with Basque *lau-* '4' means '4' in West Cauc. (*$p\check{x}ə$*), but '8' in East Cauc. (*bǖnṯe*).
[77] See, for example, Trask (1997, pp. 35, 411-415).

morphological (grammatical) similarities between the same languages. Here is how we shall apply the two tests:

Sound correspondences: There are two possible approaches to this test. One would be to compare Basque phonology with the phonology any or all of the Caucasian subgroups shown above; the other would be to compare Basque phonology directly with the phonology ancestral to all four groups: Proto-East Caucasian. Because the latter approach takes us back to an earlier chronological stage, it turns out to be simpler as well, and that is the approach we will use. To that end, I introduce the Proto-East Caucasian reconstructed by Nikolayev and Starostin,[78] and look more closely at some of the word comparisons from the above table:

BASQUE AND PROTO-EAST CAUCASIAN

	BASQUE	PROTO-EAST CAUCASIAN
'tears'	*negar, nigar*	**nĕwq̇ŭ*
'beard'	*bizar*	**bilʒV*
'mouse'	*sagu*	**c̄argwɨ*
'bird'	*txori* [čori]	**čHwīlV*
'fire'	*su*	**c̆ăjɨ*
'soot'	*kedar*	**q̇idV*
'star'	*izar*	**ʒwăhr*
'hunger'	*gose*	**gašē*
'old'	*zahar*	**swĕrho*
'thread'	*hari, hal-*	**χātV*

Some of the most obvious correspondences are already shown in **bold** type. These are the correspondences of *identical* sounds (**n = n, b = b, i = i, a = a, g = g, d = d, r = r, e = e, s = s, h = h, l = l**),[79] and sometimes these are called "trivial" correspondences, though scientifically a "trivial" correspondence is just as probative as the "non-trivial" correspondences we will look at below.

---

[78] A North Caucasian Etymological Dictionary, Moscow: Asterisk Press, 1994.

[79] Here vowels are considered equivalent, whether long or short. (In standard Basque and most of its dialects there is no vowel length contrast.) Basque z is considered equivalent to Caucasian *s, since Basque z is an unvoiced sound [s] equivalent to s in most European languages.

For the scientific test we are performing here, it is necessary to show that correspondences are not just unique occurrences (that could be due to chance), but are *recurrent,* just like the Indo-Hittite correspondences:

e.g., Sanskrit **bh** = Greek **ph** = Latin *f* = Germanic, Persian, Welsh *b*; Sanskrit, Latin, Germanic *s* = Greek, Persian, Welsh *h*; etc.

Some explanatory notes will be helpful before we continue. Traditionally, the Basque language is divided into seven or eight major provincial dialects (with common abbreviations in parentheses): Alava or Araba (extinct), Bizkaian (B), Gipuzkoan (G), High Navarrese (= alto-navarro: AN), Lapurdian (= labourdin: L), Low Navarrese (= bas-navarrais: BN), and Zuberoan (= souletin: Z). Three other distinctive dialects are or were spoken in the southeastern corner of Basque country: Salazarese, Aezkoan, and Roncalese (R). The three dialects spoken north of the French-Spanish border (L, BN, Z) are phonetically distinctive in that the phoneme *h* is still sounded in words such as *hari* 'thread' and *zahar* 'old'. In addition, these same dialects have aspirated consonants such as *kh* in *khedar* 'soot' and *lh* in *ilhar* 'peas.' In the other dialects, there is no aspiration at all and the cited words are pronounced as [ari], [šaar] or [šar], [keðar], and [ilar] or [iʎar]. In the comparisons below, the northern forms with *h* are usually cited.

Just in the ten comparisons above, three of the correspondences are already recurrent (**a** = **a**, **g** = **g**, and **r** = **r**), but for more verification we will have to turn to other Basque-Caucasian comparisons. First we'll look at Basque **n** = East Caucasian *****n*:

Basque *negar, nigar* 'weeping, tears' = PEC *$*n̆ĕwq̆ŭ$* 'tears, pus'

Basque *negu* 'winter' = PEC *$*\gamma wĭn?V$* 'winter, summer'

Basque *nahi* 'will, willingness, desire' = PEC *$*?nVhV̆$* 'shame, fright'

Basque *itain* 'tick' = PEC *$*ṭaHnā$* 'nit'

Basque *ar(h)an* 'plum, sloe' = PEC *$*\gamma ōn?V$* 'pear'

More comparisons could be cited, but these five should be sufficient for the present purpose. For **b** = ***b** we can cite:

Basque *bizar* 'beard' = PEC *$*bilʒ́V$* 'beard'

Basque *bihar* 'tomorrow' = PEC *$*b\wedge g\wedge$* 'morning, evening'
 (Rutul *biga* 'tomorrow')

Basque *belhar* 'forehead' = PEC **bɬāthŏ* 'edge, end' (Rutul *bäl* 'forehead')

Basque *behi* 'cow' = PEC **bħ^rc̣wV* 'cattle' (Avar *bóts'ts'i*)

Basque *bekho, beko, beko*-ki 'forehead' = PEC **bĕḳwo* 'part of face, mouth'

Basque *bihi* 'grain, seed, kernel' = PEC **bħĕlčinV* 'a kind of cereal'

i = *i can be verified by numerous examples, some of which are:

Basque *bizar* 'beard' = PEC **bilʒ́V* 'beard'
Basque *hil* 'dead; die; kill' = PEC **=iwλĔ* 'die; kill'
Basque *bi-zi* 'life, alive' = PEC **s̱ɨHwV* 'breath, breathe'
Basque *zikiro* 'castrated ram' = PEC **ǯɨkV̆* 'goat, kid'
Basque *hitz* 'word' = PEC **=[ɨ]mcŪ* 'speak, tell, talk'
Basque *tipi* 'little, small' = PEC **ṭiHV / *HiṭV* 'small, little'

a = *a, besides the words for 'mouse', 'star', and 'thread' in the table, there are again numerous additional examples, some of which are:

Basque *udagara* 'otter' = PEC **darq̇wV* 'weasel, marten, ermine'
Basque *sabel* 'belly, stomach' = PEC **ǯăbV* 'kidney, liver'
Basque *lasto* 'straw' = PEC **λačă* 'leaf; a kind of plant'
Basque *lamika*-tu 'to lick' = PEC **ɬamV* 'to lick'
Basque *apal* 'shelf' = PEC **ʔapVɬV* 'pole; board, cover'
Basque *gar(h)i* 'thin' = PEC **q̇warHV* 'narrow, thin'

For **g = *g**, besides the words for 'mouse' and 'hunger' in the table, we can cite:

Basque *gal-* 'to lose, corrupt, spoil,' etc. = PEC **=igwVɬ* 'to lose, get lost; steal'
Basque *gurdi* 'cart, wagon,' *gurpil* 'wheel' = PEC **gwērV* 'circle, round, roll'
Basque *egur* 'firewood' = PEC **gōrV* 'pole, piece of log'

For **d = *d**:

Basque *kedar, khedar* 'soot' = PEC **ġidV* 'soot'
Basque *hodei, odei, odai* 'cloud' = PEC **dwiHV* 'wind'
Basque *idulki* 'block of wood, pedestal' = PEC **dwāɦ̄* 'stick' (Ingush *tälg* 'chock')
Basque *lerde, lirdi* 'drivel, saliva' = PEC **ƛwirdɨ* 'manure, pus'

For **r** = **r*, there are again numerous examples. Besides 'star' and 'old' in the table, there are:[80]

Basque *erreka* 'ravine, rivulet, arroyo' = PEC **r̆iġwĂ* 'mountain, rock, cave'
Basque *erbi* 'hare', *erbi*-nude 'weasel' = PEC **r̆igwĂ* 'weasel, mouse'
Basque *herri* 'country, town, people' = PEC **ʔw˘hri* 'army, troops'
Basque *harri* 'stone' = PEC **χHĕr̆χV* 'small stone, gravel'
Basque *egur* 'firewood' = PEC **gōrV* 'pole, piece of log'
Basque *agor* 'dry' = PEC **=iGwĂr* 'dry, to dry'
Basque *har* 'worm' = PEC **fiabarV* 'worm'

For **e** = **e*, we can cite (besides the word for 'hunger' in the table):

Basque *bek(h)o* 'forehead, beak' = PEC **bĕḳwo* 'part of face, mouth'
Basque *leka* 'bean pod, husk' = PEC **lĕḳV* 'seed, grain'
Basque *bel(h)ar* 'grass, hay' = PEC **u̯elγV* 'nettle, burdock'
Basque *erdi* 'half, middle' = PEC **=ĕ/Ĕ* 'half, middle'
Basque *el(h)e* 'speech, word' = PEC **lĕHwV* 'word'
Basque *habe* 'pillar, beam' = PEC **hwĕbē* 'post, pole, tower'
Basque *sare, sale* 'net, grate; stockade' = PEC **čɦaɫē* 'enclosure, fence'

For Basque *z* [š] = **s*, besides the words for 'old':

Basque *zain* 'nerve, blood vessel, root' = PEC **sēɦmV* 'muscle, vein, intestine'
Basque *zeden* 'moth, grub, mite, weevil' = PEC **sindV* 'a kind of insect' (Tsez *zedo* 'moth')

---

[80] By the way, all the Basque examples here contain the trilled rr, as opposed to the single-flap r.

Basque *zer* 'what?', *zein* 'which?', etc. = PEC **s̱āj* 'what'
Basque *izan* 'to be' = PNC **=ā̃sV* 'to sit, stay'
Basque *bi-zi* 'life, alive' = PEC **s̱ĭHwV* 'breath, breathe'
Basque *hezur, ezur* 'bone' = PEC **rīmswe (~ *mswīre)* 'rib, side'

Besides the words for 'old', the correspondence **h** = **h* is found in:

Basque (Z) *hün* 'marrow, brain', etc. = PEC **ḫwĕʔnV* 'blood'
Basque *haga* 'long pole' = PEC **ḫăkwV* 'bush, branch, sprout'
Basque *habe* 'pillar, beam' = PEC **ḫwĕbē* 'post, pole'
Basque *nahi* 'will, willingness, desire, wish' = PEC **ʔnVḫV* 'shame, fright'
Basque *arhe, are* 'harrow' = PEC **γarhV* 'harrow'
Basque *ilhar (ilar)* 'vetch, peas, beans' = PEC **hōwɫ[ā]* 'bean(s), lentil(s)'

For **l** = **l*, besides the words for 'thread', there are:[81]
Basque *leka* 'bean pod, husk' = PEC **lĕkV* 'seed, grain'
Basque *apal* 'shelf' = PEC **ʔapVɫV* 'pole; board, cover'
Basque *txahal* [čahal], *xahal* [šahal], etc. 'calf' = PEC **Hc̣wɨlV / *Hlɨ̄c̣wV* 'heifer, calf'
Basque *(h)utsal* 'transient, ephemeral, trifling', (Z) *ütsal* 'dry, barren, sterile' = PEC **=Hīc̣Ă̌l* 'naked, bare'
Basque *gal-* 'to lose, corrupt, spoil', etc. = PEC **=igwVɫ* 'to lose, get lost; steal'
Basque *idulki* 'block of wood, pedestal' = PEC **dwāɫɨ* 'stick'
Basque *belhar* 'forehead' = PEC **b ɟ ā̄ɫhŏ* 'edge, end' (Rutul *bül* 'forehead')
Basque *belhar* 'grass, hay' = PEC **u̯elγV* 'nettle, burdock'
Basque *elhe* 'speech, word' = PEC **lĕHwV* 'word'
Basque *ilhar, ilar* 'vetch, peas, beans' = PEC **hōwɫ[ā]* 'bean(s), lentil(s)'
Basque *alha* 'grazing, pasture'; *alha-tu* 'to graze, to feed' = PEC **=iʔwVl* 'to feed on, eat, bite'

---

[81] PEC **š* was probably an allophone (positional variant) of **l*. In this list the northern Basque forms (e.g., *belhar* 'grass, hay') are cited rather than the less conservative forms (*belar, bedar*) that have lost original *h*.

Basque *bulhar* 'chest, breast' = PEC **Gwălħē* 'udder, breast'
Basque *ilhe* 'hair' ('wool' in Z) = PEC **ʔālχV* 'wool'
Basque *zelai* 'field, meadow' = PEC **ʒ^lV* 'plain, plateau'
Basque *bele, bela* 'crow, raven'; *belatz* 'sparrow hawk' = PEC **GHwV̄ɬV* 'crow, jackdaw'
Basque *zulo* 'hole' = PEC **s̱wōɫV* 'pipe, tube'

By now, you may have noticed that some of the same comparisons have been used more than once. In fact, eight of the **l** = **l* comparisons have already been used above to verify other correspondences. The 'forehead' comparison has appeared three times (for **b, l,** and **h**). We have also seen the comparison involving Basque *zahar* 'old,' which shows three correspondences (**s, h, r**), and others like this will be noted as we proceed with this test. These are good signs for the proposed Vasco-Caucasian family, because it means that the same Basque word may contain more than one recurrent correspondence with East Caucasian.

Now that we have dealt with all the "trivial" correspondences, and shown that they are recurrent, we will proceed with the "non-trivial" correspondences, that is, correspondences of *unlike* sounds. The first of these was seen in the 'tears' comparison, Basque *negar, nigar* = PEC **nĕwq̇ŭ,* where *q̇* was a **glottalized uvular stop.** Other examples include:

Basque *garhi, gari* 'thin' = PEC **q̇warHV* 'narrow, thin'
Basque *gai, gei* 'material, subject,' (archaic) 'thing' = PEC **q̇wăjē* 'thing(s), possession(s)'
Basque *egun* (*egu-, egur-*) 'day' = PEC **Hwīq̇V* 'day'
Basque *egin* 'to do, make' (also auxiliary verb) = PEC **=Hŏq̇E* 'to do, make, be, become'
Basque (BN) *jaugin* 'to come' = PEC **=Huq̇Ŭn* 'to go, come'

Here we come to our first split correspondence – cases in which the same East Caucasian phoneme corresponds sometimes to one Basque phoneme (**g**), in other cases to another (Basque **k**), as we saw in the word for 'soot': Basque *kedar* = PEC **q̇idV.* Other examples of **k** = **q̇* include:

Basque (Z) *kharats* 'bitter, sour', (R) *karats* 'bitter', (BN) *karats* 'stench'[82] = PEC

---
[82] The dialects referred to are Z = Zuberoan, R = Roncalese, BN = Basse Navarre.

*q̇ĕḥlV 'bitter'

Basque *kokots, kokotz*, '(point of) chin; snout' = PEC *q̇ăčɨ́ (> Rutul, Tsakhur *q'ats* 'chin')

Basque *ikusi* 'to see' = PEC *=Hārq̇V(n)- 'to see, find'

Basque *akain, akan* '(large) tick' = PEC *q̇ā̃nʔV 'louse, nit, worm'

Basque *jakin* 'to know (a fact)' (< *e-aki-n*) = PEC *=ĭq̇E 'to know, hear'

So we have at least six comparisons where Basque **g** = PEC *q̇*, and at least six where Basque **k** = PEC *q̇* correspond. This is a problem for future study, and we will either eventually find some conditioning factor that determines whether Basque has **g** or **k**, or we could find that PEC *q̇* derives from two originally different phonemes, and Basque reflects the older state of affairs. We will see other split correspondences as we proceed, usually in which Basque (with a simpler phonetic system) has one phoneme corresponding to more than one phoneme in the complex Caucasian system.

The next "non-trivial" correspondence was seen in the word for 'beard': Basque *bizar* = PEC *bilʒ́V. (PEC *ʒ́ was a sibilant affricate, rather similar to the consonants in Eng. judge.) Additional examples of *z* [s] = ʒ́ include:

Basque *zur*, (Bizk.) *zul* 'wood, timber, lumber' = PEC *ʒ́w[ĕ]ḥ 'twig, rod, sheaf'

Basque *hazi* 'to grow, cultivate, bring up; seed; semen' = PEC *=Vʒ́V 'to grow'

The 'bird' comparison, Basque *txori* [čori] = PEC *čHwīlV, shows the correspondence Basque č (written *tx*) = PEC *č̣, for which additional examples are:[83]

Basque (Z) *txainku* [čã́jŋkü], (G) *txanket* [čaŋket] 'lame' = PEC *č̣ãnkV 'trap'[84]

Basque (c) *txeme* [čeme] 'span of thumb and index finger' = PEC *č̣wimħV 'span'

---

[83] For each of these words some Basque dialects have the fricative [š]: *xori* [šori] 'bird,' *xanku* 'lame,' *xeme, xehume* 'demi-empan.'

[84] The semantic link is that an animal that is trapped is made lame.

The 'bird' comparison also shows a correspondence Basque **r** = PEC **l (*ł)*. However, a page or two earlier we saw a correspondence of Basque **l** = PEC **l (*ł)*, verified by no fewer than sixteen comparisons. If you (naturally) ask "which is correct?," the answer is: both are! The reason for this seemingly ambiguous answer is that these are splendid examples of conditioned reflexes – phonetic changes that produce two or more different results, depending on the phonetic environment in the word, or on morphological factors. Here I will list more examples of the correspondence Basque **r** = PEC **l*, and see if you can discover the conditioning factors:

Basque *ur,* (Z) *hur* 'water' = PEC **ħwĭlV* 'river, reservoir'
Basque *zur,* (Bizk. *zul*) 'wood, timber, lumber' = PEC **ʒw[ĕ]łĭ* 'twig, rod, sheaf'
Basque *kharats* 'bitter, sour' = PEC **q̇ĕħlV* 'bitter'
Basque *erdara* 'foreign (language)' / (combinatory form) *erdal-* = PEC **Ł̣ōlV* 'guest, neighbor'
Basque *sare,* (Bizk.*sale*) 'net, grate; stockade' = PEC **čħałē* 'enclosure, fence'
Basque *hari* / (combinatory form) *hal-* 'thread' ~ PEC **χā̇łV* 'thread'
Basque *gari* 'wheat' / (combinatory form) *gal-* = PEC **g̱ōl?e* 'wheat'
Basque *ugari* 'abundant' / *ugal-du* 'to increase, multiply' = PEC **Hā̇χułV* 'long'
Basque *azeri* 'fox' / (combinatory form) *azel-* = PEC **cEhwōĺe*
Basque *txori* [čori] 'bird' / combinatory form *txol-* = PEC **čHwī lV* 'small bird'
Basque *zorhi, zori* 'ripe, to ripen; fortune, luck,' etc., (Bizk.) *zoli* 'to mature, ripen; nimble, lively; omen' = PEC **ʒōłV* 'healthy, whole'

Could you spot the difference between this list and the earlier list for Basque **l** = PEC **l (*ł)*? In the first list Basque **l** was either (a) initial position in the word (*leka*), (b) in final position in a polysyllabic word (*apal, txahal, hutsal*), (c) at a morpheme boundary (*gal-*), (d) before a consonant (usually *k* or *h*), or (e) between vowels in the sequences *ele, ela,* or *ulo*. In the second list (immediately above), Basque **r** appears (a) in absolute final position in a monosyllabic word (*ur, zur*), or (b) between vowels in the sequences *ara, are, ari, eri*, or *ori (orhi)*. When these rules are taken into consideration, the correspondences turn out to be regular, after all.

Note also that some of the Basque words in the second list have a variant with l (for example, *hari* 'thread' beside *hal-gai* 'fabric,' *txori* 'bird' beside *txol-arre* 'sparrow'). Here the normal variant follows the rule for **r** = **l (*ł),* while the combinatory variant follows the other rule (**l** = **l (*ł)*), because the l immediately precedes a morpheme boundary. Note also that Bizkaian dialects often have **l**-forms where other Basque dialects have **r**-forms (for example, Bizk. *sale* vs. common Basque *sare*).

Conditioned reflexes are also apparent in comparisons involving PEC **c̣* = [ts'], a glottalized sibilant affricate. In our original table we had the comparison: Basque *su* 'fire' = PEC **c̆ăjɨ* 'fire'. A similar correspondence (Basque *s* or *ts* = PEC **c̣*) also holds in the following cases:

> Basque *atso* 'old woman' = PEC **c̣wŏjV* 'woman, female'
> Basque *otso* 'wolf' = PNC **bħĕrc̣ĭ* 'wolf'
> Basque *huts* 'empty; zero, nought, absence, fault, mistake,' (c) *hutsal, utsal* 'transient, ephemeral, trifling', (Z) *ütsal* 'dry, barren, sterile' = PEC **=Hĭc̣Ăl* 'naked, bare'
> Basque *oso* 'whole, complete, entire; totally, very' = PEC **=ɦŏc̣V* 'full, fill'
> Basque *toska* '(fine white) clay' = PEC **tħiVrc̣wV* 'dirt, bog'

However, in some other cases PEC **c̣* matches with Basque *z* or *tz*:

> Basque *zamar* 'fleece, shorn wool', etc. = PEC **c̣ħiwĕme* 'eyebrow'
> Basque *ziho* 'fat, tallow' = PEC **c̣ēnx̱wV* 'fat' (adj)
> Basque *ezagu*-tu 'to know (a person)' = PEC **c̣EnχV(n)* 'to search, ask'
> Basque *etzan* 'to lie down, rest, put down' = PEC **=ic̣Ă* 'to give, put'
> Basque *haitz, aitz* 'rock, stone' = PEC **ɦəmVc̣ŏ* 'stone'

The conditioning rules can be set forth as follows: PEC **c̣* corresponds to Basque dorso-alveolars /s̄/ (orthographic z) or /A/ (orthographic tz) before or after non-rounded vowels /a, e, i/ (except when a- is a fossilized prefix. as in a-tso 'old woman'); PEC *ç corresponds to Basque apico-alveolar /ś/ or /B/ (orthographic s or ts) before or after rounded vowels /o, u/.

The next correspondence is found in the 'star' comparison: Basque *izar* 'star' = PEC *ʒwăhrī* 'star'. The correspondence z [s] = *ʒ (a sound similar to [dz]) is also found in the following sets:

> Basque *zuzen* 'straight, correct, right, honest' = PEC *HăʒĔm* 'clean' ('pure' or 'good' in some languages)
> Basque *zik(h)iro* 'castrated ram' = PEC *ʒĭkV̆* 'goat, kid'
> Basque **zinagurri* 'ant' > (Lapurdian) *zinaurri* = PEC *ʒHĔmVḳĂ* 'ant'
> Basque *zelai* 'field, meadow' = PEC *ʒəlV* 'plain, plateau'
> Basque *zimitz, zimintza* 'bedbug' = PEC *miʒĂ̆* / *ʒimiʒĂ̆* 'stinging insect'
> Basque *zorhi, zori* 'ripe, to ripen; fortune, luck', (Bizk.) *zoli* 'to mature, ripen; nimble,
>   lively; omen' = PEC *ʒōɫV* 'healthy, whole'

Yet another correspondence is found in the words for 'hunger': Basque *gose* = PEC *gašē*. The correspondence s [ś] = *š can be verified by the following:

> Basque *sits* 'moth' = PEC *šwĕʒV* 'a kind of biting insect'
> Basque *pus-pulu* 'bubble' = PEC *päršwA* 'bubble, bladder'
> Basque *beso* 'arm' = PEC *wŭšV* or *bŭšV* 'finger, hand'
> Basque *-sa-/-so* (elements denoting kinship, as in *o-sa-ba* 'uncle,' *gura-so* 'parent,' *alaba-so* 'granddaughter,' etc.) = PEC *=ĭšwĔ* 'son / daughter'

Finally, let us consider the initial correspondence in the words for 'thread': Basque *hari, hal-* = PEC *χāɫV*. PEC *χ was a throaty fricative (uvular), farther back than ch in German *Bach* or Scots *loch*. The correspondence **h** = *χ is abundantly attested:

> Basque *harri* 'stone' = PEC *χHĕrχV* 'small stone, gravel'

Basque *hartz* 'bear,' (Z) *haz*-kű 'badger' = PEC *$\chi HVr[\acute{c}]V$ 'marten, otter'

Basque *ohe* 'bed' = PEC *=$a\chi Vr$ 'to fall, lie' (> Tabasaran *aχin* 'bed', Agul *aχun* 'mattress')

Basque *oihal* 'cloth, fabric' = PEC *$\chi w\breve{\imath}l\underline{L}\,V$ 'clothes'
Basque *eho* 'to grind', *eihera* 'mill' = PEC *$H\breve{e}m\chi wV$ 'to grind'
Basque *eho* 'to beat' = PEC *$H\bar{\imath}r\chi A$ 'to beat, hit, throw'
Basque *ilhe* 'hair' ('wool' in Z) = PEC *$?\bar{a}l\chi V$ 'wool'

We saw above that Basque *h* also corresponds to PEC *h, so this is a phonetic merger, in which two originally distinct sounds merge into one. Phonetic mergers are very common in historical linguistics. For example, in Danish, Swedish, Norwegian, and Faroese, the old *th* sound (a voiceless dental fricative) has merged with the ordinary *t* sound, while *th* (written in Icelandic and Old English) and *t* are still distinct in Icelandic and English. Swedish *tråd* 'thread,' *tre* 'three,' *tunn* 'thin' have the same initial consonant as *träd* 'tree' and *tenn* 'tin,' so we can say that old *þ* and *t* have merged as *t*.

Using a comparative table of ten Basque words and ten Caucasian words as a "springboard," we have managed to discover a significant number of recurrent Basque-(East) Caucasian correspondences, which may be summarized as follows. Because Proto-East Caucasian has the more complex phonetic system, it is placed to the left:

PROTO-EAST CAUCASIAN AND BASQUE EQUIVALENT

	PROTO-EAST CAUCASIAN	BASQUE EQUIVALENT
Plosives	*b	b
	*d	d
	*g	g
	*ᵃ	g / k (conditioned?)
Fricatives	*s	z [s]
	*š	s [ś]
	*h	h (silent in southern Basque)
	*χ	h (silent in southern Basque)
Affricates	*c	z [s] / s [ś] (conditioned)
	*ʒ	z [s]
	*ǯ	z [s]

	*č̣	tx [č]
Resonants	*n	n
	*l	l / r (conditioned)
	*r	rr
Vowels	*a	a
	*e	e
	*i	i

Note that this is not the complete table of correspondences – it only concerns the correspondences found in the original table of ten words. A complete table would account for all the other PEC consonants (***p, *t, *k, *m, *w**, etc.) and vowels (***o, *u, *ü**). But even this much is enough to show that the lexical parallels between Basque and East Caucasian are not chance resemblances, but real cognates.

That was the **phonological test**, and the result was positive for the genetic relationship of Basque and East Caucasian. Next, we will begin the **morphological test**, to see if the grammatical systems of these languages can be traced to a common origin.[85] A good place to begin would be the **pronouns**:

Basque *ni* 'I': cf. Lak *na* 'I,' Dargwa (Akushi dialect) *nu* 'I,' *nu-ša* 'we.' (Most Caucasian languages have a different stem for 'I,' reconstructed as **zō* by Nikolayev & Starostin.)

Basque *hi* 'thou' (familiar second-person singular); *h-* second person singular agreement prefix on verbs (e.g., *h-ator* 'you're coming'); *-k* < **-ga* second person singular agreement suffix (e.g., *daki-k* 'you know it') : cf. EC: Chechen, Ingush, Batsbi *ħo* 'thou', Dargwa (Akushi, Urakhi) *ħu,* (Chirag) *ʕu* 'thou,' Tsakhur *ɢu* 'thou,' Udi (Nidzh dial.) *hu*-n 'thou,' Khinalug *oχ* 'thee' (dative), etc. < PEC **ɢwV / *ʔŏɢwV* (ɢ or γ ̎ is/was a throaty uvular fricative, somewhat similar to the Parisian *r*).

Basque *zu* 'you' (polite second-person singular): cf. Chechen, Ingush, Batsbi *šu* 'you' (plural)', Lak *zu* 'you' (pl.), Tsakhur *šu,* Khinalug *zu-r* 'you' (pl.), etc. < PEC **źwĕ* 'you' (pl.); a cognate pronoun is also found in West Caucasian: cf. Abkhaz *šá-ra* 'you'

---

[85] This section owes much to the manuscript "North Caucasian Morphology," by S.A. Starostin.

(pl.). It is well known that Basque *zu* was originally a plural pronoun,[86] like its Caucasian cognates. Modern Basque has created a new second-person plural, *zuek,* to fill the gap left by the old plural.

Basque *gu* 'we' is mysterious. Khinalug has *kin* 'we' (inclusive), but Nikolayev & Starostin trace it (and other East Caucasian cognates) back to a proto-form with a lateral fricative, PEC **L...* 'we' (inclusive).[87]

Only western Basque dialects have third-person pronouns: *bera* 'he/she,' *berak* or *eurak* 'they.'[88] Other dialects use demonstratives for this purpose.

In regard to the declension of nouns, Basque has (among others) the following case endings, illustrated by the word *hitz* 'word':[89]

DECLENSIONS OF BASQUE NOUNS

Absolutive	*hitz* '(a) word'	*hitz-a* 'the word'
Ergative	*hitz-ek* 'word'	*hitz-a-k* 'the word'
Dative	*hitz-i* '(to a) word'	*hitz-a-r-i* '(to) the word'
Instrumental	*hitz-ez* '(by a) word'	*hitz-a-z* '(by) the word'
Genitive	*hitz-en* '(of a) word'	*hitz-a-r-en* '(of) the word'
Locative	*hitz-eta-n* '(in a) word'	*hitz-ea-n* '(in) the word'
Allative	*hitz-eta-ra* '(to a) word'	*hitz-er-a* '(to) the word'

Some of the case endings have likely cognates in the Caucasian languages:

(1) Basque **absolutive** –0 (no ending): All the Caucasian languages also lack any ending for the **nominative (absolutive)** case. (This is not universal. In Indo-European, for example, many nouns [mainly masculine or feminine] have the nominative ending *–s*.)

---
[86] Trask (1997, p. 196).
[87] *Inclusive* 'we' includes the person addressed = 'you and I'; *exclusive* 'we' = 'he (or she or they) and I'. Many languages outside of Europe have distinctive forms for both concepts.
[88] Trask (1997, p. 96).
[89] See Trask (1997, pp. 92-96) for a detailed description of the Basque cases.

(2) Basque dative –*i*: Nikolayev and Starostin reconstruct the East Caucasian dative as *-*Hi*, which manifests as Avar –*e* (dative), Hunzib –*i* (dative), etc. In some languages the case function has shifted to instrumental (Lak, Dargwa), or ergative (Dargwa, Khinalug).

(3) Basque instrumental –*z*: Nikolayev and Starostin reconstruct Proto-Caucasian *-*s*- instrumental animate; general attributive, though in most of the modern languages this ending has shifted to other closely related functions: Chechen –*sa* (ergative animate), Lak –*ssa* (attributive suffix: adjectives and participles), Lezgi –*z* (dative, infinitive), Abkhaz –*s* (transformative/adverbial case), etc.[90]

(4) Basque genitive –*en*: Proto-Caucasian genitive *-*nV*, attested as Lezgi –*n* (genitive), Chechen –n (genitive, infinitive, adjective and participial suffix), Ubykh –*na* (possessive case), etc. In some languages, the function has shifted to ablative (Avar), ergative (Udi, Ubykh), etc. Dumézil (1933) thought Basque genitive –*en* and locative (inessive) –*n* went back to the same original case ending.

(5) Basque allative –*ra*: cf. Chechen –*l, -lla* (translative), Tsez –*r* (dative, lative), Khinalug –*li* (general locative), etc. (See above for the relationship of Basque *r* and Caucasian **l*.) The terms "allative" and "lative" are generally equivalent, expressing the goal of a motion.

QUESTION WORDS (INTERROGATIVES):

Basque has two main stems for interrogatives:

(1) *ze- : zer* 'what?,' *zein* 'which?,' *zelan* 'how?,' *zerga(i)tik* 'why?,' in some cases *ze* can be used by itself (Bizkaian *ze barri?* 'What (is) new?').

(2) *no- : nor* 'who?,' *noiz* 'when?,' *non, nun* 'where?,' *nola* 'how?,' etc.

---

[90] The function in Abkhaz "probably confirms the reconstruction of an original instrumental meaning; the instrumental case is often used with a transformative sense, e.g. in Russian" (Diakonoff & Starostin 1986, p. 75). This reconstructed meaning was made without any reference to Basque.

In the Caucasian languages, a primary interrogative root is *ṣāy, which gives rise to words such as Ingush *se,* Avar *ssun-,* Lak *ssa-,* Dargwa (Akushi dialect) *se,* Ubykh *sa* 'what?.' There is also a Proto-Caucasian interrogative base *hīnV, from which we get words such as Lezgi *ni* 'who?' (erg.), Andi *innal* 'when?,' *inul* 'where?,' Bezhta *nito* 'when?,' *nā* 'where?,' etc. Note the similar formation of Basque *non* 'where?' and Tabasaran *naʔan* (*na'an*) 'where?.'

NEGATIVE MORPHEME: Negation in Basque is expressed by the particle *ez*, for example, *ez noa etxera* 'I'm not going home':

ez	n-oa	etxe-ra
not	I-go	house-to
NEG	1PERS-VB	NOUN-allative

Basque *ez* has a variant *ze* in the Bizkaian dialect, but only with subjunctive and imperative verbs, for example *ausi ze-daizun* '… that you don't break (it).'[91]

A similar negative morpheme is found in the East Caucasian languages, for example Chechen *tsa* 'not,' Avar *–č'o* 'not', Bezhta *–eč'e* 'not', Lezgi *–č* (negative particle with past tense). In Chechen (and Ingush and Batsbi) *tsa (ca)* is still a separate word, as in Basque, but in the other languages it has become a suffix (sometimes combined with other negative morphemes).

So what can we conclude about the validity of the proposed language family that includes Basque and the Caucasian languages? Basque words that are similar to Caucasian words have been found and remarked upon by linguists for over a century. But this in itself is not enough to firmly establish a language family. It is further necessary to show that there is a *systematic* or *patterned* relationship between the sounds of the languages compared, and this was exemplified by the phonetic correspondences we outlined in some detail above.

The linguist Ilia Peiros suggests a "working definition of genetic relationship. Languages are genetically related if:

1) there is a sufficient number of comparisons consisting of [lexical] resemblances found in these languages;

---

[91] See Trask (1997, p. 209). The variant *ze* is found only in early Bizkaian texts, and is still spoken in some Bizkaian villages (Bermeo, Gernika, Mundaka, Plenzia), according to the Basque lexicographer Azkue.

2) it can be demonstrated that these comparisons are etymologies in the strict sense and not borrowings or chance similarities. As the only accepted way to demonstrate the genetic nature of a comparison is to show that its resemblances are connected by systematic phonological correspondences ..., a list of ... correspondences is another necessary element for proof of genetic relationship."[92]

Later in his article, Peiros also mentions that "[f]or the families with old morphology we should also be able to reconstruct common grammatical morphemes on the basis of comparisons between daughter language grammatical morphemes."[93] I would add this as a third characteristic of genetic relationship. For example, when the classification of the Hittite language was being discussed about a century ago, the fact that Hittite had an alternation of the grammatical morphemes *r* and *n*, as in (nominative) *watar* 'water' vs. (genitive) *wetenas*, was one of the decisive features that finally convinced linguists that Hittite was indeed Indo-European in character. In regard to Basque and Caucasian, the concordance of dative –*i*, instrumental –*s*, and genitive –*n* in both families is a comparable bundle of features that is highly unlikely to have come about by chance.

So to summarize, languages that are genetically related have:

I. a significant number of basic words of common origin (*cognates*);

II. *recurrent phonological correspondences* embedded in the cognate sets; and

III. *grammatical morphemes* of common origin.

In the case of Basque and the Caucasian languages, all three criteria have been met. I suggest that there is no longer any basis to the claim that there is "not the slightest shred of evidence" that Basque is related to the Caucasian languages.

---

[92] Peiros (1997, p. 272).

[93] Peiros (1997, p. 272, footnote 5) mentions that he does not mention grammatical morphemes as a criterion, mainly because of his extensive work with Southeast Asian languages, where "developed grammatical systems" are rare. The same caveat would also apply to languages in other parts of the world where grammatical morphemes are rare or nonexistent. For such languages, the lexical and phonological criteria are all that can be used.

A GENETIC COMPARISON OF BASQUE AND CAUCASIAN VOCABULARY

Scientists who are not linguists may be surprised to learn that there are scientific methods for determining the *genetic* classification of a language or set of languages. The *genetic* classification or affiliation of a language is understood as that of its core or kernel. For example, English has many words "borrowed" (the usual linguistic term) from French, Old Norse, and other languages, but its *core* element is derived from Anglo-Saxon, and thus English is genetically a Germanic language, and closest to Frisian, Dutch, German, etc.

The brilliant paleo-linguist Morris Swadesh devised the method known as *glottochronology* for measuring the time-depth of linguistic relationships. Since historical linguists have found that languages which are closely related (such as Dutch and German) share many words in common, and languages that are more distantly related (say, Dutch and Russian, or Dutch and Greek) share fewer words with the same origin and meaning, it should be possible to quantify, at least roughly, the amount of core vocabulary shared by any two languages, and therefore to measure the degree of relationship, and also the time-depth of their divergence. Swadesh's method was based on "a vocabulary turnover process analogous to radioactive decay" (Embleton 1986: 43). Swadesh assumed that the rate of vocabulary replacement, or *morpheme decay,* was constant over time, so that it could be quantified in the way Carbon-14 decay is used to quantify the age of organic matter.

Glottochronology, according to the classic method devised by Swadesh, is not done by comparing just *any* words in any two or more languages, but by focusing on the words that are known to be the most stable, and historically resistant to change over time. "The model claims that a test-list of N meanings can be constructed which are likely to be found in all cultures ... now generally known as a *Swadesh-list* ..." (Embleton, *ibid.*) The meanings on this list are those which are universal to human experience and everyday life, for example, 'belly, bone, foot, earth, fire, water, star, man, woman,' etc. Words such as 'table' and 'chair' (for example, in English, both words come from French) pass easily from language to language, but words like 'bone, water, woman' are demonstrably far more resistant to borrowing (in English, for example, these latter three words are still of Anglo-Saxon origin). Linguists have determined which of these types of words comprise the 100 and 200 (more or less) most basic (stable, or core) words, and have compiled rosters commonly known as the "Swadesh 100-word list," with many later modifications.

The following study of Basque and Caucasian vocabulary is modified from an earlier study published in *Mother Tongue* (volume V, 1999). The objective of this study is not to make a precise glottochronological calculation, but to use the Swadesh-list of Basque words provided by Trask (1997) as a basis for comparison with attested Caucasian words and the reconstructed Caucasian forms posited by Nikolayev & Starostin (1994) and Chirikba (1996). By focusing on the most stable (core) meanings in these languages, there is a greater chance of finding words that may be cognate (of common origin) in both languages, than if one compared words at random. In the *Mother Tongue* article, I concluded that the word comparison confirmed many earlier proposals of genetic connection between Basque and Caucasian, because I found about a 21% correlation between Basque and Caucasian basic vocabulary. According to Swadesh, 12-36% of retention is typical of a linguistic stock with about 25 to 30 centuries of divergence, and a relationship that should be "obvious to the linguist." I concluded that "Basque and the (North) Caucasian language[s] have a significant amount of basic vocabulary in common, and ... this evidence points in the direction of a genetic relationship."

The tables below summarize the lexical evidence for these conclusions. The first table (Table 1) is the most conclusive, since (a) the semantic equations are precise (e.g., Basque *mihi* 'tongue' = Tindi *mic:i* 'tongue,' etc.), and (b) the Caucasian words cited are traceable to Proto-Caucasian, not just one subfamily or one language.

The evidence cited in Table 2 is somewhat less conclusive, since (a) some of the semantic equations are inexact (e.g., Basque sabel 'belly' = Bezhta šebo liver'), and/or (b) some of the Caucasian words are restricted to East Caucasian (PEC), West Caucasian (PWC), or even a single language (e.g., Basque *hertze* 'guts' = Avar ʕorčo / ʕarča- 'guts', etc.).

BASQUE, CAUCASIAN, AND CAUCASIAN RECONSTRUCTION I:

In the following table, the meanings of the Basque words are the same as the Caucasian words compared (semantic exactness), and the

Caucasian words are common to both West Caucasian and East Caucasian, thus traceable to Proto-Caucasian. In the table, the first column consists of the English gloss. The second column is the Basque word of the same meaning, first as a proto-Basque reconstruction, second as the common literary forms (e.g. **hoc* 'cold,' literary forms *hotz* and *otz*).[94] The third column contains a representative present-day Caucasian word (or words), and the fourth column has the Proto-Caucasian (PNC) reconstruction by Nikolayev & Starostin.

Meaning	Basque word	Caucasian: Representative word	Caucasian: Reconstruction
'cold'	**hoc* = hotz, otz	H. -*oč'č'u*	**rHEčwV*
'come'	**e-augi-n* = jaugin	A. -*áʕn-*	**huq̇Un*
'die'	**hil* = hil, il	K. -*ilʔ-*	**-iwʎE*
'dog'	**hor* = or, hor	B. χor	**χwěje*
'dry'	**agoṝ* = agor	A. -*aq'ʷːara-*	**-iGwAr*
'ear'	**be-laṝi* = belarri, beharri[95]	C. *lerg ~ lerig ~ larig*	**łĕHɨ*
'earth'	**luṝ* = lur	A. *ratl'ː*	**lhĕmʎwɨ*
'eye'	**be-gi* = begi	C. *bʕärg*	**ʔwīlʔi*
'fire'	**śu* = su	L. *ts'u*	**c'ăjɨ*
'fall' (verb)	**e-rori* = erori	L. *tːiri*-xːi-	**HrałwE*
'know' (a fact)	**e-akin* = jakin	Ak. -*eq'-*	**-ïq̇E*
'old'	**sahaṝ* = zahar	Lz. *sur*	**swĕrho*
'sister'	**a-his-* = ahizpa, aizta 'sister (of a woman)'	Bz. *isi* 'sister', *is* 'brother'	**-ićī* 'brother/sister'

---

[94] Aspiration /h/ is commonly lost in the southern (Spanish) dialects of Basque but retained in the northern (French) dialects. Standard Basque (Euskara Batua) restores the /h/ in written form, but h-less forms are still commonly seen.

[95] Northern Basque *beharri* has been influenced by the verb *beha-* 'listen, look.'

Meaning	Basque word	Caucasian: Representative word	Caucasian: Reconstruction
'sit'	*e-aŕi = jarri	Ts. ǵ-i-ʔar	*-eʔ(w)Vr
'skin'	*asa-l = azal 'skin, bark'	Ab. čʷa 'skin, bark'	*ʔwā̆rćwə
'sleep'	*lo = lo (egin)	Ak. tl':unu-	*-HVƛ̱wAn
'small'	*ti- = tipi, ttipi	A. hi-t'ína-b	*t̞iHV / *Hit̞V
'squeeze'	*herći = hertsi	R. -ir(i)č'a-	*HičAn
'star'	*i-saŕ = izar	T. ts:aru	*ʒwă̄hrī̆
'that'	*hori 'that' (mesial) *hura 'that' (distal)	K. ho- Ak. hu-	*hu
'thou'	*su = zu 'thou' (unmarked) < 'you' (pl.)	C. šu 'you' (pl.) L. zu "	*źwĕ
'tongue'	*minhi = mihi, mii, mi	T. mits:i	*mē̆lc̱ǐ
'two'	*bi = bi	U. p:a̱	*q̇Hwā̃
'what?'	*se-r = zer	I. se	*s̱āj
'where?'	*no-n = non	Tb. naʔan	*hīnV
'who?'	*no-r = nor	Lz. ni 'who?' (erg.)	*hīnV
'woods'	*oihan – oihan, oian	C. ħun	*fã̄nV

Key to languages cited: A Avar Ak Akhwakh B Budukh Bz Bezhta C Chechen H Hinukh I Ingush K Karata L Lak Lz Lezgi R Rutul T Tindi Tb Tabasaran Ts Tsakhur U Udi

BASQUE, CAUCASIAN, AND CAUCASIAN RECONSTRUCTION II:

These word comparisons are somewhat less definitive than those in Table 1, either because of slight semantic differences, or because the Caucasian words are restricted to one branch of Caucasian, or even one language. On the other hand, at least some of these comparisons reflect the fact that meanings of words frequently change over time, and that old words frequently pass out of use in subgroups of a family, or even in most languages of a family.

Meaning	Basque word	Caucasian: Representative word	Caucasian: Reconstruction
'back'	*bi-ska-r̄ = bizkar	Ab. a-zkʷa	*zakʷa (PAb)
'belly'	*śabe-l = sabel	Bz. šebo 'liver'	*ǯăwV
'bird'	*čori = txori, xori	Ch. č'or ~ č'oru	*čhwī̆lV (PEC)
'bone'	*ħä(N)sur̄ = hezur, ezur, azur	R. sur 'part, side'	*rɨmswe / *mswɨre 'rib' (PEC)
'breast'	*bulha-r̄ = bulhar, bular, budar	A. ɣʷári 'udder'	*ɢwălfḯč̃(PEC)
'day'	*egun	L. q'ini	*Hwī̆ɢV (PEC)
'fall' (verb)	*e-auśi = jausi	C. –oss- 'to godown'	*-ŭśV (PEC)
'far'	*hur̄un = hurrun, urrun	R. χiri-dɨ	*-ārχV (PEC)
'fat' (grease)	*sinho = ziho	T. ts'inɬu- 'fat' (adj)	*čēnxwV (PEC)
'father'	*aita = aita	Ub. tʷə	*(a)tʷə (PWC)
'few'	*guti	Lz. güt'ü 'narrow'	*kwHəṭV
'fly' (verb)	*hegas = hegaz (egin)	Ts. al-iχas	*HiχV (PEC)
'foot'	*hoin = oin, huin	L. niq:a 'heel'	*ʔĭnɢwV̆ (PEC)
'four'	*lau-r	Ub. p'tl'ə	*ṗx̌ə (PWC)
'go'	*e-oHan = joan	K. -oʔan	*-VʔwVn (PEC)

49

Meaning	Basque word	Caucasian: Representative word	Caucasian: Reconstruction
'guts'	hertze ~ heste	A. ʕorčo / ʕarča-	-
'hair' (1)	*ülhe = ilhe, ile, ule	Ts. arχ 'autumn wool'	*ʔālχV (PEC)
'hair' (2)	*bilho = bilho, bilo	L. p'iħulli 'feather'	*ṗVħVɫV
'hand'	*eśku = esku	Kh. čigin 'shoulder'	*ćəgwV (PEC)
'head'	*buru = buru	U. bul	-
'hear'	*e-ncun = entzun	D. -umc'- 'to search'	*-ămçE
'here'	*heben = heben, hemen	Tb. hamu 'this'	*hă (PEC) + *mV (PNC)
'hit'	*e-o = jo	Ch. -uγ	*-Hiγwe(r)
'horn'	*a-daṙ = adar	A. tl:ar	*ƛwɨrV (PEC)
'I' (first person singular)	*ni = ni	D. nu	*nɨ (PEC)
'male'	*aṙ = ar	I. ärh 'ungelt'	*ʔīrɫwV (PEC)
'man'	*gison / *gisa- = gizon, giza-	Abk. χać'a	*qaća (PAb)
'many'	*aśko = asko	L. č'ạu	*čHəqwV
'night'	*gau = gau	Ts. χam	*χ:am: (PL)
'not' (verbal negation)	*es = ez	K. -č'e	*ʒ́ə / *ćə (PEC)
'sand'	*fionda-ṙ = ondar, hondar	Kh. ant 'earth, ground'	*ʔantV (PEC)
'see'	*e-kuśi = ikusi	B. irq-	*-Hărq̇V(n)- (PEC)
'sew'	*e-ośi = josi	An. -eš:- 'to weave'	*-irsE-
'sharp'	*soṙoc = zorrotz	Ab. ts'ara	*ćarə (PAb)

Meaning	Basque word	Caucasian: Representative word	Caucasian: Reconstruction
'skin'	*lar̄u = larru, narru 'skin, hide, leather'	A. tl':er 'color'	*λŏli
'snow'	*e-lhu-r̄ = elhur, elur, edur	C. lō̃	*jĩwɬV / *ɬĩwV (PEC)
'stone'	*har̄i = harri, arri	Ak. χaχi 'gravel'	*χHĕrχV (PEC)
'tail'	*bustan = buztan	Ts. bi̯t	*p:o̯c̣:V (PL)
'this'	*hau-(r) = haur, aur	C. ha-ra	*hẵ (PEC)
'thou'	*hi, *-ga = hi, i, -k	C. ħo	*γwṼ (PEC)
'tooth'	*hor̄c = hortz, ortz	L. k:arč:i	*gə[r]ǯwē̃ (PEC)
'tree'	1. *haice = zuhaitz, zugatz, atze 2. *hamu = zuhamu, zuhain	1. K. eže-la 'pine tree'	1. *Hẵ(r)ǯwĩ
'turn'	*e-culi = itzuli	Ag. iltsan-	*-ĩrcVl (PEC)
'twenty'	*hogei = hogei, ogei	A. q':ó-go	*Gə (PEC)
'warm'	*bero = bero	Khw. bobolu 'hot'	-
'water'	*hur = ur, hur	A. ħor 'lake, pond'[96]	*ħwirɨ (PEC)
'woods'	*baśo = baso	Ak. beča 'mountain'	*wɨce (PEC)
'worm'	*haNar̄ = har, aar, ar (Roncalese ãr)	A. ħapára	*fiabarV (PEC)

---

[96] Alternatively the Basque word for 'water' can be compared with Lezgi hül 'sea, liquid,' etc. < PEC *ħwĩlV.

Additional languages cited: Ab Abaza Abk Abkhaz Ag Agul An Andi Ch Chamalal D Dargwa Kh Khinalug Khw Khwarshi Ub Ubykh

Proto-Languages cited: PAb Proto-Abkhazian PEC Proto-East Caucasian PL Proto-Lezgian PWC Proto-West Caucasian [undesignated reconstructions are PNC = Proto-(North) Caucasian]

BASQUE, CAUCASIAN, AND CAUCASIAN RECONSTRUCTION III:

The following comparisons involve meanings that are not on the Swadesh 100-word or 200-word lists, but nevertheless are meanings that are very basic. Most of these comparisons are those listed by the Russian Caucasianist Sergei A. Starostin (1996) with the designation of "quite plausible, both phonetically and semantically, correspondences" between Basque and Caucasian.

Meaning	Basque word	Caucasian: Representative word	Caucasian: Reconstruction
'aunt'	*ise- = izeba, izeko	C. d-ētsa 'paternal aunt'	*-ĩḉwī (PEC)
'be'	*isa-n = izan	C. -is- 'to stay'	*äsA
'beard'	*bisa> = bizar	Bz. bizal-ba 'mustache'	*bilӡ̌V (PEC)
'bitter'	*kerać = kerats, karats	Kh. q'al	*q̇ěfilV
'blind'	*IĆU = itsu	T. -ets:u-	*-VċV (PEC)
'brain, marrow'	*muin = mun, muin	Tb. maʔ	*mäfinū (PEC)
'dung'	*Koroc = korotz ~ gorotz	Ar. k'urč' 'dung of sheep'	*k[u]rčV (PEC)
'firewood'	*e-gu> = egur	U. gor ~ gorgor 'pole'	*gōrV (PEC)
'forehead'	*beko = beko	Ts. bok' 'muzzle'	*běḳwo

Meaning	Basque word	Caucasian: Representative word	Caucasian: Reconstruction
'fox'	*ɦaseɣali = azegari, azeri, hazeri, axeri, etc.	T. *sari*	*chwōlĕ
'goat' (castrated)	*sikiro = zikiro	An. *ts':ek'ir* 'kid'	*ʒĭkV̆
'half/middle'	*e>di = erdi	Bz. *-atlo* 'middle', *-atlo-kos* 'half'	*-ĕλE
'hunger'	*gośe = gose	Ag. *gaš*	*gašē
'lap'	*maga-l = magal	K. *bakʷal* 'belly'	*bVnḳwV
'lose'	*gal- = galdu	Ag. *gul-* 'to lose, get lost'	*-igwVɫ (PEC)
'milk'	*eSne = esne, ezne	Ch. *s:ĩw*	*šänʔu
'mite'	*siga-> = zigar	D. *ts'ika ~ ts'eka* 'flea'	*ćäkwə
'moth'	*śić = sits	L. *suts'* 'tick'	*šwĕʒV (PEC)
'mouse'	*śagu = sagu	Ts. *sok* 'weasel'	*cārgwɨ
'nape'	*kokot = kokot	Ch. *qʷaq'a* 'gullet'	*ɢwVnɢwV (PEC)
'neighbor'	*ɦauso = hauzo, aizo	C. *ħāša* 'guest'	*HV̄čwE
'nerve, blood vessel'	*sain = zain, zañ	Ch. *s:ē* 'sinew, muscle'	*sēħmV (PEC)
'nut'	*hu> = hur 'hazelnut'	Bz. *hetle* 'nut, walnut'	*ʔwōrλV
'old woman'	*aćo = atso	L. *ts:u-* 'female'	*cwŏjV
'people, inhabited place, country'	*he>i = herri, erri	L. *ara-l* 'army, troops'	*ʔwəhri

Meaning	Basque word	Caucasian: Representative word	Caucasian: Reconstruction
'put'	*e-bini = ipini, ibeni, imiñi	Tb. *imi*-di xuz 'to stay'	*ʔima(n)- (PEC)
'root (of hair)'	*čo>u = txorru	Kh. *č'ar* 'hair'	*ćħwərə (PEC)
'tear' (eye water)	*n[e]ga-> = negar, nigar	D. *nerɣ*	*něwq̇ŭ (PEC)
'tick' (1)	*a-kain = akain, akan, lakain	D. *q'i* 'nit'	*q̇ā̃nʔV (PEC)
'tick' (2)	*i-tain = itain	Ak. *t'ani* 'nit'	*ṭaHnā
'whole, complete'	*ośo = oso	Tb. *ats'u* 'full'	*-ɦŏc̣V
'wolf'	*oćo = otso	An. *bots'o*	*bħěrčě

THE PROBLEM OF "ISOLATES" II: BURUSHASKI

There is another mysterious "isolate" language spoken high in the mountains of northeastern Pakistan by some 60,000 people. This is the language formerly known by names such as Kanjut, Khajuna or Werchikwar, and now usually as Burushaski. It is spoken in the Hunza, Nager, and Yasin valleys, a mountainous environment best known in the West as a legendary haven of health and long life. The possible connections of this language with Basque and the Caucasian languages have been explored throughout the twentieth century, by, for example, the scholars Robert Bleichsteiner, Karl Bouda, and Hermann Berger. The following table lists some of the most promising proposed cognates. Footnotes indicate meanings that vary from the canonic meaning in the left column, dialectal provenance of words cited, and other notes.

This table only lists some of the cognates common to all three branches. Other possible lists would show cognates common only to Basque and Burushaski, or to Caucasian and Burushaski. Again, as in the Basque-Caucasian table, most of the words are basic, only the last two ('thread' and 'house') having any cultural content. The words for 'milk,' 'goat' ~ 'sheep,' and 'horse' ~ 'donkey' may bear witness to the beginnings of animal husbandry before the three groups diverged.

And what of the tests applied earlier to the Basque-Caucasian case, phonology and grammar? Rather than discussing the phonology in detail, as we did in the Basque-Caucasian case, I will just mention a few of the correspondences. Some "trivial" correspondences ($b = b = b$; $n = n = n$) are readily apparent in several of the comparisons. More interesting are comparisons such as these:

('stomach') Bur. –*phaṭ* = Bsq. *eperdi* = Cauc. *$pHVrtwV$
('slime') Bur. ɢiṭ = Bsq. *lerde* = Cauc. *$\underline{\lambda}wirdi$
('narrow') Bur. *čhaḍ-úm* = Bsq. *estu* = Cauc. *$čHVrdV$

In these words, Burushaski has **retroflex** plosives – voiceless /ṭ/ in word-final position, voiced /ḍ/ between vowels. The contrast between **dental** plosives /t/, /d/ and **retroflex** plosives /ṭ/, /ḍ/ is typical of languages in the South Asian (Greater Indian) linguistic area. It is found in Indo-European (Indo-Aryan) languages such as Hindi and Bengali (and ancient Sanskrit), in some Iranian languages (such as Pashto), in Dravidian languages such as Tamil and Malayalam, and even in some Munda (Austroasiatic) and Sino-Tibetan languages of the region. Therefore it is thought that Burushaski, like Indo-Aryan, acquired the contrast through contact with languages that were in India before them. In the three words shown above, it appears that the Burushaski retroflex plosives developed out of the older clusters of /r/ + /t/ or /r/ + /d/, which are preserved as such in Basque and Proto-Caucasian. This type of change also took place in Indo-Aryan languages, for example, Hindi āṭh 'eight' < Old Indic aṣṭā < PIE *oktō; Sanskrit nīḍá 'resting place.' Indo-Iranian *niždas < PIE *nizdó-s 'sitting place, nest' (cf. Lat. nòdus, Lith. lìzdas, Arm. nist, Eng. nest, etc.); in the Vedic texts this word has instead a retroflex lateral /ḷ/: nīḷá.

BURUSHASKI, BASQUE, CAUCASIAN, AND PROTO-CAUCASIAN:

(Gloss)	Burushaski[97]	Basque	Cauc-asian[98] (modern)	Proto-Caucasian
'face'	buk[99]	beko[100]	buk'ʷʰ	*bĕkwo
'stomach'	-phaṭ[ff]	eperdi[103]	pạrt'i[104]	*pHVrṭwV
'abdomen'	-úl	urdail[105]	b-etl'tl'u[106]	*=īraṭ̣V

---

[97] Dialects are designated as Hunza (H), Nager (N), and Yasin (Y).

[98] In this column, representative words are cited from actual Caucasian languages. The next column is made up of reconstructions, usually Proto-Caucasian, but occasionally lower level reconstructions, as indicated in footnotes.

[99] 'throat'; cf. meanings in Basque and Caucasian: 'mouth' in Nakh languages, 'muzzle' in Tsakhur, 'lip' in Kryz and Budukh. And cf. the IE cognates Eng. *mouth* = Latin *mentum* 'chin,' for the type of semantic shift.

[100] 'forehead'

[101] Rutul 'part of face' (lips + nose)

[102] (Y) *phaṭ* 'stomach (of fowl),' (H,N) *-pháṭ* 'viscera (of fowl).' [ṭ] is a retroflex plosive.

[103] 'rump, buttocks'

[104] Archi 'large intestine'

[105] 'stomach, abomasum, rennet'

[106] 'stomach, abomasum, rennet'

(Gloss)	Burushaski	Basque	Cauc-asian (modern)	Proto-Caucasian
'back'	-sqa[107]	bizkar	azkʷa[108]	*zəkʷa[109]
'fur'	bišké	bizar[110]	bizal-ba[111]	*bilӠV
'pus, tears'	nagéi[112]	negar[113]	notʼqʼa[114]	*něwq̇ŭ
'slime'	ɢiṭ	lerde, lirdi[115]	xʷerd[116]	*λ̣wirdɨ
'milk'	ṣiŋ	ezne	šin[117]	*s̈̃amʔV
'goat'	tshigír[118]	zikiro[119]	tsʼtsʼikʼer[120]	*ӡ̌ikV̆
'horse'	čhardá[121]	asto[122]	čada[123]	*čada[124]
'rodent'	čargé[125]	sagu[126]	sok[127]	*cārgwɨ̄
'flea'	Khin, khen[128]	akain[129]	Gēnig[130]	*ġā̈nʔV

[107] 'on one's back' – must be used with a possessive prefix, such as á-sqa 'on my back'.

[108] Abkhaz

[109] Proto-Abkhaz-Tapant (a subgroup of West Caucasian)

[110] 'beard'

[111] Bezhta 'mustache'

[112] (H) nagéi, (N) magéi 'boil, ulcer'

[113] 'tears, weeping'

[114] Chechen 'pus'

[115] 'drivel, saliva'

[116] Avar 'pus'

[117] Chechen 'udder'

[118] (N) '(she-)goat'

[119] 'castrated ram'

[120] Karata 'kid' (young goat)

[121] (H,N) čhardá, (Y) čardé 'stallion'

[122] 'ass, donkey'

[123] Abkhaz 'ass, donkey'

[124] Proto-Abkhaz-Tapant (a subgroup of West Caucasian)

[125] (Y) 'flying squirrel'

[126] 'mouse'

[127] Tsakhur 'weasel'

[128] (H,N) khin, (Y) khen

[129] '(large) tick'

[130] Chechen 'louse'

(Gloss)	Burushaski	Basque	Cauc-asian (modern)	Proto-Caucasian
'fruit'	Gaíŋ[131]	ar(h)an[132]	géni[133]	*γōn?V
'forest'	hun[134]	oihan	ħun[135]	*fãnV
'stone'	xóro[136]	harri	χirχem[137]	*χHĕrχV
'slope'	hurgó[138]	hegi[139]	urqi[140]	*ħwərgē
'fire'	ši[141]	su	ts'u[142]	*čǎjɨ
'bitter'	Gaqáẏ-um[143]	kharats[144]	q'ala[145]	*q̇ĕfilV
'narrow'	čhaḍ-úm[146]	estu	č'a̱rt'a[147]	*čHVrdV
'to know'	-ki-[148]	jakin[149]	=iq'ᵇᵇᵇ	*=ɨ̃q̇E
'thread'	Gaẏ, hari	hal-	χal[151]	*χātV
'house'	-yeéš[152]	etxe [eče]	ts'a[153]	*c[ĩ]ju

---

[131] 'grapes'

[132] 'plum, sloe'; I analyze the word as *ar-han,* the first element being a fossilized class prefix, as seen in Tibetan *r-gun* 'grape, vine'.

[133] Avar 'pear'

[134] (Y) 'wood, firewood', (H,N) 'wood, timber, beam, hewn trunk'

[135] Chechen 'forest'

[136] (Y) 'small stones'

[137] Lezgi 'small stones, gravel'

[138] 'steep slope, uphill, up the mountain'

[139] 'top, summit, ridge; border, corner, edge'

[140] Dargwa (Akushi) 'mountains'

[141] (II,N) 'fireplace, hearth'

[142] Lak

[143] (H,N) Gaqáẏ-um, (Y) qaqám 'bitter'

[144] Zuberoan 'bitter, sour'

[145] Archi

[146] (N) čhaḍ-úm; (H) čhan-úm, (Y) čan-úm (influenced by the verb *du-čhan?*)

[147] Dargwa (Akushi)

[148] 'to learn'

[149] 'to know (a fact)' (< **e-aki-n*)

[150] Bezhta 'to know'

[151] Chechen 'a piece of thread'

Another interesting non-trivial correspondence is seen in the following comparisons:

('bitter')Bur. ɢaqáy̰ -um = Bsq. k(h)arats = Cauc. *q̌ĕfilV
('thread') Bur. ɢay̰ = Bsq. hari = Cauc. *χā̆ƚV

Burushaski /y̰/ is a very unusual and peculiar sound,[154] heard – as far as I know – only in two of the three dialects of Burushaski (Hunza and Nager), and in Dumaki, an Indo-Aryan language spoken in the same area (Gilgit). The correspondence of Bur. /y̰/ = Bsq. /r/ = Cauc. *l ~ *ƚ may also be verified by:

('sheep') Bur. huy̰óo = Bsq. ahari 'ram' = Cauc. *ʔīlχU 'sheep, lamb'
('leaf') Bur. khiy̰ = Cauc. *k̲əwƚV 'sheaf'
('stones') Bur. qhiy̰é = Cauc. *q̇wiƚə 'rock, cliff, stone'

Apart from the above, other evidence shows that Bur. /y̰/ comes from an /l/-like sound (lateral). For example, the place name Námay̰ is otherwise known as Nomal (a village between Gilgit and Hunza).

These comparisons exemplify another recurrent pattern:

('rodent') Bur. čargé = Bsq. sagu = Cauc. *cārgwɨ
('slope') Bur. hurgó = Bsq. hegi = Cauc. *fiwə̄rqē

The rule can be stated as "Bur. /rg/ = Bsq. /K/ = Proto-Cauc. *rK," where *K represents "velar or postvelar plosive." At least two other Basque-Caucasian comparisons confirm this pattern:

('border') Bsq. muga = Cauc. *mŏrqwV̆ 'stripe, line'

---

[152] 'dauernder Wohnsitz; Seßhaftigkeit, Beständigkeit' (H. Berger: 'lasting dwelling-place; sedentariness, permanence').

[153] Chechen 'house, room'

[154] The Norwegian linguist Morgenstierne described /y̰/ (which he transcribed as /ɽ/) as "a fricative r, pronounced with the tongue in the retroflex ... position." The American linguist Greg Anderson describes /y̰/ as "a curious sound whose phonetic realizations vary from a retroflex, spirantized glide, to a retroflex velarized spirant." Besides /y̰/ and /ɽ/, it has also been transcribed as /ly/ and /gh/. Hermann Berger finds /y̰/ similar to the Tamil sound commonly transcribed as /ḷ/.

('temple') Bsq. *loki* = Cauc. *∜ arq̇wĕ 'forehead, cap'

Here Basque is least conservative, losing /r/ before velar plosives, while in the case of /rd/, above, Burushaski was innovative in merging /rt/, /rd/ as /ṭ/, /ḍ/. (Note that some Caucasian languages – independently but convergently – have undergone the same change as Basque, for example, Chechen *moGa* 'line, row', Khwarshi *tl'oq'o* 'forehead'.)

These comparisons show yet another correspondence:

('fire')   Bur. *ši*   = Cauc. *c̣ăji̋*
('house') Bur. *–yeé š* = Cauc. *c̣[ī]ju*

Overlooking the Basque reflexes for the moment,[155] the correspondence Bur. /š/ = Cauc. *c̣* /ts'/ is confirmed by other cases:

('blind')   Bur. *šon* = Cauc. *c̣A̋wnV* 'dark'
('driftwood') Bur. (Y) *šul* = Cauc. *c̣wīłfiV* 'stick, branch'
('wool')[156] Bur. *še* (pl. *šémiŋ*) = Cauc. *c̣ɦwĕme* 'eyebrow'

Finally, note these parallels:

('horse') Bur. *čhardá* = Bsq. *asto* = Cauc. *čada*
('narrow') Bur. *čhaḍ-úm* = Bsq. *estu* = Cauc.*c̣HVrdV*

Here Burushaski and Caucasian have clear vowels between the first and second consonants, while Basque has clustered the consonants and placed a vowel initially. The same tendency is seen in some other comparisons, all involving sibilant affricates: /č/ as in church; /čh/ is the aspirated version, /č'/ the glottalized, /c̣/ the retroflex. In Basque the original sibilant affricates have uniformly become /ś/, written s:

---

[155] The Basque reflexes are "conditioned" (vary depending on phonetic environment), as discussed above in the comparison of Basque and Caucasian.

[156] The semantic connection of 'wool' and 'eyebrow' is seen clearly in the Sino-Tibetan language Kanauri: *tsam* 'wool, fleece' and *mik-tsam* 'eyebrow' (lit. 'eye-wool'). By the way, I consider Proto-Sino-Tibetan *tshām* 'wool, head hair' to be cognate with Caucasian *c̣ɦwĕme* 'eyebrow', Burushaski *še[m]* 'wool', and Basque *zamar* 'fleece'.

('measure') Bur. -*čuq*¹⁵⁷ = Bsq. *aska*¹⁵⁸ = Cauc. **c̨ä̃qwă / c̨ä̃qwă*¹⁵⁹

('all') Bur. *ç̌iq*¹⁶⁰ = Bsq. *asko, aski*¹⁶¹ = Cauc. **čH∧qwV*¹⁶²

I believe these examples are sufficient to show that the basic lexicon of Burushaski is intimately connected with the basic lexicons of Basque and the Caucasian languages, and this is further verified by the recurrent sound correspondences between and among the three groups of languages.

MORPHOLOGY: We shall also explore some grammatical correspondences between Burushaski and its Vasco-Caucasian cousins, Basque and Caucasian. Let us begin with the pronouns.

Both Burushaski and the reconstructed Proto-Caucasian have suppletive pronoun stems in the second person singular. According to Nikolayev and Starostin, the original Proto-Caucasian paradigms were very complicated and difficult to reconstruct with much certainty. For the present purpose, let us compare Hunza Burushaski (as described by Berger, 1998) with two East Caucasian languages, Khinalug and Tsakhur (and Proto-East Caucasian)[163]:

---

[157] (H) –*čuq*, (N) –*čóq* 'a measure of grain,' (Y) *čiq* 'sifting tray'

[158] 'crib, manger, trough'

[159] 'scoop, spoon, wooden vessel'

[160] (Y) 'all, altogether'; H and N have different words.

[161] *asko* 'much, many'; *aski* 'enough'

[162] 'big' ('many' in Lak)

[163] Here the symbol /ɢ/ is used to represent the voiced uvular fricative (otherwise /ɣ/ or /ʁ/).

SECOND PERSON SUPPLETIVE PRONOUN STEMS:

	Direct	Genitive	Dative
1st person singular ('I – me'):			
Burushaski	je, já	áa	áar
PEC	*zō(-n)	*ʔiz(V)	*ʔez(V) (erg.)
	Khinalug zɨ (**nom.**)	i, e	as
	yä (**erg.**)		
	Tsakhur zu	yiz-ɨn	za-
2nd person singular ('thou – thee'):			
Burushaski	un	góo	góor
PEC	*u̯ō(-n)	*ʔeu̯V/*ʔiu̯V	*ʔŏGwV (erg.)
	~ *GwV̄		
	Khinalug wɨ (**nom.**)	wi	oχ
	wa (**erg.**)		
	Tsakhur wu ~ Gu	y-ɨG-	wa-

In spite of some rearrangements of the original paradigms, much similarity can still be seen. Both Burushaski and East Caucasian have two different allomorphs of the word for 'thou.' What is more, the allomorphs are phonetically as well as functionally similar, i.e., un = *u̯ō(-n), and góo = *GwV̄. The Burushaski word for 'thou' (direct), un, is identical with those of the East Caucasian languages Archi and Udi (un 'thou'; cf. Lezgi and Agul wun 'thou'). The Khinalug and Tsakhur forms cited above lack the final –n.

A note on **suppletion**: Suppletion means the coexistence of lexically unrelated variants (allomorphs) of the same morpheme. A common example is the paradigm of English 'to go':

present tense: *go*   past tense: *went*   participle: *gone*

Though English speakers unconsciously think of *went* as the "same" word (in the past tense) as *go*, it was originally the past tense form of another verb, *to wend*, that replaced the earlier past tense of *go* (Old English *éode*, itself a suppletive form! German [*ging*] and

Swedish [*gick*] preserve the original Germanic past tense forms). Suppletion is also found in the paradigm of *good:*

	Positive	Comparative	Superlative
English	good	better	best
German	gut	besser	(der/die/das) beste
Swedish	god	bättre	bäst

All three languages (as well as other Germanic languages) use a different stem for the comparative and superlative forms of 'good.'[164] Joseph H. Greenberg cited these forms as examples of superior evidence of genetic relationship.[165] Complete paradigms showing shared irregularities of this type are highly unlikely to have come about by chance, and thus far more probative than the comparison of the single words good/gut/god by themselves. Likewise, the pattern of r/n alternation discussed above was viewed by linguists as a valuable piece of evidence for genetic relationship of Hittite with the Indo-European languages.

I suggest that the suppletive pronouns found in Burushaski and East Caucasian should also be considered strong evidence of genetic relationship:

Burushaski *un* / *góo* 'thou' = PEC *$*\underline{u}\bar{o}(-n)$ / *$*_Gw\bar{V}$ 'thou'

Both languages have two different allomorphs of the word for 'thou.' What is more, the allomorphs are phonetically as well as functionally similar, i.e., *un* = *$*\underline{u}\bar{o}(-n)$, and *góo* = *$*_Gw\bar{V}$. This, coupled with the many lexical parallels and recurrent sound correspondences listed above, can only be the result of genetic relationship.

As we saw above, there is a tendency over time to even out irregularities. Thus children say things like *gooder*, *goodest*, and eventually some of these neologisms become accepted. We saw, for example, that the Germanic languages generalized either the *–r* form or the *–n* form of the word for 'water'. In the Vasco-Caucasian family, two widely separated languages – Basque and Dargwa – have independently leveled out the suppletion of first and second person singular pronouns in the same way:

---

[164] Those who have studied the classical languages will recall that Latin and Greek also have irregular comparative and superlative forms of 'good' (and some other adjectives), though with totally different stems than are used in Germanic. Sanskrit also has a few such cases.

[165] "Agreement in irregularities and evidence from survivals of grammatical markers that have become petrified are worthy of special consideration [in the genetic classification of languages]." Greenberg, "Principles of Genetic Classification" (p. 30), in Language in the Americas (Stanford University Press, 1987).

Basque   *ni* 'I' : *hi* 'thou'
Dargwa (Akushi, Urakhi)   *nu* 'I' : *ħu* 'thou'

The *nV* stem is preserved only in Dargwa and Lak (*na*) among the Caucasian languages (as well as in Basque), while the *ħu/hi* 'thou' stem (presumed cognate with Burushaski *góo*, Tsakhur *ɢu*, etc.) has been generalized at the expense of the *$u̯ō(-n)$* allomorph.

Another morphological pattern is found when we look into the grammatical gender (or class) system of nouns in Burushaski. Most Indo-European languages have a three-gender or two-gender system, or have merged all genders and thereby lost their grammatical significance:

Three genders: masculine (M) / feminine (F) / neuter (N): Sanskrit, Greek, Latin, German, Icelandic, Norwegian

Two genders: M / F: French, Spanish, Italian, etc., or common (M+F) / neuter (N): Swedish, Danish

No genders: English

Since Hittite had a two-gender system (animate / inanimate), many linguists think that the three genders of Indo-European are an innovation (a split of the animate gender), and the older Indo-Hittite system was two-gender. In Burushaski, there are *four* genders (or classes):

	Class	Singular	Plural
1a	Human masculine	i-	u-
1b	Human feminine	mu-	u-
2	Non-human animate	i-	u-
3	Non-human inanimate	i-	i-

The phonetic elements in the right column are third-person possessive prefixes corresponding to each class. Most Caucasian languages also have a multiple-gender system, and the following system is reconstructed for Proto-East Caucasian:

	Class	Singular	Plural
1	Animate (masculine)	*u̯	*w
2	Animate (feminine)	*y	*w
3	Inanimate (non-collective)	*w / *b	*r
4	Inanimate (collective)	*r / *d	*r

The phonetic elements in the right column are the markers associated with each class. Depending on the language, they may appear attached to adjectives, or to verbs, or to nouns, for example:

> Bagwali *w-ass* 'brother'; *y-ass* 'sister'; *w-aša* 'son'; *y-aš* 'daughter'
> Tindi *w-aha* 'son'; *y-aha* 'daughter'; *b-etl'tl'u* 'stomach'; *b-atl'tl'i* 'in the middle'
> Dargwa *w-aħ* 'face (of a man)'; *r-aħ* 'face (of a woman)'; *b-aħ* 'face (of an animal)'

In some Caucasian languages, the prefixes have been retained sporadically in some words even though the original class distinctions are forgotten. Elements such as these are called **petrified** or **fossilized.**

> Lezgi *ru-fun* 'belly'; Tsakhur *wu-xun* 'belly'; Ubykh *t-χamə́* 'skin, fur'; *t-χʷa* 'ashes'; *b-ɬa* 'eye'; *b-ɓa* 'top,' etc.

The Burushaski possessive prefixes are fully functional, and (roughly) similar to the Dargwa examples above:

Bur. *á-sqa* 'on my back', *gó-sqa* 'on your back', *í-sqa* 'on his back', *mú-sqa* 'on her back'

And what of the "third leg" of our trifecta, Basque? In contrast to Burushaski and Caucasian, modern Basque has no grammatical gender or class distinctions whatsoever, but there are some interesting prefixed elements that have attracted linguists' attention. The original prefixal nature becomes clear when we compare Basque words with their proposed cognates in Caucasian and Burushaski:

1. o- / u-

Basque *olho, olho* 'oats' (< **o-ɫo*): cf. Cauc: PNC **λw̃ɨwV* 'millet'

Basque *oihal*, 'cloth, fabric' (< **o-xal*): cf. Cauc: PEC **χwĭlɬ̣V* 'clothing'

Basque *ohe (o-he)* 'bed': cf. Cauc: Tabasaran *aχin* 'bed', etc.

Basque *oihan (oi-han)* 'forest': cf. Cauc: Chechen *ḥun* 'forest,' etc.

Basque *oski (o-ski)* 'shoe': cf. Cauc: Tabasaran *šaq'ʷ* 'heel'; Bur. *ṣoq* 'sole of shoe'

Basque (Bizkaian) *uzen* (*u-zen)* 'name': cf. Bur. *sén-* 'to say, name'; *sénas* 'named'

Basque *urdail* (*u-rdail)* 'stomach': cf. Cauc: Tindi *b-etl'tl'u*, Karata *m-etl'u* 'stomach'; Bur. *–úl* 'belly'

Basque *ukondo* (*u-kondo)* 'elbow': cf. Cauc: Hinukh *q'ontu* 'kncc,' etc.

2. e- / i-

Basque *elhur, elur* (< **e-ɫu-r*) 'snow': cf. Cauc: PEC **λĭwV* 'snow' > Chechen *lō*, etc.

Basque *egur (e-gur)* 'firewood': cf. Cauc: Udi *gor, gorgor* 'pole,' etc.

Basque (Z) *ekhei* (*e-khei)* 'material': cf. Cauc: Lak *q'aj* 'thing(s), ware(s),' etc.

Basque *esne* (*e-sne)* 'milk': cf. Cauc: Chechen *šin* 'udder'; Bur. *ṣiŋ* 'milk'

Basque *ele, elhe* (*e-lhe*) 'word': cf. Cauc: Inkhokwari *loje* 'word, sound, voice,' etc.

Basque *izar (i-zar)* 'star', etc.: cf. Cauc: Tindi *tstsaru* 'star,' etc.

Basque *ihintz (i-hintz* < **i-xinc*) 'dew': cf. Cauc: Lak *xunts'a* 'bog,' etc.

Basque *ilindi, ilhinti* (*i-lhinti*) 'firebrand, ember': cf. Cauc: Andi *ɬudi* 'firewood,' etc.

Basque *idulki (i-dulki)* 'block of wood': cf. Cauc: Archi *dali* 'long stick, pole,' etc.

Basque *itain, ithain* (*i-thain*) 'tick': cf. Cauc: Akhwakh *t'ani* 'nit,' etc.

Basque (common) *izen (i-zen)* 'name': cf. Bur. *sén-* 'to say, name'; *sénas* 'named'

Basque *izerdi (i-zerdi)* 'sweat, sap': cf. Cauc: PEC **c̣āɬwV* 'blood, life'

3. be- / bi-

Basque *behatz (be-hatz)* 'thumb, toe' (vs. *hatz* 'finger, paw'): cf. Cauc: Avar *kʷač'* 'paw', etc.

Basque *belarri* (*be-larri*) 'ear': cf. Cauc: Batsbi *lark'* < **lari-ḳ* 'ear', etc.

Basque *belaun, belhaun, belhain* (*be-lhaun*) 'knee': cf. Cauc: Akhwakh *etlelo* 'elbow,' etc.

Basque *behazun* (*be-hazun*) 'bile': cf. Cauc: Archi *ssam* 'gall,' etc.; Bur. *-sán* 'spleen'

Basque *bizkar (bi-zka-r)* 'back': cf. Cauc: Abkhaz *azkʷa* 'back'; Bur. *-sqa* 'on one's back'

Basque *bizi* (*bi-zi*) 'life, alive': cf. Cauc: Lak *ssiħ* 'breath, vapor,' Chechen *sa* 'soul,' etc.

Basque (G) *bilder* (*bi-lder*) 'drivel, drool' (vs. *helder, herde* in other dialects): cf. Cauc: PNC **fiăm ʯă* 'sweat'

4. a-

Basque *ahizpa* (*a-hiz-pa*) 'sister (of a woman)': cf. Cauc: Bezhta *is* 'brother,' *isi* 'sister,' etc.; Bur. *-ċo* 'brother (of a man), sister (of a woman)'

Basque *atso* (*a-tso*) 'old woman': cf. Cauc: Batsbi *pst'u* 'wife', Lak *tstsu-* 'female,' etc.

Basque *abere* (*a-bere*) 'domestic animal, cattle': cf. Cauc: Udi *bele* 'cattle,' etc.

Basque *ahuña* (*a-huña*) 'kid': cf. Cauc: Andi *kun* 'ram,' etc.

Basque *akain* (*a-kain*) 'tick': cf. Cauc: Chechen *gēnig* 'louse,' etc.; Bur. *khen, khin* 'flea'

Basque *ametz* (*a-metz*) 'gall oak': cf. Cauc: Chechen *naž* 'oak tree' etc.; Bur. (H) *meṣ*, (Y) *no ṣ* 'bush, shrub, sapling'

Basque *aho* (*a-ho*) 'mouth': cf. Cauc: PNC *χwi-* in *χwi m(V)ṗV* 'mouthful'

Basque *ahur* (*a-hur*) 'hollow of the hand': cf. Cauc: Dargwa *kur* 'pit,' etc.

Basque *adar* (< **a-rdar*) 'horn': cf. Cauc: Avar *tltlar* 'horn,' etc.; Bur. *-ltúr, tur* 'horn'

The original separability of these apparent prefixes is shown also by internal evidence. Some Basque words have different prefixes in different dialects, or a prefix in some dialects but not in others, or prefixed and unprefixed words can co-exist (see *hatz* vs. *be-hatz*, below):

Basque (c) *izen* (*i-zen*) 'name' vs. Basque (B) *uzen* (*u-zen*) 'name'

Basque (c) *k(h)e* vs. Basque (AN, BN, R) *e-ke* 'smoke'

Basque (AN, BN, L) *(h)erde*, (B, BN, L, R, Z) *(h)elder* 'drivel' vs. (G) *bilder* (< **bi-* + *helder*)

Basque (c) *gai, gei* 'material, subject, topic' vs. (BN, Z) *e-khei* id.

Basque *hatz* vs. *be-hatz*: (Meanings vary widely depending on dialect, e.g. in Bizkaian, *atz* 'finger' vs. *beatz* 'toe'; in Zuberoan, *hatz* 'finger' or 'paw' vs. *behatz* 'thumb')

Even though these prefixed elements no longer carry any grammatical function in modern Basque, some linguists have speculated that they formerly did, and represent what Joseph Greenberg called "stage III articles." Clear examples of stage III articles are seen in Haitian Creole, for example /latab/ 'table,' /deze/ 'egg' (< French *la table, des oeufs*), where the former articles are no longer separable but have fused with the noun roots. The same thing has happened with the Caucasian fossilized prefixes mentioned above. For example, in Lezgi *rufun* 'belly' (< *ru-fun*) the old class prefix (*ru-*) has fused with the noun stem (*fun*), just as in the Haitian

Creole examples. (However, the class system is still alive in Tsakhur and Rutul, which have *wu-xun* and *u-xun*, respectively, belonging to the third class.)

In sum, I think the most likely explanation of the Basque prefixes is that they are fossilized remnants of what formerly were class markers. In this light the Basque fossilized prefix **be- / bi-** resembles the Caucasian 3-class marker **w / *b*:

> Basque **be-**larri 'ear,' **bi-**zkar 'back': cf. Cauc: Tindi **b-**etl'tl'u 'stomach'; Dargwa **b-**ạħ 'face (of an animal)'; Tsakhur **wu-**xun 'belly'; Ubykh **b-**ӡa 'eye,' etc.

If so, Basque **o- / u-** could correspond to the Caucasian 1-class marker **u̯*, and Basque **e- / i-** could be related to the Caucasian 2-class marker **y*:

> Basque **o-**saba 'uncle,' **o-**he 'bed,' **u-**rdail 'stomach,' etc.: cf. Cauc: Bagwali **w-**ass 'brother', **w-**aša 'son'; Tindi **w-**aha 'son'; Dargwa **w-**ạħ 'face (of a man)'
>
> Basque **i-**zeba 'aunt,' **i-**hintz 'dew,' **e-**l(h)ur 'snow,' etc.: cf. Cauc: Bagwali **y-**ass 'sister,' **y-**aš 'daughter,' Tindi **y-**aha 'daughter'; Chechen **y-**üħ 'face, end,' etc.

This hypothesis is supported by the opposition of Basque *o-saba* 'uncle' vs. *i-zeba* 'aunt,' possibly an old but rare parallel to the Caucasian opposition of **u̯* (masculine) vs. **y* (feminine).

To summarize the grammatical evidence for classes (genders) in the Vasco-Caucasian family: Burushaski and Proto-East Caucasian agree in having a 4-class system; modern Basque has no grammatical genders or classes, but the lexical evidence of fossilized prefixes points to the earlier existence of a multiple-class system.

BASQUE AND CAUCASIAN WORDS FOR 'BLUE ~ IRON'

In both Basque and Caucasian there is a lexical connection between words for 'blue' and words for 'iron':

Basque: *urdin* 'blue': *burdin(a)* 'iron' (in Zuberoan: *úrdīn: bürdǘña*, resp.)

Caucasian: PNC **nHǟX̱'wV* 'blue; (blue metal) > iron' (NCED 851). E.g., Nikolayev & Starostin posit the developments: PEC **nHǟX̱'wV* 'blue' > Tsez *niga* 'blue, gray,' Hinukh *nik*-diju 'blue, green, gray,' vs. PEC **hnǟX̱'ū* '(iron) horseshoe' > Tsez, Hinukh *hiX̣u*, Hunzib, Bezhta *heX̣* 'horseshoe.' In West Caucasian, words for metal are commonly a compound including a word for color. They posit West Caucasian **ɣʷəX̣'ʷV* (<*ɣʷə + *X̣'ʷV 'blue'), becoming Adyge *ʁʷəč'ə*, Kabardian *ʁʷəś*, and Ubykh *wəc'ʷá* 'iron'.

Now, can the Basque and Caucasian words be reconciled phonologically? Clearly, it will not be easy, but the first step is the recognition that Basque *-rd-* corresponds regularly to Proto-Caucasian medial *-X̣'- (or, in fact, any PNC/PEC lateral affricate, including -λ- or -ɬ-, the first being the [dl] type and the second being [tɬ], with *-X̣'- representing the glottalized [tɬ']), e.g.:

Basque **erdi* 'half, middle' = PNC **=ĕX̱'E* 'half, middle' (NCED 412)
Basque **urde* 'pig' = PNC **wHārX̱'wə* 'boar, pig' (NCED 1047)
Basque **fierde* 'drivel' = PNC **ɦămX'ă* 'sweat' (NCED 509)
Basque **i-särdi* 'sweat, sap' = PEC **ć'āλwV* 'blood, life' (NCED 376)
Basque **urdail* 'stomach' (dial. also 'rennet' or 'womb') = PEC **=ɨɨraλV* 'stomach, abomasum, rennet' (NCED 670)

The last of these five comparisons requires metathesis and assimilation or dissimilation: thus a PEC *=ɨɨλalV would fit better with the Basque word. Metathesis is well known in Caucasian: for example, in Tindi *t'uk̓a* and *k̓ut'a* 'he-goat' coexist in free variation (NCED 1004), and many other roots have to be reconstructed with metathetic variants, e.g.: *s̠ēħmV / *ħēms̠V 'muscle, vein, intestine' (NCED 959), *t'iHV / *Hit'V 'small, little' (NCED 1001), and others. In Basque as well metathesis is not unknown, e.g. common Basque *gibel* 'liver', beside *bigel* 'liver' in Alto Navarro.

Several Basque-Caucasian lexical comparisons require metathesis on one side or the other, for example, Basque negu 'winter' is probably cognate with PNC *γwĭnʔV (NCED 482: > Chechen ʕa / ʕäna- 'winter', Lak γʷi- / γin- 'summer,' etc.), but a metathesized PNC *nʔĭγwV would fit perfectly with the Basque *negu*.

So PNC *nHā̈λ̠'wV is 'blue.' If we posit a hypothetical form *HwVλ̠'ǟn, which has all the same proto-phonemes, only in a different order, it is perfectly compatible with Basque $urdin$ 'blue':

PNC
*nHā̈λ̠'wV ~ *HwVλ̠'ǟn   'blue'
Basque
u   rd   i   n   'blue'

Then Basque burdin 'iron' could be a compound *b(u)- '*metal' + urdin 'blue,' like the West Caucasian example above (*ɣʷə 'metal' + *λ̓ʷV 'blue'). Whether the Basque *b(u)- is positively to be identified with PWC *ɣʷə 'metal' is yet another question, but the two forms seem phonetically compatible. One other Basque word for metal begins with *b-*: *berun* 'lead,' which may be connected in some way with Latin *plumbum*.

GENETIC AND CULTURAL LINGUISTIC LINKS BETWEEN BURUSHASKI AND THE CAUCASIAN LANGUAGES AND BASQUE[166]

Abstract: The Burushaski language of northeastern Pakistan has long eluded a generally agreed classification among the language families of the world. Recently the careful application of multilateral comparison has led to the hypothesis that Burushaski is probably most closely related to the (North) Caucasian languages and Basque (confirming earlier suggestions by Berger, Bleichsteiner, Bouda, and others). This hypothesis is supported by lexical evidence (cognates of basic vocabulary) as well as by morphological similarities, and further confirmed by recurrent phonological correspondences. Cultural vocabulary shared by the same languages indicates a dispersal of the proposed proto-language, variously termed Euskaro-Caucasian or Macro-Caucasian, at a time when domestication of sheep and goats and cultivation of grain crops were well in place.

This paper is divided into two major parts: (a) the presentation of some of the evidence for the genetic relationship of Burushaski to the Caucasian languages and Basque, and (b) the presentation of some of the cultural vocabulary shared by the same languages. In the first section, genetic evidence is divided into lexical cognates, morphological evidence, and phonology.

Lexical evidence: Burushaski-Caucasian-Basque comparisons.

In each etymological entry, the Burushaski word or words are listed first, with dialectal designations (H = Hunza, N = Nager, Y = Yasin) where appropriate. Next, proposed Caucasian cognates, if any, are cited, then Basque cognates, if any, and finally, there may be notes, following the symbol §.

Body parts:

báćin (H,N) 'shank; (animal's) hind leg above the hock'

~ Cauc: Avar *púrc:i* 'ham', Tabasaran *bac* 'paw', etc. < PEC **b[ə]cV* (NCED 291)

---

[166] Based on a paper given at the 3rd Harvard Round Table on Ethnogenesis of South and Central Asia, Harvard University, May 12-14, 2001.

bumbálten (Y) 'ankle' < **bum(b)la-lten* (old compound of ? + *-lten* 'bone')
~ Cauc: PEC **bĭmɫV̆* 'hoof, foot' (> Tsez *bula* 'hoof,' etc.: NCED 307) + PEC **X̱'wVnʔV* (see the entry for *ten* 'bone,' below)

bur (H,N,Y) '(single) hair,' *-l-pur* (H) ~ *-r-pur* (N) ~ *-mú-r-puli-ań* (Y) 'eyelid' (where *-l-* ~ *-r-* = 'eye'), *-ś-pur-ań* (H) ~ *-ṣ-pur-ań* (N) ~ *-ṣ-puri-ań* (Y) 'mane (of animals)' (where *-ś-* ~ *-ṣ-* = 'neck')
~ Basque *buru* 'head,' *be-p(h)uru* 'eyebrow' (*be(t)-* = *begi* 'eye')
§ Bur. and Basque compared by Berger (1956, p. 9, note 16).

galgí (H,N,Y) 'wing, fin'
~ Cauc: Lak *qa* 'wing,' Lezgi *γil* hand,' etc. < PEC **qĭlʔi* (NCED 895)
~ Basque *hegal* 'wing'
§ Bur. and Basque compared by Berger (1956: 7).

-ġáan (H,N) ~ *-ġán* (Y) 'heel'
~ Cauc: Avar *eγé* 'heel,' Lak *niq:a* 'heel,' etc. < PEC **ʔĭnɢwV̆* (NCED 248)
~ Basque *oin* 'foot' (*huñ* in the Zuberoan dialect)
§ Bur. and Basque compared by Berger (1956: 10).

-húṭes (Y) ~ *-úṭis, -úṭ* (H,N) 'foot'
~ Cauc: Avar *ħet'é / ħet'* 'foot,' Chechen *t'a* 'front leg (of animal),' etc. < PEC **t'wīfiV̄ (~ *fiwīt'V̄)* (NCED 1007)

jaláalimiń 'long hair (of people)'
~ Cauc: Karata *žale* 'mane,' Lak *zulū* 'nap, pile,' etc. < PEC **ǯāɫhɨɨ* (NCED 1101)

-kin (H,N) ~ *-ken* (Y) 'liver'
~ Cauc: Chamalal *k'ũũ* 'liver', Andi *k':unu* 'kidney', etc. < PEC **k̲'unHV* (NCED 728)
~ Basque ? *kun- / gun-* in the dialectal words *kuntzurrun ~ guntzurrun* 'kidney' (Bizkaia, Gipuzkoa), elsewhere *giltzurrin*, etc. In all cases, an old compound with obscure components.

kúur 'finger-joint, toe-joint'; *kurón* 'bone'

~ Cauc: Chechen *k'uram* 'bone (for playing dice)', Lezgi *k'ur* 'hoof, leg (of animal),' etc. < PEC **k'wĭrV* (NCED 736)

-*mélc̣* (H,N,Y) 'jaw, jawbone'

~ Cauc: Tabasaran *melz* 'tongue,' Khinalug *mic'* 'tongue', etc. < PNC **mĕlc̣'ĭ* (NCED 802)

~ Basque *mihi (> mii, mi)* 'tongue'

§ For phonology, see Bengtson (1999).

-*miṣ* (H,N) ~ -*meṣ* (Y) 'finger, toe'

~ Cauc: Kryts *mič'*-ek 'hoof, nail, claw,' Lak x:i-*mič'* 'hoof,' etc. < PEC **mič'V* (NCED 819)

-*móqiṣ* (H,N) 'cheek' ~ -*móqiṣ* (Y) 'face,' -*móqoṭ* 'cheek'

~ Basque *moko ~ mokho* 'beak, forehead,' *mok(h)oz-mok(h)o* 'face-to-face'

-*múltur* (H,N) 'nostril'

~ Basque *mutur ~ muthur* 'snout, muzzle'

§ Bur. and Basque compared by Berger (1959, p. 33, note 57). Caucasian forms such as Batsbi *marƚŏ* 'nose,' Bezhta *moλ'o* 'beak' could be related (cf. NCED 1041).

-*múś* (H,N,Y) 'nose, snot'

~ Cauc: Chechen *marš* 'snot,' Andi *maču* 'snot,' etc. < PEC **mHărčwV* (NCED 816)

~ Basque (Gipuzkoa) *musu* 'nose' (in other dialects: 'snout, face, lip, kiss,' etc.)

-*pat* (H) ~ -*phat* (N) ~ -*p(h)at* (Y) 'side, flank'

~ Cauc: Lezgi *p:ad* 'side,' etc. < PEC **bVdV* (cf. Urartian *bedə* 'side; (postpos.) on the part of, by'; NCED 315)

pholġó (Y) ~ *phulġúuẏ* (H) ~ *phurġúuẏ* (N) 'feather'

~ Cauc: Lak *p'iƕulli* 'feather,' Dargwa (Akushi) *paḥala* 'feather,' etc. < PNC **p'VƕVƚV* (NCED 879)

~ Basque *bilho* 'hair, mane'

-qat (H) ~ *-qhat* (N) ~ *-qet*-arań (Y) 'armpit'
~ Cauc: Avar me-*héd* 'brisket (chest of animal),' Bezhta *γade* 'brisket' < PEC **qVdV* (NCED 897)

-qháśiń (H,N) 'hind end, arse' ~ *-xáśań* (Y) 'female sex organ'
~ Cauc: Udi *qoš* 'behind,' etc. < PEC **-VqV* (? NCED 1026)
§ Comparison by Bouda (1954, p. 229, no. 28).

-qhát (H,N) ~ *-xát, -xat* (Y) mouth'
~ Cauc: Lak *qʷi̯t'* 'Adam's apple, beak,' etc. < PEC **qwi̯t'i* (NCED 905)

-qhúrpat (H,N) ~ *-xórpet* (Y) 'lung'
~ Cauc: Tsez *χot'ori,* Archi *χurt:ur*-t:i, etc. 'lung' < PEC **q̱wəlθV(rV̄)* (NCED 901)
~ Basque *hauspo* (~ *haspo* ~ *hausko*) 'bellows' ('lung' in the Bizkaian dialect)
§ Bur. and Basque compared by Berger (1959: 21).

-sán (H,N,Y) 'spleen'
~ Cauc: Tindi *s:imi* 'gall (liver bile); anger,' Archi *s:am* 'gall,' etc. < PNC **c̱wäjmě* (NCED 329)
~ Basque *behazun (*be-ha-zun)* 'bile'

-sú (Y) ~ *-súi* (H,N) 'navel, umbilical cord'
Cauc: Dargwa (Chirag) *zu* 'navel,' Tindi *c:ũũ* 'navel,' etc. < PEC **ǯŏnʔŭ* (NCED 1096)

-súsun (H,N) ~ *-sésen* (Y) 'elbow'
~ Cauc: Udi *sun* 'elbow', Lak *s:an* 'foreleg, paw, pad,' etc. < PEC **s̱inŏ* (NCED 963)

tal (H) 'stomach, belly'
~ Cauc: Avar *t'ul* 'liver', Lak *t:ilik'* 'liver,' etc. < PEC **Hläƛ'V* (NCED 586)
§ Note recurrent correspondences of Burushaski *t-* with Caucasian lateral affricates (λ, ƛ, ƛ') and Basque *l-,* see the next four entries, and the Phonology section of this paper.

táno (H,N) 'colon, rectum' (probably related to *táno, tanéelo* 'illegitimate child, of low birth')
~ Cauc: Avar *t'ínu* 'bottom,' Khinalug *k'an-i*k' 'under,' etc. < PNC *$H\bar{\lambda}'\breve{o}n\breve{u}$ (NCED 590)

tar-íŋ '*skin' > 'bag made from animal hide (for containing fluids, or for rafts)'
~ Cauc: Avar *λ̃:er* 'color' (< *'skin'), Dargwa *guli* 'skin, hide, sheepskin,' etc. < PNC *$\underline{\lambda}\breve{o}li$ '*skin' (NCED 789)
~ Basque *larru* 'skin, hide, leather'
§ Bur. and Basque compared by Berger (1959, p. 26, note 34).

ten (Y) 'bone' ~ *-ltín, tin* (H,N) 'bone'
~ Cauc: Avar *λ̃':an* 'groin', Agul *k:un* 'ankle,' etc. < PEC *$\underline{\lambda}'wVnʔV$ (NCED 785)

tur (Y) ~ *-ltúr, tur* (H,N) 'horn'
~ Cauc: Avar *λ̃:ar*, Chechen *kur* 'horn,' etc. < PEC *$\underline{\lambda}ʮɨrV$ (NCED 771)
~ Basque *adar* 'horn' (< *a-rdar*)
§ Bur. and Basque compared by Berger (1959, p. 34, note 57).

-úl (H,N,Y) 'belly, abdomen, bowels'
~ Cauc: Tindi b-*eλ̃':u* 'stomach, rennet, abomasum' (*b-* = class prefix), Dargwa (Akushi) *-arg* 'stomach, inside,' etc. < PEC *-$ɧra\underline{\lambda}V$ (NCED 670)
~ Basque *urdail* 'stomach,' (in Bizkaian also 'rennet; womb')

-yáldir (H) ~ *-yáldin* (N) 'the part of the ribs under the armpit; middle part of the breast'
~ Cauc: Akhwakh *raλ̃':iča* 'belt, girdle,' Hunzib *ɔλ̃e* 'belt', etc. < PEC *$j\breve{e}r\underline{\lambda}'wV$ (NCED 678)
§ For the regular correspondence of Burushaski *-lt-* (*-ld-*) to Caucasian *-λ̃-
(*-λ̃'-), see the Phonology section of this paper. For semantics, cf. Greek ζῶνη [zōnē] 'waist, loins; belt, girdle'.

Nature:

baṅ (N) ~ *baṅgí* 'resin (of trees)'
~ Cauc: Chechen *baga* 'pine tree,' Lezgi *muk'*-rag 'fir tree,' etc. < PEC **bḧĭnk'wV* (NCED 296)

bar (H,N,Y) 'small valley, ravine, gorge'
~ Basque *ibar* 'valley'
§ Bur. and Basque compared by Berger (1956: 7; 1959: p. 28, note 39).

bun, (pl.) *bundó* (H,N) 'mountain pasture, mountain grove; boulder; wild, mountain-' ~ *bun,* (pl.) *bundó* ~ *bunjó* (Y) 'boulder'
~ Basque *mendi* 'mountain'
§ Bur. and Basque compared by Berger (1959, p. 28, note 41).
díltar 'buttermilk'
~ Cauc: Avar *rax* 'milk,' Hunzib *reɬ* 'butter,' etc. < PNC **rḧăƛwV̆* (NCED 949)
§ For the regular correspondence of Burushaski -*lt-* (-*ld-*) to Caucasian **-ƛ-*
(*-ƛ'-), see the Phonology section of this paper

duldúm 'rising cloud (of dust, smoke, etc.)' < *dul* + *dúm* ?
~ Cauc: Archi *diɬʷ* 'cloud,' Lak *t:urlu* 'cloud,' etc. < PEC **dilₜwV* (NCED 400)

ge ~ *gye* (H,N,Y) 'snow'
~ Cauc: Khinalug *q:i* 'cold' (n.), Lak -*ǝ-q:i* 'to grow cold, catch cold,' etc. < PNC
*-HīGA (NCED 568)

gon (H,N,Y) 'dawn'; cf. *gunċ* (H,N,Y) 'day'
~ Cauc: Lak *q'ini* 'day,' Avar *q':o* 'day,' etc. < PEC **Hwīq'ī-(nV)* (NCED 622)
~ Basque *egun (egu-, egur-)* 'day'
§ Burushaski and Basque compared by Berger (1956: 16).

ġónderes ~ *ġondoles* (Y) 'water, that runs over many stones'

~ Cauc: Botlikh γadaru 'stream, brook,' Lak ǧtara 'mountain stream,' etc. < PEC *γHwadVrV (NCED 478)

§ Note: Burushaski ġ and Caucasian γ are the same sound (voiced uvular fricative).

haménç (Y) 'curds, cheese'
~ Cauc: Chechen morza 'whey, buttermilk,' Lezgi č'em 'butter', Khinalug mic 'butter, oil,' etc. < PEC *Hȝ́ĕmɨ (NCED 624)

hun (H,N) 'wood, timber, beam, hewn trunk,' (Y) 'wood, firewood'
~ Cauc: Chechen ḥun 'forest,' Khwarshi hun 'mountain,' etc. < PNC *fãnV (NCED 425)
~ Basque: oihan 'forest, woods'

mal (H,N,Y) 'field'
~ Cauc: Archi maɬ:i 'winter pasture,' Avar márxi 'farmstead,' etc. < PNC *malxwē (NCED 795)

phétiṅ (H,N,Y) 'ashes'
~ Cauc: Dargwa pat:a 'excrement,' Akhwakh beda 'dirt', etc. < PEC *pidV (NCED 871)

phunċ (H,N,Y) 'dew'
~ Cauc: Lak pic' 'dew, sweat,' Dargwa penc' 'resin', Ubykh bzə 'water,' etc. < PNC *pĭnc̣'wA (NCED 871)

*-śare ~ *-śere '*night,' in: gó(i)n-śare (H,N) ~ gón-śere (Y) 'the whole night, all the night through' (gon = 'dawn')
~ Cauc: Avar sordó 'night,' Chechen süjrē 'evening,' etc. < PNC *śwErV (NCED 977)

śi (H,N) 'fireplace, hearth'; cf. śútum (Y) id.
~ Cauc: Ingush c'i, Lak c'u, etc. 'fire' < PNC *c'äjɨ 'fire' (NCED 354)
~ Basque su 'fire'
§ Bur. and Basque compared by Berger (1956: 17).

taγ (Y) 'branch, shoot'

~ Cauc: Hinukh λ'iχ 'bough,' Lak k'urχ 'sprout,' etc. < PEC *λ'ōrχwV (NCED 780)

tap (H,N,Y) 'leaf'; *-ltápu-* (H,N) ~ *-ltápi-* (Y) 'to wither'
~ Cauc: Lak č'ap'i, Adyge tħāp 'leaf,' etc. < PNC *λ'ăpi (NCED 774)

tápi (H,N) 'stone terrace'
~ Cauc: Avar λ'eb 'stone', etc. < PEC *λ'ĕpV̄ (NCED 777)
~ Basque (Zuberoan) *lape* 'shelter under the eaves of a shed'

ter (H,N,Y) 'high pasture, summer mountain pasture'
~ Basque *larre* 'grassland, pasture'
§ Bur. and Basque compared by Berger (1959, p. 26, note 34).

tik (H,N,Y) 'earth, ground; rust'
~ Basque *leku* ~ *lekhu* 'place'

tiṣ (H,N,Y) 'wind'
~ Cauc: Tsez ɬaci 'wind,' Akhwakh λãc':o 'voice, shout,' etc. < PEC *λ[a]rc̣'V (NCED 767)

tumáẏ (H,N) 'nutshell, shell of fruitstone' ~ *tumá* (Y) 'hard shell (of nut, egg), fruit stone'
~ Cauc: Chechen t'um 'marrow; kernel (of a fruit, nut),' Abkhaz a-t'amá 'peach,' etc. < PNC *t'ümhV (NCED 1004)

ther (H,Y) ~ *ther-k* (N) 'dirt'
~ Cauc: Akhwakh tereti 'ashes, dust,' Bezhta tär 'sheep's dungm' etc. < PEC *türV (NCED 993)

yáltar (H,N) 'upper leafy branches' ~ *galtár* (H,N,Y) 'small branch, twig'
~ Cauc: Avar ʕarλ':él 'branch, bough,' etc. < PEC *ɦălχ'VɬV (NCED 508)
§ For the regular correspondence of Burushaski *-lt-* to Caucasian *-λ- (*-λ'-)*, see the Phonology section of this paper.

Wild animals:

balás (H) ~ *baláć* (N) '(larger) bird'
~ Cauc: Avar *γálo* 'jackdaw,' Adyge *q:ʷaʟa-ź* 'crow,' etc. < PNC **GHwV̄ɬV* (NCED 460; ʟ denotes a voiced lateral fricative)
~ Basque *bele ~ bela ~ belatzaga*, etc. 'crow, raven,' *belatz* 'sparrow hawk'
§ Assumes **Gw > b* in Burushaski and Basque.

ćargé (Y) 'flying squirrel'
~ Cauc: Chechen *šat'q'a* 'weasel,' Andi *sarX̌':u* 'weasel,' Adyge *cəγʷa* 'mouse,' etc. < PNC **cārgwɨ* (NCED 322)
~ Basque *sagu* 'mouse'; *sagu-zahar* 'bat' ('mouse-old'); combinatory form *sat-*, as in *sator* 'mole' ('mouse-dog'?), *satitsu* 'shrew' ('mouse-blind')

çhin (H,N) ~ *çen*(Y) ('small) bird'
~ Cauc: Abaza *c'i-s* 'small bird, sparrow,' Avar *ḥinč':* 'bird', Archi *noc'* '(small) bird, sparrow,' etc. < PNC **finɨć'(w)ĭ* (NCED 525)
§ The comparison assumes metathesis (the Avar form is virtually the reverse of the Bur. forms).

ġúrqun (H) ~ *ġúrquć* (N) ~ *ġórkun* (Y) 'frog'
~ Cauc: Tindi *q':orq':u*, Khinalug *q'urq'or*, Kabardian *ḥandər-q:ʷāq:ʷa*, etc. 'frog' < PNC **q̇'wVrVq'V̄* (NCED 942)

har (H,N) 'corn worm'
~ Cauc: Avar *ḥapára*, Tsakhur *ab̰ra*-wuč'e 'worm' < PEC **ḥabarV* (NCED 508)
~ Basque *har* 'worm'
§ Bur. and Basque compared by Berger (1956: 7).

haúlal (Y) ~ *hoólalas* (H,N) 'butterfly, moth'
~ Basque *euli* 'fly' (insect)
§ Bur. and Basque compared by Berger (1956: 16), citing Zarubin's transcription of Yasin *ahúlal*. There is also an isolated Caucasian word: Archi *hiliku* 'fly'.

khin (H,N) ~ *khen* (Y) 'flea'
~ Cauc: Chechen *γēnig* 'louse,' Dargwa *q'i* 'nit', etc. < PEC **q'ǟnʔV* (NCED 911)
~ Basque *akain* 'tick'

khíśo (H,N) ~ *khíśu* (Y) 'mosquito'
~ Basque *kokoso* ~ *kukuso* 'flea'

pherán (Y) 'moth' ~ *phirán* (H,N) 'spider'
~ Cauc: Chechen *polla* 'butterfly,' Andi *pera* 'bee', etc. < PEC **pŏrV* (NCED 875)
~ Basque *pinpirin* ~ *pinpilin* 'butterfly'

phin (H,N) ~ *phen* (Y) 'fly' (insect)
~ Cauc: Avar *púq:na* 'drone,' Dargwa (Akushi) *mirqi* 'bee,' etc. < PEC **pänqwV* (NCED 868)

qarúuyo (H) ~ *ġarúuyo* (N) 'heron'
~ Cauc: Adyge *q:araw* 'crane,' Dargwa (Akushi) *q'anq'* 'heron, bustard,' etc. < PNC **q'ǝǝrǝǝq'wV* (NCED 914)

tal (H,N,Y) 'dove'
~ Cauc: Avar *ƛ':iƛ':i* 'a kind of songbird', Budukh *kakɨl* 'partridge,' etc. < PEC **ƛ'eƛ'ē* (NCED 776)
§ Note recurrent correspondences of Burushaski *t-* with Caucasian lateral affricates (λ, ƛ, ƛ'): see Phonology section of this paper.

tur-ćún (Y) ~ *tur*-śún (H,N) 'marmot' (old compound of *tur-* + ?)
~ Cauc: Ingush *ler*-g 'hare,' Andi *ƛ':an*-k'ala, Ubykh *La* 'hare,' etc. < PNC **λǎrV* (NCED 788)
§ Marmot and hare are both rodents. See Phonology section for initial correspondence.

Human relations:

-*ço* (N,H) ~ -*çu* (Y) 'brother (of a man), sister (of a woman); husband of a man's sister'

~ Cauc: Chechen *w-aša* 'brother,' *j-iša* 'sister,' Agul *ču* 'brother,' *či* 'sister,' Adyge *šə* 'brother,' etc. < PNC *-ič̌ī̆* (NCED 669)

~ Basque *ahizpa (a-hiz-pa)* 'sister (of a woman)'

ġul (H,N) 'grudge, enmity, hatred'
~ Cauc: Avar *γʷel* 'gossip, rumor; abuse,' Khinalug *qol* 'offence,' etc. < PEC *ɢwāɬho* (NCED 465)

hir (H,N,Y) 'man; male (of animals)'
~ Cauc: Chechen *ēra* 'ungelt,' Akhwakh *b-eɬ:o* 'male,' etc. < PEC *ʔīrɬwV* (NCED 210)

~ Basque *ar (arr-)* 'male'

-is (Y) 'child; (animal's) young' ~ *-sk* (H,N) '(animal's) young; (jokingly) human child'
~ Cauc: Avar *w-as* 'son,' *j-as* 'daughter,' Bezhta *ožo* 'son, boy,' etc. < PNC *-ĭšwE* (NCED 671)

jaám (H,N) ~ *jâm* (Y) '(distant) kinsman'
~ Cauc: Chechen *zamō* 'best man', Lak *mač:a* 'kinsman,' Rutul *q'u-ǯäm* 'brother-in-law,' etc. < PEC *ǯ̆ămV / *mǟǯ̆V (NCED 1101)

~ Basque *seme* 'son'; cf. *senhar* 'husband'

§ cf. Kartvelian: Megrelian *žima*, Georgian *ʒma* 'brother' (< Cauc?).

sis (H,N) ~ *ses* 'persons, people'
~ Cauc: Ubykh *ć́ə́ć́a* 'persons, people,' Avar *či* 'man,' etc. < PNC *ćwījo (NCED 336)

Descriptives:

babárum (babár-um) (Y) 'hot, pungent' (of food), (H,N) 'pungent (taste); burning (pain); hot-tempered, irascible (person)'
~ Cauc: PWC *bla/ə* 'to burn' (Chirikba 1996: p. 393); Tsez *boboru*, Khwarshi *bobolu* 'hot'

~ Basque *bero* 'hot'

§ Bur. and Basque compared by Berger (1959: 30).

ġaqáy-um (H,N) ~ *qaqám* (Y) 'bitter; unsweetened; sour'
~ Cauc: Chechen *q'äħa* 'bitter,' Ubykh *q'aq'ə* 'sweet,' etc. < PNC **q'ĕfilV* (NCED 912)
~ Basque *karats* 'bitter; foul-smelling'
§ Bur. and Basque compared by Berger (1956: 10).

hultáṣ (Y) 'barefoot'
~ Basque *orthuts* 'barefoot'
§ Compared by Berger (1959, p. 27, note 35).

ṣuqúrum (ṣuq-úr-um*)* (H,N) ~ *iṣqórum (iṣq*-ór-um*)* 'sour, bitter'
~ Cauc: Chamalal *s'ik'u*-b 'sour,' Archi *c'eg^w*-du 'rank, bitter,' etc. < PEC **c̠'ǟk'wV* (NCED 356)

tharén-um (H,N) 'narrow (of clothes)'
~ Cauc: Avar *t'eréna*-b, Khinalug *k'ɨr* 'thin,' etc. < PNC *-iX̌'ɨlV* (NCED 639)
~ Basque *lirain* 'slender'

Morphological evidence: Pronouns

Pronouns: Both Burushaski and the reconstructed Proto-(North) Caucasian have *suppletive* pronoun stems in the first and second person singular. According to Nikolayev and Starostin (1994, pp. 402, 483-84, 855, 1014-15, 1084-85), the original Proto-Caucasian paradigms were very complicated, and difficult to reconstruct with much certainty. For the present purpose, let us compare Hunza Burushaski (Berger 1998, vol. I, p. 80) with two East Caucasian languages, Khinalug and Tsakhur (and PEC):

FIRST AND SECOND PERSON SUPPLETIVE PRONOUN STEMS:

	Direct	Genitive	Dative
1st person singular ('I – me'):			
Burushaski	je, já	áa	áar
Khinalug	zɨ (nom.) jä (erg.)	i, e	as
Tsakhur	zu	jiz-in	za-
(PEC	*zō(-n)	*ʔiz(V)	*ʔez(V) (erg.)))
2nd person singular ('thou – thee'):			
Burushaski	un	góo	góor
Khinalug	wɨ (nom.)	wi	oχ
Tsakhur	wu ~ γu	j-iγ-	wa-
(PEC	*u̯ō(-n) ~ *γwV̄	*ʔeu̯V/*ʔiu̯V	*ʔōγwV (erg.))

Clearly, a great deal of rearrangement has taken place, in all of these languages, since the original paradigms of thousands of years ago. Note also that the Hunza word for 'thou' (direct), *un*, is identical with those of the East Caucasian languages Archi and Udi (*un* 'thou'; cf. Lezgi and Agul *wun* 'thou'). Interestingly, another East Caucasian language, Dargwa (Akushi and Urakhi dialects), has rearranged the first and second person paradigms to coincide with those of Basque:

Dargwa (Akushi, Urakhi)   *nu* 'I'   *ħu* 'thou'
Basque   *ni*   *hi*

Here the *nu/ni* stem is preserved (in Caucasian) only in Dargwa and Lak, while the *ħu/hi* 'thou' stem is presumed cognate with Burushaski *góo*, Tsakhur *γu*, etc.

Phonological Correspondences:

Correspondences of stops: In general, Burushaski unaspirated *p, t, k, q* correspond to Proto-Caucasian (glottalized) **p', *t', *k', *q'*, respectively; and Burushaski aspirated *ph, th, kh, qh* correspond to Proto-Caucasian (aspirated) *p, *t, *k, *q, respectively. See the following examples from the above comparisons:

-kin (H,N) ~ -ken (Y) 'liver' ~ Cauc: Chamalal k'ũũ 'liver,' etc. < PEC *ḵ'unHV

kúur 'finger-joint, toe-joint'; kuróṅ 'bone' ~ Cauc: Chechen k'uram 'bone (for playing dice),' etc. < PEC *k'wĭrV

khor (H,N) 'large wicker basket' ~ Cauc: Akhwakh koro 'trough, gutter,' etc. < PEC *ḵwərV

pherán (Y) 'moth' ~ phirán (H,N) 'spider' ~ Cauc: Andi pera 'bee,' etc. < PEC *pŏrV

phétiṅ (H,N,Y) 'ashes' ~ Cauc: Akhwakh beda 'dirt,' etc. < PEC *pidV

phin (H,N) ~ phen (Y) 'fly' (insect) ~ Cauc: Avar púq:na 'drone,' etc. < PEC *pänqwV

phunć (H,N,Y) 'dew' ~ Cauc: Lak pic' 'dew, sweat,' etc. < PNC *pĭnc̣'wA

qaqám (Y) 'bitter; unsweetened; sour' (but ġaqáẏ- [H,N]) ~ Cauc: Ubykh q'aq'ə 'sweet,' etc. < PNC *q'ĕfilV

qarúuẏo (H) (~ ġarúuẏo [N]) 'heron' ~ Cauc: Adyge q:araw 'crane,' etc. < PNC *q'əərəəq'wV

-qhás̀iṅ (H,N) 'hind end, arse' ~ -xás̀aṅ (Y) 'female sex organ' ~ Cauc: Udi qoš 'behind,' etc. < PEC *-VqV

-qhát (H,N) ~ -xát, -xat (Y) mouth' ~ Cauc: Lak qʷi̯t' 'Adam's apple, beak,' etc. < PEC *qwɨ̈t'i

-qhúrpat (H,N) ~ -xórpet (Y) 'lung' ~ Cauc: Tsez χot'ori, etc. 'lung' < PEC *q̇wəlθV(rV̄)

tókur (H,N) 'wooden chest (for grain, etc.)' ~ Cauc: Rutul *t'ak* 'basket (for berries),' etc. < PNC **t'āqV*

tumáy̯ (H,N) 'nutshell, shell of fruitstone' ~ *tumá* (Y) 'hard shell (of nut, egg), fruit stone' ~ Cauc: Chechen *t'um* 'marrow; kernel (of a fruit, nut),' etc. < PNC **t'ŭmhV*

ther (H,Y) ~ *ther-k* (N) 'dirt' ~ Cauc: Akhwakh *tereti* 'ashes, dust', etc. < PEC **türV*

Correspondences to Caucasian lateral affricates: As already pointed out in some of the notes to the above lexical comparisons, there are recurrent correspondences between Burushaski initial *t-* *(th-)* and medial *-lt-* *(-ld-)* and the Proto-Caucasian lateral affricates (**λ, *ƛ, *ƛ'*), as shown in the following examples. The corresponding reflexes in Basque are initial *l-* and medial *-rd-*, respectively. (Comparisons already listed above will be cited in abbreviated form) :

(a) examples with Burushaski initial *t-* *(th-)*:

Bur. *tal* 'dove' ~ PEC **ƛ'eƛ'ē*

Bur. *tal* (H) 'stomach, belly'~ Cauc: Avar *t'ul* 'liver,' etc. < PEC **Hläƛ'V*

Bur. (H,N) *tápi* 'stone terrace' ~ PEC **ƛ'ĕpV̄* ~ Basque *lape*

Bur. *tur-ćún* ~ *tur-śún* 'marmot' ~ PNC **λărV*

Bur. *tar-íŋ* 'skin bag' ~ PNC **ƛŏli* '*skin' ~ Basque *larru*

Bur. (Y) *taγ* 'branch, shoot' ~ PEC **ƛ'ōrχwV*

Bur. *ter* (H,N,Y) 'high pasture, summer mountain pasture' ~ Basque *larre*

Bur. *tik* (H,N,Y) 'earth, ground; rust' ~ Basque *leku* ~ *lekhu*

Bur. *tiṣ* 'wind' ~ PEC **ƛ[a]rc̣'V*

Bur. (H,N) *tharén-um* 'narrow' ~ PNC **-iƛ'ĭlV* ~ Basque *lirain*

(b) examples with Burushaski alternation of (initial) *t-* / (medial) *-lt-*:

Bur. (Y) *ten* 'bone' / (H,N) *-ltín* 'bone' (bound form) ~ PEC **ƛ'wVnʔV*

Bur. (Y) *tur* 'horn' / (HN) *-ltúr* (bound form) ~ PEC **ƛwĭrV* ~ Basque *adar*

87

Bur. *tap* 'leaf' / du-*ltápi-* (*-ltápu-*) 'to wither' ~ PNC **ƛ'ăpi*

Bur. (Y) *té-* / *-lté-* 'to swear' ~ PEC **Hiƛ̱V* 'to say' (NCED 572)

Bur. (Y) *túl-* / *-ltúl-* 'to saddle' ~ PEC **ƛ̱'wiłē*

Bur. *tá-* / *-ltá-* 'to put on (shoes, stockings)' ~ PEC **-ōmƛV* 'to put on (trousers, shoes)' (NCED 861)

Bur. (Y) *túl*-um / *-ltúl*-um 'the same, like' ~ PEC **-ăƛ̱wVn* 'to resemble, similar' (NCED 261)

(c) examples with Burushaski medial *-lt-* (*-ld-*):

Bur. (Y) *baltí* 'front room of house' ~ PEC **bŭlƛ̱'V*

Bur. *-ltar-*, *-ltir-* 'to show' ~ PEC **ʔiƛ̱V* 'to look' (NCED 209)

Bur. *díltar* 'buttermilk' ~ PNC **rħăƛwV̆*

Bur. (H,N) *giyált* 'spoon, scoop' ~ PEC **jă[l]ƛwV*

Bur. (N) *daltán-* 'to thresh' (< **raƛan-*) ~ PEC **-V̄rƛV*

Bur. *yáltar* (H,N) 'upper leafy branches', etc. ~ PEC **ɦălƛ̱'VłV*

Bur. (H) *-yáldir* ~ (N) *-yáldin* 'part of the ribs,' etc. ~ PEC **jĕrƛ̱'wV*

Bur. (Y) (ba)-*hált-* 'to wash' ~ PEC **-Vƛ̱'Vn* 'to wash, pour, weep' (NCED 1023)

Cf. also cases where one East Caucasian language, Avar, partially converges with Burushaski in the development [t'] < **ƛ'*:

Avar *t'ul* 'liver' (< **ƛ'äHlV*) = Bur. *tal* 'stomach, belly'

Avar *t'ínu* 'bottom' (< **Hƛ'ŏnŭ*) = Bur. *táno* 'rectum'

Avar *t'eréna*-b 'thin' (< **-iƛ'ĭlV*) = Bur. *tharén*-um 'narrow (of clothes)' = Bsq. *lirain*

Further examples are given in Bengtson (2005).

Cultural vocabulary: words for domestic animals:

aćás (H,N,Y) 'sheep, goat, sheep and/or goat(s) = Kleinvieh, small cattle'

~ Cauc: Adyge *āča* 'he-goat,' Dargwa (Akushi) *ʕeža* ~ (Chirag) *ʕač:a* 'goat,' etc. < PNC **ʔēǰʒ̂wē* (NCED 245)

§ Note the semantic variation 'sheep' ~ 'goat,' which recurs in several of the comparisons below. Cf. *huyés,* below.

buć (H,N) '(ungelt) male goat, 2 or 3 years old'

~ Cauc: Lak *buχca (< *buc-χa?)* 'he-goat (1 year old),' Rutul *bac'i* 'small sheep,' Khinalug *bac'ɨz* 'kid,' etc. < PEC **b[a]c'V* (NCED287)

§ Note variation between the meanings 'young goat' and 'young kid' within the East Caucasian family. Berger (1998: 60) notes a similar word in Wakhi, *buč* (< Burushaski?).

ćigír (Y) ~ *ćhigír* (N) ~ *ćhiír* (H) '(she-)goat'

~ Cauc: Karata *c':ik'er* 'kid,' Lak *c'uku* 'goat,' etc. < PNC **ʒ̄īkV̆ / *k̄ɨʒ̂V̆* (NCED 1094)

~ Basque *zikiro ~ zikhiro* 'castrated goat'

ćhindár (H,N) ~ *ćuldár* (Y) 'bull' (Yasin form influenced by *ćulá*? See next entry.)

~ Cauc: Chamalal, Bagwali *zin,* Tindi, Karata *zini* 'cow,' etc. < Proto-Avar-Andian **zin-HV* (NCED 262-263)

~ Basque *zezen* 'bull'

ćhulá (H,N) ~ *ćulá* (Y) 'male breeding stock': (H) 'drake,' (N,Y) 'buck goat'

~ Cauc: Andi *č'ora* 'heifer,' Agul *luč* 'heifer,' Chechen *ēsa* 'calf,' etc. < PEC **HċwīlV̆ / *Hl̄ɨċwV* (NCED 556)

~ Basque *txahal* [čahal] ~ *xahal* [šahal] > *txaal,* etc. 'heifer, calf'

du (H,N,Y) 'kid, young goat up to one year'

~ Cauc: Chechen *tō* 'ram,' Lak *t:a* 'sheep, ewe,' Kabardian *t'ə* 'ram,' etc. < PNC **dwăn̄ʔV* (NCED 405)

ḍágar (N) 'ram'

~ Cauc: Avar *deʕén* 'he-goat,' Hinukh *t'eq'ʷi* 'kid (about 1 year old),' etc. < PEC **dVrq'wV* (NCED 403)

élgit (N) ~ *hálkit* (Y) 'she-goat, over 1 year old, which has not given birth'
~ Cauc: Agul, Tsakhur *urg* 'lamb (less than a year old),' Chamalal *barg*ʷ 'a spring-time lamb,' etc. < PEC **ʔwɨlgɨ* (NCED 232)

huyés (H,N,Y) 'Kleinvieh, small cattle, sheep and/or goats'
~ Cauc: Avar *ʕi* 'sheep flock', Lak *ja-* 'sheep flock' < PEC **ɦVʔV̆* (NCED 532)
§ Cf. *aćás,* above.

thugár (H,N) 'buck goat'
~ Cauc: Karata *t'uka* 'he-goat,' Bezhta *t'iga* 'he-goat,' etc. < PNC **t'ūgV̄* (NCED 1003)

Cultural vocabulary: the horse:

haġúr ~ haġór 'horse'
~ Cauc: Kabardian *xʷāra* 'thoroughbred horse,' Lezgi *χʷar* 'mare,' etc. < PNC **farnē* (NCED 425)
~ Basque *behor ~ bohor* 'mare' (if < **(H)weH(w)or,* or sim.)
§ Berger (1998: 185) notes resemblance to Turkish *aiġır* 'stallion'.

-ltúl (H,N,Y) 'to saddle (a horse), prepare mount,' *tilíañ* (H,N) ~ *tilíhañ ~ teléhañ* (Y) 'saddle' (n.)
~ Cauc: Avar *X̌':ilí* [tɬ':ilí], Lak *k'ili,* etc. 'saddle' < PEC **X̱'wilē* 'saddle' (NCED 783)

Cultural vocabulary: grain cultivation and production:

baẏ (H,N: double plural *baçéñ ~ báẏiñ*) ~ *ba* (Y) '(small-grained) millet' (Panicum miliaceum)
~ Cauc: Chechen *borc* 'millet,' Karata *boča* 'mille,' etc. < PNC **bŏlćwĭ* (NCED 309)

ćha (H,N) ~ ća 'millet' (Setaria italica)
~ Cauc: Bezhta č'e 'a species of barley,' Andi č'or 'rye,' etc. < PEC *č'[e]ħlV (NCED 384)

daltán- (N) 'to thresh (millet, buckwheat)' (< *r-aƛa-n-)
~ Cauc: Ingush ard-, Batsbi arl- 'to thresh,' Tindi rali 'grain ready for threshing,' etc. < PEC *-V̄rλV 'to thresh,' *r-ĕλō 'grain ready for threshing' (NCED 1031)

darċ 'threshing floor, grain ready for threshing'
~ Cauc: Dargwa daraz 'threshing floor,' Lak t:arac'a-lu id., Tabasaran rac: id., etc. < PEC *ħrənʒū (NCED 503)
§ Comparison by Bouda (1954, p. 228, no. 4: Burushaski + Lak).

gur (H,N,Y) 'whea,' gurgán (H,N) 'wheat sown in autumn'
~ Cauc: Tindi q':eru, Archi qoqol, etc. 'wheat' < PEC *ɢōlʔe (NCED 462)
~ Basque gari 'wheat' (combinatory form gal-)
§ Berger (1998: 161) notes the similar Tibetan word, gro 'wheat.'

harṣ (H,N) ~ harṣ ~ haṣċ (Y) 'plow'
~ Cauc: Akhwakh ʕerc:e 'wooden plow,' Lak qa-ras id., etc. < PNC *Hrājcū (NCED 601)

Cultural vocabulary: other artifacts:

baltí (Y) 'front room of house' ~ baldí (H,N) 'veranda'
~ Cauc: Hinukh buƛe 'house,' Lak burč'a-lu 'threshold', etc. < PEC *bŭlX̱'V (NCED 312)

ċhágur (H,N) 'chest or box for grain or meal'
Cauc: Avar caɣúr 'corn bin, barn,' Chechen cχar 'penthouse,' etc. < PEC *cVɢVrV̆ (NCED 328)

giyált (H,N) 'spoon, scoop'
~ Cauc: Hunzib ẽgu 'wooden shovel,' Lezgi jirf id., etc. < PEC *jă[l]ƛwV (NCED 673)

khor (H,N) 'large wicker basket'
~ Cauc: Akhwakh *koro* 'trough, gutter,' Lezgi *k:ʷar* 'a big jar (for carrying water),' etc. < PEC *$\underline{k}$wərV* (NCED 706)

tókur (H,N) 'wooden chest (for grain, etc.)'
~ Cauc: Ingush *t'aqa* 'tub (for cheese brine),' Rutul *t'ak* 'basket (for berries),' etc. < PNC *t'āqV* (NCED 997)

-yeéś (H,N) 'lasting dwelling place, permanent residence'
~ Cauc: Tsakhur *jic'a* 'sty, cattle shed,' Ubykh *cʷəjá* 'house, roomk' etc. < PNC *c'[ī]ju (/ *j[ī]c'u)* (NCED 364)
~ Basque *etxe* [eče] 'house'
§ Bur. and Basque compared by Berger (1956: 18, 24).

Abbreviations:
H = Hunza,
N = Nager,
Y = Yasin (dialects of Burushaski);
NCED = Nikolayev & Starostin 1994
PEC = Proto-East Caucasian,
PNC = Proto-North Caucasian,
PWC = Proto-West Caucasian

CONCLUSIONS:

On the basis of more than 70 cognate sets in basic vocabulary, together with the regular phonological patterning of the cognates and the shared morphological patterns, a genetic relationship among Burushaski, the North Caucasian languages, and Basque is the best hypothesis for explaining these similarities.

Cultural vocabulary shared by the same languages, including words for domestic sheep and goats, for cultivated grain crops (and processes connected with them), and for other artifacts, suggests that the speakers of the proto-language ancestral to these languages (Euscaro-Caucasian or Macro-Caucasian) dispersed as early as 7000 to 9000 years BP in association with the spread of animal domestication and the cultivation of grain.

BASQUE PHONOLOGY IN THE LIGHT OF THE DENE-CAUCASIAN HYPOTHESIS[167]

The genetic classification of the mysterious Basque language has been a topic of vigorous discussion throughout the Twentieth Century, and this discussion continues to the present day. Some of the latest exchanges in this discussion are found in the journals *Mother Tongue* (especially issues I and V) and *Dhumbadji!* (see References). Impelled by severe criticism (especially by R.L. Trask) as well as by gentle criticism and encouragement (see, *e.g.*, Blažek 1995, Starostin 1996), I have worked intermittently for several years at establishing regular phonological correspondences between Basque and the languages I consider most closely related to it, namely the (North) Caucasian languages, and Burushaski. In several articles previously published, I have used the terms "Macro-Caucasian" or "Vasco-Caucasian" for this language family, which I consider to be a subgroup of the larger family (macro-family) "Dene-Caucasian" (Starostin's "Sino-Caucasian") that also includes the Sino-Tibetan, Yeniseian, and Na-Dene families. In the present paper, comparisons will primarily be made within the Macro-Caucasian family (Basque + Caucasian + Burushaski), with occasional references to other Dene-Caucasian languages. Lexical comparisons involving only Caucasian and Burushaski (and not Basque) will be set aside for the time being.

THE PHONOLOGICAL SYSTEM OF BASQUE

A common Basque consonant inventory is as follows (modified from Hualde, 1991):

---

[167] The present paper is an extensive revision of a paper completed and privately circulated in 1997, entitled "Some Observations on Macro-Caucasian Phonology." It was revised in 2004-05 while I was working with the of the Evolution of Human Language Project (EHL - Santa Fe Instutute). I am grateful for the support of EHL and especially for extensive discussions with the late Sergei A. Starostin.

Labial	Dental/Alveolar[168]		Palatal	Velar
p	t		c	k
b	d		ɟ	g
f	s̄	ś	š	x
	c̄	ć	č	
m	n		ñ	
	l		ʎ	
	r			
	r̄			

In standard Basque orthography, the phonemes /**p, t, k, b, d, g, f, m, n, ñ, l, r**/ are written with the corresponding Latin or Spanish letters: *p, t, k, b, d, g, f, m, n, ñ, l, r*. The remaining phonemes are represented as follows:

c = tt   as in *ttipi* 'very small, tiny' (dim. of *tipi*)
ɟ = dd   as in *onddo* 'toadstool, fungus'
s̄ = z   as in *zazpi* 'seven'
c̄ = tz *as in* hotz *'cold'*
ś = s   as in *sei* 'six'
ć = ts   as in *huts* 'fault, empty'
š = x   as in *xexen* 'small bull' (dim. of *zezen*)
č = tx   as in *txitxar* 'grasshopper, cicada'
ʎ = ll   as in *bello* 'hot' (dim. of *bero*)
r̄ = rr   as in *harri* 'stone'
x = j   as in *jan* 'to eat' (but only in western Basque, mainly Gipuzkoa)
Elsewhere the grapheme *j* is pronounced [dž] (Bizkaia), [j] (Alto Navarro), [j] (Lapurdi, Basse Navarre), [ž] (Zuberoa), or even other variants.[169]

Northern ("French" Basque) dialects (Lapurdi, Basse Navarre, Zuberoa) also have a phoneme /**h**/, generally corresponding to orthographic *h*. These same dialects lack the phoneme /**x**/, and also tend to have aspirated consonants, such as Zuberoan *phiper* 'pepper' (but BN, L *bipher*), *thu* 'spit,' *khedarre* 'soot,' *anhua* 'provisions,' *iñhar* 'a little,' *alhaba* 'daughter,' *ürhe* 'gold,' etc.

---

[168] /**t, d**/ are dental; /**l, n, r, r̄**/ are alveolar; /**s̄, c̄**/ are dorso-alveolar (= lamino-alveolar); /**ś, ć**/ are apico-alveolar.

[169] See the map presented by Trask (1997, p. 86).

The voiced obstruents written *b, d, g* have stop [b, d, g] or fricative [β, ð, γ] allophones, depending on their position in the word or phrase.[170] Trask (1997) prefers to call the latter "continuants" (approximants with no audible friction).

The Basque vowel system is a simple 5-vowel system: /a, e, i, o, u/. Only the Zuberoan (Souletin) dialect differs in also having the front-round vowel /ü/. Zuberoan and Roncalese also have a contrastive set of nasal vowels /ã, ẽ, ĩ, õ, ũ, ü̃/.

THE PHONOLOGICAL SYSTEM OF PROTO-CAUCASIAN

In this paper, the Proto-Caucasian (PNC) reconstruction by Nikolayev and Starostin is accepted as a baseline while recognizing that some details are open to correction or modification. Nikolayev and Starostin (1994: 40) postulate the following consonant phonemes:[171]

labial	p	b	ṗ			w	m	u̯
dental	t	d	ṭ			r	n	j
hissing	c	ʒ	c̣	s	z			
palatal (hissing-hushing)	ć	ʒ́	ć̣	ś	ź			
hushing	č	ǯ	č̣	š	ž			
lateral	λ	ƛ	λ̣	ɬ		l		ɫ
velar	k	g	ḳ	x				
uvular	q		q̇	χ	ʁ			
laryngeal			ʔ	h	ɦ			
emphatic laryngeal			ʔ̣	ḥ	ʕ			

For explanations of the phonetic symbols, see Appendix C.

Nikolayev and Starostin (NCED, p. 72) reconstruct 9 vowels for Proto-Caucasian, each of which may be short or long:

---

[170] This pattern is similar to, but not identical with, the pattern in Castilian Spanish. (See Hualde 1991.)

[171] "Two more very rare voiced fricatives are reconstructed for PEC (lateral L and velar γ), as well as the supposedly interdental fricatives ϑ and ϑ:. These phonemes have no correspondences in PWC, and their existence in PNC is dubious." (NCED, p. 41)

i	ü	ɨ	u
e		o	
ä		a	

NATIVE OR BORROWED?

In a study of comparative phonology, it is necessary to distinguish native words from borrowed words, since only the former bear witness to the regular patterns typical of genetic relationship.[172] Of the roughly 300 Basque words discussed in this paper, a preponderance (about 260) are indisputably of native Basque origin, and for these there are no serious hypotheses of borrowed origin. For just over a tenth of the total (about 35), there have been more-or-less serious etymological proposals deriving the words from other languages, usually Latin/Romance, but occasionally other (or "unknown") sources. In each case, I have carefully considered phonetic, semantic, and historical factors to determine whether a Basque word is most likely native or borrowed.

It is undisputed that many Basque words, even some basic ones, are loanwords. A clear example is the basic word *luma* 'feather.' Because the Romance languages surrounding Basque have a similar word (Spanish, Portuguese *pluma*, from Latin *plūma*), it is obvious that Basque borrowed the word from a Romance source, and there are no likely candidates for cognates in Dene-Caucasian languages. Other cases, in which we find likely parallels both in Romance and in Dene-Caucasian, are more difficult to resolve. Some examples will be mentioned here, and others will be found elsewhere in this paper.

As an example of phonetic factors, the internal clusters /lh/ and /rh/ (in northern Basque dialects) are usually characteristic of native Basque words.[173] For this reason and others I consider Basque words such as *bilho 'hair, mane,' *mulho 'heap,' *śorho 'field, meadow' most likely to be native Basque and not borrowed as commonly supposed. The proposed Caucasian cognates of these words (*ṗVħVɨV, *muħalV, *čHäɨu, respectively) all have laryngeals that account for the (northern) Basque /h/. As shown elsewhere in this paper, several other (undisputed native) Basque

---

[172] Of course, once a word enters a language it thereafter undergoes the same regular changes as words native to the language or borrowed earlier.

[173] At least in the noun stem of the type (C)VRHV. There are some loanwords of the type (Z) *gelhari* 'maidservant, governess' (< Latin *cellaria*), with accent after the *-lh-*.

words show the same regular correspondence: see *belhaī 'grass,' *ilhaī 'peas,' *bulhaī 'chest,' *gorhi 'butter,' etc.

As an example of semantic factors, there is the Basque word *abere* 'domestic animal, cattle,' in which I differ from most vasconists who derive this word from Latin *habere* 'to have.' The huge semantic discrepancy is explained as the *reverse* of Latin *pecu, pecus* 'sheep, cattle' > *pecunia* 'property, money,' though no typological parallels for the change 'to have' > 'animal' have been offered. In this paper, I suggest a semantically exact alternative. Because Basque *abere* has a stem variant *abel-* (*abel-gorri* 'bovine stock,' lit. 'cattle-red,' etc.), I posit the earlier form **a-bele,* which can be straightforwardly compared with Udi *bele* 'cattle,' Hunzib *bala* 'chamois,' etc. < Proto-Caucasian **bŭłV* (see **1. 23**).

As an example of historical factors, it is widely supposed (Michelena, Trask) that Basque *kaiku* 'wooden bowl used for milking sheep' is borrowed from Latin *caucus* 'drinking vessel.' In investigating this Latin word, I found it to be very obscure – it is not even cited in standard Latin dictionaries. In modern Romance languages, its only descendant is Rumanian *cauc* 'ladle,' with no attestation at all in Iberia.[174] I find it highly unlikely, from a historical standpoint, that the Basque shepherds would even have heard of this arcane foreign word, let alone adopted it to denote an object they had used for untold centuries of milking sheep. And since Dene-Caucasian has an etymology of suitable phonetic shape and semantic content (Caucasian **qwăqwV*, Sino-Tibetan **guăk,* Yeniseian **q ^ k-,* Tlingit *qákw,* etc.), I regard it as more likely that Basque has retained this old DC word (see **6.3**).

Each of the etymologies below is a hypothesis, and as such, is subject to further testing of the types mentioned above. If it turns out that my judgments are faulty, and any or all of the ±35 disputed words turn out to be loanwords after all, we still have the ±260 indisputably native words as a firm basis for the phonology described below.

THE ETYMOLOGIES

The etymologies are arranged according to the Proto-Dene-Caucasian phonemes being compared, in the following order: occlusives and affricates (labial, dental, hissing, hissing-hushing, hushing, lateral affricate, velar, uvular, laryngeal); fricatives (labial, hissing, hissing-hushing, hushing, lateral, velar, uvular, laryngeal); resonants and glides (**m, *n, *r, *l, *w, *j*); vowels.

---

[174] Meyer-Lübke 1935: no. 1773.

Lexical material is presented in the following order: Proto-Basque[175] words, followed by attested forms: (c) indicating common Basque (or the form found in most dialects), then dialectal forms with indications such as (B) = Bizkaian, etc. (See Table of Abbreviations, at the end of the main text.) Caucasian comparanda are presented second, and then Burushaski.

Altogether, about 330 Basque words are discussed in this article. They are indexed in Appendix D under the usual spellings in Basque orthography.

1. Labial Occlusives

PDC *p:* While I agree with Trask (1997, p. 126) that "the evidence for **p** in Pre-Basque is decidedly scanty," there are some examples of **p* both initially and medially, and I think the evidence below calls into question the statement that "fortis/lenis contrast [here, /p/ vs. /b/] was entirely confined to intervocalic position."

1.1. Basque **pinc (> *binc > *minc):* (L,Z) *phintz,* (BN) *p(h)intz(a),* (B,G,AN,R) *mintz* 'membrane (covering an egg or nut)'[176] ~ Cauc: Proto-Lezgian **pinc^w* 'eyelash, feather' > Agul (Keren) *bic'bic'* 'eyelash,' *pinc'* 'feather,' Agul (Burshag) *pinc'* 'eyelash' (cf. NCED 365) ~ Burushaski **phenVs-* > (Y) *-phénas* 'brow, forehead hair,' (H,N) *-phínis, -phíniṣ* (sg.) 'a braid that lies on the ear', (pl.) 'head hair (only of women, close cropped)'

1.2. Basque **pinpiRin* > (L) *pinpirin,* (AN, L) *pinpilin-posa, -pauxa* 'butterfly' ~ PEC **pŏrV* ~ **părVpăłV* > Chechen *polla* 'butterfly,' Andi *pirinpa* 'butterfly,' Tindi *pera* 'bee,' etc. (NCED 875) ~ Burushaski (H, N) *phirán* 'spider', (Y) *pherán* 'moth, soul,' *phéru* 'maggot'[177]

---

[175] Proto-Basque forms are my own reconstruction, which differs in some respects from that of Michelena.

[176] The form *mintz* secondary by nasalization < **binc* <**pinc.* Cf. the parallel process in Agul dialects: Fite *murc'*'feather'; the Burkikhan dialect has both *purc'* and *murc'* 'feather.' The claim of "Latin origin" of Bsq **pinc* (Trask 1995: 58) is hardly tenable, since there is no Latin antecedent. The semantic commonality of 'skin ~ fur ~ hair' is well attested. Cf. Ainu **kAp* 'skin, fur'; **ur* 'fur coat, skin, hair of body,' etc. (Vovin 1993).

[177] Apparently of phonosymbolic origin, but attested in all three Macro-Caucasian families, and thus archaic.

1.3. Basque **puś-* > (B) *puspulu, puspulo* 'bubble,' (B) *pustilla, puxila* 'bubble,' (B, G) *pusla, puslo,* (B) *puxilu* 'blisters,' (B) *puxika* [pušika], *pusiga, puxiga* 'bladder'[178] ~ Batsbi *puš* 'bump, lump,' Dargwa (Kaitag) *puš-lik'* 'bladder,' (Akushi) *pušaʕ* 'bubble, bladder' < PNC **päršwA* (NCED 868)

1.4. Basque **pun-pul-* > (BN) *punpula* 'tear,' (L, R) *punpuilla* 'bubble,' etc. ~ PNC **pHulq̇ɨ* 'dirt; secretion in the eye' > Agul *p'ạr* 'secretion in the eye,' Lezgi *bürq'ü* 'blind', etc. (NCED 871)[179]

1.5. Basque **e-purdi* > (AN, B, BN, G) *ipurdi*, (L) *iphurdi*, (AN) *epurdi*, (B) *eperdi, iperdi* 'rump, buttocks'[180] ~ Archi *pạrt'i* 'large intestine,' Bezhta *pirt!i* 'bladder, lung,' etc. < PEC **pHVrṭwV* (NCED 871) ~ Burushaski (Y) *phaṭ* 'stomach (of fowl),' (H,N) *-phát* 'viscera (of fowl)' ~ cf. ST: PST **Pat* > Burmese *phat* 'to vomit,' etc. (ST I: 98) ~ Na-Dene: Eyak *wətʼ* 'vomit'; PAth **wəṭʼ* 'belly' > Kutchin *vəd,* Kato *-bətʼ,* Navajo *-bìd,* etc.

1.6. Basque **apal* > (B, G) *apal* 'shelf' ~ Avar *epel* 'lid, cover,' Inkhokhwari *apar* 'pole (for planking the ceiling)' < PEC **ʔapVɨV* 'pole; board, cover' (NCED 202)

1.7. Basque **tupV* 1 barrel, cask, 2 pot, kettle, 3 copper > (Z) *tüpa, thüpe* 1, (G) *tupi* 2, *tupiki* 3, (AN, BN, L, R) *tupin(a)* 2, etc. ~ Hunzib *t'ɨpi* 'a small barrel,' Tsakhur *t'opi* 'jug, jar,' etc. < PNC **tʼāpV* (NCED 996)

PDC **pʼ*: There are few examples of Proto-Caucasian **pʼ*, and it is possible that /pʼ/ did not exist in Proto-Dene-Caucasian. These examples suggest that **pʼ* became Basque /b/ initially, /p/ medially. Final labials do not exist in Basque.

1.8. Basque **bilho* > (BN, Z) *bilho,* (AN, BN) *bilo, billo* 'hair, mane'[181] ~ Cauc: Lak *p'iħulli* 'feather,' Dargwa (Akushi) *pạħạla*

---

[178] There has probably been some influence from Romance words for 'bladder' (Spanish *vejiga,* etc. < Latin *vēsīca*), but the element **puś-* is clearly Dene-Caucasian: cf. Dargwa *pušlik'* 'bladder,' for which Latin influence is hardly thinkable.

[179] Here only the sequences **pul-* ~ **pHul-* are compared, with affective changes, common in words of this sort, on both sides.

[180] See Appendix A for the fossilized prefix *i-/e-*.

[181] Attempts have been made to derive this word from Latin *pilu-* 'hair,' but this clearly would have become Basque **biru.* The cluster *-lh-* indicates native Basque origin. (See the discussion under **l.*)

'feather,' Abkhaz á-*bra* 'mane,' etc. < PNC **ṗVħVɬV* (NCED 879) ~ Burushaski *pholġó* (Y), *phulġúuẏ* (H), *phurġúuẏ* (N) 'feather'

1.9. Basque **apo* > (B) *apo* 'hoof' ~ Bezhta, Hunzib *ap'a* 'paw,' Ubykh *-p'a* (in q'*ā-p'á* 'hand'), etc. < PNC **HapV̆* (NCED 545)

1.10. Basque **apa* > (AN, B, BN) *apa* 'kiss' ~ Chechen *oba, uba* 'kiss,' Khinalug *p'a* 'kiss,' etc. < PNC **pắʔV* (NCED 878)

1.11. Basque **lape* > (Z) *lape* 'shelter under the eaves of a shed' ~ PEC **λ̆čṗV* 'stone plate or shed' > Chechen *laba* 'shed; peak of cap,' Avar *λ̇'eb* 'stone,' etc. (NCED 777) ~ Burushaski (H, N) *tápi* '(smaller) stone terrace'

PDC **b:* There is abundant evidence that PDC **b* generally becomes Basque /b/ [b ~ ;]. When followed by a nasal cluster, **b* > Basque /m/ (*makila, magal*). However, the sequence /bo/ > Basque /o/ (*ontzi, otso*).

1.12. Basque **biha-r̄* > (BN, L, Z) *bihar,* (G) *bigar,* (B, G, R) *biar* 'tomorrow'[182] ~ Rutul *bi̯ga* 'tomorrow,' Lezgi *p:ak:a* 'tomorrow,' *p:ak:a*-ma 'morning, dawn,' etc. < PEC **b ʌ g ʌ* 'morning, evening' (NCED 292) ~ cf. Yen: PY **pVk-* 'morning' > Ket *hígem,* etc. (SSEJ 254)

1.13. Basque **belfia-r̄* > (BN) *belhar,* (Sal, Z) *belar* 'forehead'[183] ~ Rutul *bäl* 'forehead,' Tindi *bala* 'edge, end, corner,' etc. < PEC **b ꟻ āłhŏ* (NCED 285) ~ Burushaski *bal* 'wall'(< '*edge') ~ cf. ST: Tibetan *dpral* 'forehead' (< **d-r-pal?)*

1.14. Basque **bisa-r̄* > (c) *bizar* 'beard'[184] ~ Hunzib *bilaž*-ba 'beard,' Bezhta *bizal*-ba 'mustache,' Agul *mužur* 'beard,' etc. < PEC **bilǯV* (NCED 303) ~ ? Burushaski (H, N, Y) *biške* '(animal) hair, fur' (if *-ke* is a suffix)

1.15. Basque **borc / *bośt* > (AN, BN, L, R) *bortz,* (R) *borz,* (B, G, Z) *bost* 'five,' (B, G) *boste*-ko 'hand' (Azkue: 'cualquiera de las manos'; Aulestia & White: 'n. (mus.) quintet). n. hand. n. five (of a suit of cards). adj. having five parts or members of five;

---

[182] PDC **bVkV-* > Proto-Basque **biha-,* PEC **b ʌ g ʌ* (with progressive assimilation), etc.

[183] See Appendix A for explanation of the element *-r.* **belfia-r̄* 'forehead' contrasts with **belha-r̄* 'grass, hay' (q.v.).

[184] See Appendix A for the final element *-r,* likely cognate with the same suffix in Caucasian: Agul *mužur,* etc.

made up of five.') ~ PEC *b[^]cV > Avar púrc:i 'ham,' Tabasaran bac 'paw', etc. ~ Burushaski (H,N) bácin 'shank, (animal's) hind leg above the hock'

1.16. Basque *behi > (BN,L,Z) behi, (B,G,R) bei 'cow'[185] ~ Cauc: Godoberi

purc:i 'cattle,' Andi buc'ir 'cattle,' Avar bóc':i 'cattle,' Lezgi barc'ak 'young

buffalo', etc. < PEC *bħ^ rcwV (NCED 296)

1.17. Basque *beko > (BN, L) bek(h)o,[186] (AN, B, L) beko-ki 'forehead' ~ PEC *bĕḳwo 'part of face, mouth' > Tsakhur bok' 'muzzle,' Chechen baga 'mouth,' etc. (NCED 289)

1.18. Basque *bihi > (BN,L,Z) bihi, (AN-Baztan) bigi [biɣi] 'grain, seed, kernel'[187] ~ Chechen borc 'millet', Avar muč, Andi beča, etc. < PNC *bŏlćwi

'millet' NCED 309)[188]

1.19. Basque *bero > (c) bero 'hot'~ Cauc: PWC *bla/ə 'to burn' (CWC 393); Tsez boboru, Khwarshi bobolu 'hot' ~ Burushaski babárum (babár-um) (Y) 'hot, pungent' (of food), (H,N) 'pungent (taste); burning (pain); hot-tempered, irascible (person)'

1.20. Basque *mak- > (c) makila, (Z) makhila 'cane, stick,'[189] (B) maket 'club, very thick pole' ~ Bezhta maq 'stake', Abkhaz a-bə́q'ʷ 'post, pillar,' etc. < PNC *bħə̄nġV̆ (NCED 295)

1.21. Basque *maga-l > (B, G, R) magal 'lap, breast' ~ Abkhaz á-mgʷa 'belly,' Avar bak'ʷáli 'belly,' etc. < PNC *bVnḳwĂ (NCED 318)

1.22. Basque *onci > (AN, B, G, R) ontzi, (BN, L, Z) untzi 'vessel, container; boat, ship' ~ PEC *bōnʒ(w)V 'vessel' >

---

[185] See Appendix B for elucidation of the correspondence of Basque behi = PEC *bħərc'wV, etc.

[186] Usually in the phrase bek(h)oz-bek(h)o 'face to face.' The word is traditionally explained as Late Latin *beccu-, though no true Latin antecedent exists. Rather, the Vasconic word was borrowed by other European languages, including French bec, English beak.

[187] See Appendix B for elucidation of the correspondence of Basque bihi < *bixi = Caucasian *bŏlćwi, etc.

[188] Cf. also Chechen božan 'rye,' Godoberi beč'in 'rye,' Avar (Chadakolob) boč'ón 'fruit stone,' Tindi, Karata beč'in 'barley,' etc. < PEC *bħĕlčinV (NCED 294)

[189] Many have tried to derive makila from Latin bacillum, but the latter would have become *bakilu, not makila, and the dialectal maket clearly cannot be derived from Latin. Simply a chance resemblance, and the DC etymology explains the initial m-.

Chechen *batt*-am 'brass water-jar,' Karata *muc':i* 'jar, pot,' etc. (NCED 311)

1.23. Basque **oćo* > (c) *otso* 'wolf,' Aquitanian OXSON, OSSON (in proper names) ~ Andi *boc'o,* Lak *barc',* Chechen *borz* 'wolf,' etc. < PNC **bh̃ěrcĭ* 'wolf' (NCED 294) ~ cf. ST: Old Chinese **prāts* 'mythical predator' ~ PY **pes-* in **pestap* 'wolverine' > Kott *feštap,* etc. (SSEJ 247)

1.24. Basque **a-bele* > (c) *abere* 'domestic animal(s), cattle'/ *abel-buru* 'head of cattle'[190] ~ Udi *bele* 'cattle,' Hunzib *bala* 'chamois,' Chechen *bula* 'aurochs,' etc. < PNC **bǔtV* (NCED 314)

1.25. Basque **habe* > (c) *habe, abe* 'pillar, beam' ~ PEC **hwěbē* > Avar *ħubí* 'post, pole, stem,' Tsez *hibo* 'stick,' etc. (NCED 497)

1.26. Basque **śabe-l* > (c) *sabel* 'belly'[191] ~ Bezhta *šebo* 'liver,' Chechen *žim* 'kidney,' Abkhaz á-*z* 'gall,' etc. < PNC **ǯǎbV* (NCED 1106) < PDC **čabV*[192]

1.27. Basque **bete* 'full' > (c) *bete,* (BN,Z) *bethe* ~ Chechen *butū* 'hard, tough,' Kabardian *bəda* id., etc. < PNC **bVtV* (NCED 320) ~ Burushaski *buṭ* 'much, many'

1.28. Basque **mendi* 'mountain' > (c) *mendi* ~ ? Khinalug *mta* 'mountain' (isolated in Cauc.)[193] ~ Burushaski **bun[d]-* 'mountain pasture, mountain grove, boulder; wild, mountain-' > (H,N,Y) *bun* / (pl.) *bundó* (Y pl. also *bunjó*)

---

[190] It is commonly supposed (*e.g.,* Trask 1995, p. 12; 1997, pp. 169, 295, etc.) that Basque *abere* comes from Latin *habere* 'to have' (cf. Spanish *haberes* 'property'), but the Basque word *only* applies to animals, and the allomorph *abel-* (as in *abel-buru* 'head of cattle,' *abel-tegi* 'stable') clearly indicates the original form **abele.* Latin *habere* is simply a chance resemblance, and not even semantically close.

[191] Assuming a suffix *-l:* cf. *azal, magal* (*q.v.*). Cf. Yeniseian: PY **tVpVʎ* / **tVbVʎ* 'spleen' (SSEJ 292).

[192] Starostin (1996, 106) cites the reconstruction **ǯǎbV,* vs. **ǯǎwV* in NCED. The initial of PNC **ǯǎbV* seems to reflect voicing assimilation (*č* > *ǯ*). Basque *s* /š/ corresponds to Caucasian **č,* not **ǯ.* Further Dene-Caucasian cognates confirm the primacy of **D:* PST **ć(h)uap* 'lung,' PY **tVpVʎ* / **tVbVʎ* 'spleen' (ST IV: 13; SSEJ 292).

[193] Cf. Georgian *mta* 'mountain,' also isolated in Kartvelian, borrowed from Cauc. (Khinalug), or *vice versa*? Latin *mōns* / *montis,* Welsh *mynydd,* etc., are either chance resemblances, loanwords < DC, or remnants of a very old Nostratic-Dene-Caucasian unity. The Burushaski form points to PDC **bVndV.*

2. Dental Occlusives

PDC *t:* PDC *t* becomes Basque /t/ in most positions (often *th* in the aspirating dialects). There are few examples.[194]

2.1. Basque **tu-(ka)* > (c) *tu, thu* 'to spit,' (AN, BN, L) *t(h)uka* 'spitting,' (G) *itoi* 'drop' ~ PEC **tw ^ jV* 'spit, spittle' > Avar *tuj* 'spittle,' *tu(j)-* 'to spit,' Ingush *tug* 'spittle,' etc. (NCED 994) ~ Burushaski *thu* 'to spit' ~ cf. ST: PST **thōj* 'spit,' **thok* 'saliva' (ST II: 163, 164); Yen: PY **duK* > Kott *tuk* 'saliva' (SSEJ 224); Na-Dene: Tlingit *tuχ* 'to spit'

2.2. Basque **tośka* > (c) *toska,* (BN, L, Z) *thoska* '(fine white) clay'[195] ~ Hunzib *tac'* 'bog,' Chechen *t'q'arš* 'slush, mire,' etc. < PEC **tɬiVrcwV* (NCED 992)

2.3. Basque **tini* > (BN, Z) *thini* 'summit, top' ~ Burushaski *-thán* 'point, summit, peak' ~ cf. ST: PST **tēŋH* 'top' > Tibetan s-*teŋ,* etc. (ST II: 121)

2.4. Basque **fionda-r̄* > (L) *hondar* 'sand, bottom,' (BN) *hondar* 'bottom,' (AN) *ondar* 'bottom,' (B, G) *ondar* 'sand, beach,' (Z) *undar* 'remnant, residue'[196] ~ PEC **ʔantV* > Tsez *atu* 'dirt, mud,' Khinalug *ant* 'earth, ground' (NCED 201)

PDC **t':* In most positions PDC **t'* > Basque /t/ (often *th* in aspirating dialects). The internal cluster **-rt'-* > Basque *-rd-*(as in *ip(h)urdi).*

2.5. Basque **ti-,* **ti-pi* > (AN, L) *tipi* 'little, small,' (B) *tintin* 'poquito, très peu,' *-tilla* 'little' (diminutive suffix) ~ Avar *hit'ina-b* 'small,' Lezgi *t'i*-mil 'few,' Ubykh *t'a* 'less, smaller,' etc. < PNC **t̩iHV / *Hit̩V* (NCED 1001)

---

[194] The paucity of **t*-words may seem troubling, but cf. the NCED, which has only fourteen etymologies with initial **t-,* versus 33 with initial **t̩- = *t'-.* Conversely, it has 33 with **p-,* but only 6 with **ṗ- = *p'-.*

[195] The supposed derivation from Latin *tuscu-* 'unrefined, dissolute' (Trask 1995, p. 62) is wildly improbable. By the accepted phonetic rules, *tuscu-* would become Basque **duzku,* not *toska,* and the meanings have even less in common. *Toska* is the fine white clay used to make porcelain.

[196] **(H)ondar̄* 'residue, dregs' may be a homonym of distinct origin. And there may be contamination with *ondo* 'side; residue' and *hondo* 'bottom' (? < Spanish *hondo* < Latin *fundu-*). See Appendix A for the fossilized ending *-r.*

2.6.a. Basque **toki* > (B, AN, L) *toki* 'place, location' ~ Proto-Circassian **t'ak'ʷə* 'place' > Adyge *t'ak'ʷ*, etc. (Kuipers 1975)

2.6.b. Basque **tupV* 1 barrel, cask, etc. ~ Hunzib *t'ipi* 'a small barrel,' etc. < PNC **t'āpV* (= **1.7.**)

2.7. Basque **tanka, *tinka* > (R, Z) *tanka*, (B) *tanga* 'drop (of liquid) / gota / goutte,' (R) *tinka* 'a little (of liquid)' ~ Rutul *t'ank'* 'drop,' Avar *t'ink'* 'drop,' etc. < PNC **ṭHänḵŏ* (NCED 1000)

2.8. Basque **i-tain* > (R) *itain*, (BN, Z) *ithain* 'tick' ~ PNC **ṭaHnā* 'nit' > Akhwakh *t'ani*, Lak *t'u*, etc. (NCED 995)

2.9. Basque **e-tori* > (AN, B, G, L) *etorri*, (L) *ethorri* 'to come,' ('to adapt, get along,' and other meanings in B,G) ~ Avar *t'ur-* 'to run away,' Udi *t:ist:un* 'to run,' etc. < PEC **ĭṭVr* (NCED 659)

2.10. Basque **e-te-n* > (AN, B, G, L) *eten*, (BN, L, Z) *ethen* 'to break, cut' ~ PEC **ĭṭV* 'to cut, divide' > Hunzib =*it'-* 'to divide,' Tsakhur =*et'a-* 'to break,' etc. (NCED 660)

2.11. Basque **guti* > (AN, BN, L) *guti*, (Z) *güti* 'few, little'[197] ~ Lezgi *güt'ü* 'narrow,' Lak *kut'a-* 'short,' etc. < PNC **ḵHə̆twV / *ḵwHə̆tV* (NCED 690)

2.12. Basque **lotu* > (AN, B, G) *lotu*, (BN, L, Z) *lot* 'to tie' ~ Lezgi *iliṭ-iz* 'to bind around,' Kryz *ju-ṭul-* 'to tie, bind,' etc. < PNC **jeṭal-* 'to tie, bind; untie' (NCED 679: implicitly ~ **jelaṭ-* > Lezgi)

2.13. Basque **i-s-ta-* 1 groin, 2 thigh, 3 hamstring in (B) *iztegi, iztei, iztai* 1, *izter, iztar* 2, (AN) *izta-tu* 3, (Z) *ixter* [íšter] 2, *ixtezáñ* 3, etc.[198] ~ Chechen *t'a* 'front leg (of animal),' Avar *ħet'é / ħet'* 'foot,' etc. < PEC **twĭħV ~ *ħwĭṭV* (NCED 1007) ~ Burushaski -*úṭ* ~ -*úṭis* ~ -*húṭes* 'foot' ~ cf. ST: PST **t ˇH* > Old Chinese **təʔ* 'foot, heel' (ST II: 123) ~ Na-Dene: Haida s-*t'áay*, s-*t'a-* 'foot,' *t'aa-* 'to step,' Sarsi -*t'ás*, -*t'àz* 'to move one's own foot,' etc.

2.14. Basque **a-s-tapa-* in (AN, BN, R, Z) *aztapar* 'paw,' (AN, G, L) *atzapar* 'leg or claw (of bird),' (B) *atzamar* 'finger'[199] ~

---

[197] Other variants are palatalized: (L) *gutti* [guci], (G) *gutxi*, (B) *gitxi*. Simply affective palatalization, or influence of Coptic *kuǯi, kūy* 'small'?

[198] See Appendix A for explanation of the fossilized segments **i-, *-s-, *-r.*

[199] External evidence indicates that *aztapar* is original, with secondary *atzapar* (influenced by *hatz*, q.v.), and *atzamar* (probably contaminated with *(h)amar* 'ten', q.v.). See Appendix A for

Dargwa *t'up'* 'finger,' Lezgi *t'ub* 'finger,' *tup'al* 'finger-ring,' etc. < PEC **twɨbi* 'finger' (NCED 1007)

2.15. Basque **e-purdi* 'rump, buttocks' ~ PEC **pHVrṭwV* (= **1.5.**)

PDC **d:* PDC **d* manifests as Basque /t/ initially (and in the cluster /śt/), /d/ medially (and in the cluster /rd/).

2.16. Basque **tak-* '*back (part),' in (L) *takoin,* (B) *takoi* 'heel (of a shoe)' (lit. 'back [of] foot' > Span. *tacón,* Port. *tacão*) ~ PNC **dHāqwĀ* > Rutul *daq* 'back of head,' Ubykh *tʷəq* 'neck,' etc. (NCED 399) ~ cf. ST: PST **tūk* 'neck' > Garo gi-*tok,* etc. (ST II: 148) ~ PY **tuɢV* > Ket *tū* '(upper) back,' Pumpokol *tuk* 'back(wards)' ~ Na-Dene: Tlingit *déχ* 'back,' *daχ* 'place behind one,' -*daχ* 'from'; Navajo *dah* 'off, down off'

2.17. Basque **tutu* '* tube' > 1 horn, bugle, 2 spout, neck (of jar), 3 feeding tube, feeding bottle, 4 vulva, 5 anus > *tutu* (B) 4,5, (G) 1,5, (AN) 1,2,3, (BN) 1, (L) 1, 3 ~ Lak *dudu* 'speaking pipe, megaphone,' Lezgi *t:üd* 'throat, gullet,' etc. < PEC **dfiwōdwō* 'tube, pipe' (NCED 400) ~ Burushaski *ḍóḍo* 'throat, gullet'

2.18. Basque**tuntun* > (AN, B, BN, G, L) *tuntun* 'Basque drum, tambourine, small drum' ~ Agul *damdam* 'drum', Lezgi *daldam,* etc. < PNC **dwə̆n?V* (NCED 406) ~ Burushaski *TaTá-* 'a kind of big drum,' *TamTám* 'to drum'

2.19. Basque **tak-* > (B) *tako* 'circular piece of wood, chock,' (Aulestia & White 'wedge, block, chock, stopper'), (AN, B, G) *taket* 'stake, post' (Aulestia & White 'stake; wedge, block, chock, stopper') ~ Adyge *t:āq:a* 'stump, block,' Dargwa *duk'i* ~ *duk'* 'log, beam,' etc. < PNC **dwĭq(w)V̂* (NCED 408) ~ Burushaski (H, N) *ḍáko* 'wooden pillar, roof-post, tent-pole,' (Y) *ḍáku* 'walking stick'

2.20. Basque **u-dagera* > (BN, L, Sal) *udagara,* (B) *uagara, ugadera, igarabi, ugabere,* (G) *igabera,* (AN) *igaraba,* (B, L) *ugadera,* (Z) *ügadera*[200] 'otter' ~ PEC **darq̇wV* > Andi *darɢʷa*

---

explanations of the initial elements *a-z-* and the final element *-r.*

[200] External evidence indicates that *udagara* is probably the oldest variant (others being metathesized variants and the folk-etymologized *ugabere* 'water animal'). **u-* is a combinatory form of **hur* 'water.'

'weasel, marten,' Lak *t:arq'a* 'weasel, ermine' (NCED 399) ~ cf. Yen: PY **täχVr* 'otter' > Ket *ta:ʌ*, Kott *thēgär*, etc. (SSEJ 283)

2.21. Basque **keda-r̄* > (B) *kedar, kedarra*, (Z) *khedárre*, (BN) *kedar, keder, kelder, kerrada*, (L) *kheder, kelder*, (G) *kedar, kear, kelar*, (R) *gedar* 'soot' ~ Akhwakh *q':ēt'a* 'soot,' Lak *q'it* 'soot; flour dust,' etc. < PEC **q̇idV* (NCED 927) ~ cf. Na-Dene: Haida *Gayt* 'ashes', Tlingit *kɛl't'* 'wood ashes'[201]

2.22. Basque **ĥodäi* > (BN, Z) *hodei*, (AN, B, G, R) *odei*, (B, G) *odai*, (B,R) *odoi* 'cloud' (also 'thunder' in B,G,AN,BN,R) ~ Dargwa (Akushi) *daʕ* 'wind,' Archi *di* 'odor, scent' < PEC **dwiHV* 'wind' (NCED 407)

2.23. Basque **o-dol* > (c) *odol* 'blood' ~ cf. PST **t(h)˜lH* 'meat, flesh' > Lushai *tāl* 'flesh, muscle,' etc. (ST II: 158) ~ Na-Dene: Eyak *deɬ* 'blood'; Chipewyan *dèɬ*, Navajo *diɬ* 'blood,' etc.[202]

2.24. Basque **i-dul-ki* > *idulki* (B) 'block of wood,' (G) 'pedestal' *(< *i-dul-ki)*[203] ~ Ingush *tälg* (< **tāl-ik'*) 'chock,' Archi *dali* 'long stick, pole,' etc. < PEC **dwāɬi* 'stick' (NCED 405)

2.25. Basque **lerde* > (AN, BN, G) *lerde*, (G) *lirdi* 'drivel, saliva'[204] ~ PEC **λwirdɨ* > Archi *ɬ:ʷit* 'manure, dung,' Avar *xʷerd* 'pus,' etc. (NCED 763) ~ Burushaski *γit* 'slime' ~ cf. ST: PST **lV̌t* > Tibetan *lud* 'phlegm, mucus; manure, dung,' etc. (ST III: 51) ~ Na-Dene: PAth **ɬu·t'* > Kutchin *ɬíd* 'scar,' Navajo *ɬóód* 'sore,' etc.

2.26. Basque **eśtu* > (AN, B, G) *estu* 'narrow, cramped, exhausted' ~ Dargwa *č̣arṭa*, Andi *č̣:iṭir* 'narrow,' etc. < PEC **č̣HVrdV* (NCED 387)

---

[201] A mysterious lateral + dental cluster appears in widely separated languages: Basque (BN, L) *kelder* and Tlingit *kɛl't'*.

[202] The semantic connection 'blood ~ flesh' is well known: cf. Russian кровь 'blood' ~ Greek κρέας 'flesh'. See Appendix A for the fossilized prefix *o-*.

[203] See Appendix A for the fossilized prefix *i-*.

[204] This word has been associated, and in some places contaminated, with the similar word **fierde / *fielde-r̄*, which is of an entirely different origin (*q.v.*).

3. Sibilant Affricates

Proto-Caucasian (according to NCED) had a rich inventory of sibilant affricates, with three points of articulation, and for each of the three points, three laryngeal features (plain voiceless, glottalized, and voiced). (See the chart in the Introduction.) It is uncertain whether the three points, or just two (as apparently in Na-Dene), can be projected back to Proto-Dene-Caucasian. The Basque evidence favors a split into three points of articulation, because the reflexes are different, at least in the plain voiceless column (*c, *ć, *č*); in the glottalized column, the reflexes of *c'* are distinct from those of *ć'* and *č'*, which fall together. In the voiced column the Basque reflexes of *ʒ, *ʓ,* and *ǯ* fall together as dorso-alveolar /s̄/ (orthographic z) or /c̄/ (orthographic tz). The three-way split may be restricted to the Vasco-Caucasian subgroup.

PDC *c:* In most positions, PDC *c* [ts] corresponds to Basque apico-alveolars: /ś/ (orthographic s) or /ć/ (orthographic ts). In nouns with fossilized prefixes (see Appendix A), the reflex is dorso-alveolar /s̄/ (orthographic z), and in final position, the Basque reflex is dorso-alveolar /c̄/ (orthographic tz). The Basque words *eśan* 'say' and *hic* 'word' seem to reflect different reflexes of the same PDC root:[205]

3.1.a. Basque *śagu > (c) sagu, (BN-Aldude) sabu 'mouse', (c) sagu-zar 'bat' (lit. 'old mouse'), sat-itsu 'shrew' (lit. 'blind mouse'), etc. ~ PNC *cārgwī̆ > Adyge cəɣʷa 'mouse,' Tsakhur sok 'weasel,' etc. (NCED 322) ~ Burushaski (Y) ćargé 'flying squirrel' ~ cf. ST: PST *sraiŋ(H) > Old Chinese *sreŋ 'weasel,' etc. (ST IV: 105) ~ Yen: Ket saʔqa 'squirrel' > Kott šaga, etc. (SSEJ 268) ~ Na-Dene: Tlingit calg 'squirrel,' Eyak cəɬk', PAth *cələx 'squirrel'

3.1.b. Basque *śuśt(V)r(V) 'root' > (B) sustar, (B,G) sustrai ~ Burushaski *cherés̄ 'root' > (Y) cerés̄, (H,N) chiris̄, -chíris̄ [206]

---

[205] In the word for 'five' there is variation between eastern *bortz* and western *bost*. Cf. *lasto*.

[206] Starostin tentatively reconstructs PDC *[c]Vr(V)čV, including the evidence of PY *čīǯ- 'root'.

3.2. Basque *ɦośin 1 deepest part of a river, 2 abyss, 3 sea, 4 whirlpool > (L) hosin 1,2, (B, AN, BN, Z) osin 1, (G) osin 1,3,4 ~ Tindi hinc:i 'spring', etc. < PEC *ʔwīnc̣V̆ < *ʔwic̣inV 'well, spring' (NCED 232) ~ cf. ST: PST *cĕŋH > Old Chinese * ceŋʔ 'well,' etc. (ST IV: 3) ~ PY *sin- > Kott šinaŋ 'spring', etc. (SSEJ 274)

3.3.a. Basque *baśo, *baśa 1 forest, 2 desert, 3 wild > (B, G, AN, Z) baso 1, (L, Z) basa 2,3, etc. ~ Akhwakh beča 'mountain', Tindi besa 'mountain', Archi sob 'mountain pasture,' etc. < PEC *wīce (NCED 1053)[207]

3.3.b. Basque *eśan 'to say' > (B,G,AN) esan ~ Andi =osan-, Karata =asan- 'to say, tell,' etc. < PNC *=[ī]mcŪ (NCED 642) ~ Burushaski *-s-/*-ś- 'to say (to someone)'

3.4. Basque *ićú > (c) itsu, (Z) ütsü, (R) utsi 'blind' ~ PEC *=Vc̣V > Tindi =ec:u-b 'blind,' Akhwakh =ec:o-da 'blind, dark,' Khwarshi sajsu 'dark', etc. (NCED 1017)

3.5. Basque *ɦaseli ~ *aseɦali > (B) azegari, azagari, azari, azeri, (G, AN) azari, azeri, (BN, L) hazeri, (Z, R) axeri [ašéri, ašéi] 'fox'[208] ~ Tindi sari, Akhwakh šari, Tsez ziru, Archi s:ol 'fox,' etc. < PNC *chwōlĕ < *cEhwōlĕ 'fox, jackal' (NCED 324) ~ Burushaski hal 'fox'

3.6. Basque *beHa-sum(a)[209] in (L, Z) beazuma, (BN) behazun, (G) beazun, (B) beaztun 'bile, gall' ~ PNC *c̣wãjmĕ > Dargwa (Chirag) sume, Avar c:in 'gall, anger,' Archi s:am 'gall,' etc. (NCED 329) ~ Burushaski -sán 'spleen' ~ cf. ST: PST *sĭn 'liver' > Tibetan m-čhin, etc. (ST IV: 103) ~ PY *seŋ 'liver' > Ket śēŋ, etc. (SSEJ 272) ~ Na-Dene [*sVN-T]: Eyak -saht 'liver'; Galice -saʔɬ, Navajo -zid, etc.

---

[207] The semantic connection of 'forest' and 'mountain' is well known. Cf., e.g., Lithuanian gìria "forest' ~ Slavic gora 'mountain', and the etymology of Basque oihan, q.v.

[208] In light of this evidence, the attempt to derive the Basque word for 'fox' from a personal name Asenariu (Trask 1995, p. 19; 1997, p. 299) hardly requires comment. Most pertinently, there is no trace of a nasal vowel in Zuberoan or Roncalese. Nor does the Asenariu hypothesis account for the initial h- in Lapurdian, nor the fricative –g- [γ] in parts of Bizkaia. The archaic and quadrisyllabic Bizkaian forms, allowing for metathesis, match very well with the archaic Caucasian form *cEhwōlĕ ~ Basque *ɦaseli ~ *aseɦali.

[209] The exact composition of Basque behazun is mysterious, but the element -zun, -zuma can be identified with the Caucasian word for 'gall, anger' ('spleen' in Burushaski, 'liver' in Sino-Tibetan and Yeniseian).

3.7. Basque **asaro* 1 autumn, 2 seedtime, 3 October, 4 November > *azaro* (Sal) 1, (B, G, BN, R) 2, (BN, R) 3, (G, AN, L,Z) 4 ~ PNC **cōjwīlfiV* > Tindi *c:ibar* 'winter,' Khinalug *cuwa-ž* 'autumn,' etc. (NCED 327) ~ cf. ST: Old Chinese **chiw* 'autumn' ~ PY **sir₁-* > Ket *šīʎi* 'summer,' etc. (SSEJ 275)

3.8. Basque **hic* > (c) *hitz, itz* 'word,' *hitz egin, itz egin* 'to speak, talk' ~ Chechen *=ic-* 'to tell', Khwarshi *=is-* 'to say, speak,' etc. < PNC **=[ī]mcŪ* (NCED 642) ~ Burushaski **-s-/*-ś-* 'to say (to someone)'

3.9. Basque **borc / *bośt* 'five,' etc. ~ PEC **b[ə]cV* ~ Burushaski (H,N) *bácin* (= **1.15**)

3.10. Basque **e-cułi* > 1 turn over, upset, 2 turn around, return, 3 turn one's head, 4 turn sour (milk), 5 convert (religion), 6 return, repay > (B) *itzuli* 1, 2, (G) 1, (AN) 1,2,3,4,6, (BN) 1,2,3,4,5,6, (L) 1,2,5,6, (Z) *ützüli* 2,5,6, (R) *utzuli* 2,4,6 ~ Agul *ilcan-* 'to turn (on an axis),' Tabasaran b-*ilcun*-ag 'whirligig, humming-top', etc. < PEC **=īrcVl* 'to twirl, turn round' (NCED 649)

PDC **c':* The reflexes of this sound are conditioned by position and surrounding vowels: Basque dorso-alveolars /š/ (orth. *z*) or /č/ (orth. *tz*) before or after non-rounded vowels /a, e, i/;[210] dorso-alveolar /č/ in the cluster /nč/ (orth. *ntz*); apico-alveolar /ś/ or /B/ (orth. *s* or *ts*) before or after rounded vowels /o, u/.[211] For the peculiar development of the PDC clusters **-lc'- / -rc'-* to Basque **h-* see Appendix B.

3.11. Basque **sama-r̄* (diminutive **čama-r̄*) 1 fleece, shorn wool, 2 zamarra (animal hide used as raincoat), 3 mane, 4 (men's) jacket or vest, 5 blouse, 6 apron worn by reapers > (B,G) *txamarra* 6, (AN, BN) *zamar* 1,2, (L) *txamar* 5, (Z) *zamar* 2,3, also (Larrasquet) 'herbe jaunie dont on rembourre les matelas ... longs poils d'une bête de somme mal soignée'[212] ~ PEC **cfiwĕme* 'eyebrow' > Lezgi r-*c'am,* Lak *c'ani,* etc. (NCED 364) ~

---

[210] Except when /a/ is a fossilized prefix, as in *atso* 'old woman', *q.v.*

[211] I am grateful to Sergei A. Starostin for detecting the conditioning factors.

[212] As seen here, Basque *zamar, txamar(ra)* has many meanings depending on dialect. Out-comparison indicates that the meaning 'hair' is oldest, with specializations to 'wool', 'eyebrow', etc. Via the Basque diminutive form *txamar,* this is the ultimate source of Spanish *chamarra* 'wool, sheepskin, or leather jacket'. See Appendix A for the final element -*r*.

Burushaski *śe[m] 'wool' ~ cf. ST: PST *chām 'hair (of head)' > Garo mik-*sam* 'eyebrow,' Kanauri *cam* 'wool, fleece,' etc. (ST IV: 19) ~ Yen: PY *c ^ ŋe* 'hair' > Kott *heŋai*, etc. (SSEJ 213) ~ Na-Dene *c'Ṽ(χ)* > Tlingit *s'ì* 'eyebrow'; Eyak *c'ã·χ* 'eyebrow'

3.12. Basque *si(n)ho > (BN, Z) *ziho,* (AN-Baztan) *zigo* 'fat, tallow', (R) *zĩa-tu* cover oneself with grease, (oil) to coagulate'[213] ~ Tindi *c'inVu-,* Dargwa *c'erx:-* 'fat' (adj) < PEC *c̄ēnxwV* 'fat' (adj) (NCED 362)[214]

3.13. Basque *e-sagu- > (c) *ezagu-tu,* (Z) *ezagü-t* 'to know (a person) = conocer, connaître,' *ezagun* 'evident, known'[215] ~ Avar *c'eχ:é-* 'to search, ask,' Ubykh *ʒ"a-* 'to ask,' etc. < PNC *c̄EnχV(n)* 'to search, ask' (NCED 359)

3.14. Basque *ecan > (c) *etzan* 'to lie down, rest (intr.); put down (tr.)' ~ Abkhaz a-*c'a*-rá 'to lay eggs', Agul *c'a-* 'to give,' etc. < PNC *=ic̄Ă* (NCED 626)

3.15. Basque *encun > (c) *entzun,* (Z) *entzün* 'to hear, listen' (B, BN [Baigorri] also 'to smell') ~ PNC *=ămc̄Ĕ > Batsbi *=abc'-* 'know, get to know,' Dargwa *umc'-es* 'to search,' etc. (NCED 262) ~ Burushaski *-jḗc- > (H,N) -yḗc-, (Y) –yéc- 'to see'

3.16. Basque *i-hinc > (L) *ihintz,* (Z) *ihitz* [ĩhĩts], (BN) *ihitz,* (G, AN, R) *intz,* (B) *euntz, iruntz, irauntz, iñontz* 'dew' ~ PEC *xwɨ̆mc̄wɨ̄* > Lak *xunc'a* 'bog,' Tindi *hic:u* 'bog, marsh,' etc. (NCED 1065) ~ Burushaski *huṣ* 'moisture (of field, ground)' (? loan < Tibetan or Balti) ~ cf. ST: PST *χŭ(s)* > Tibetan *hus* 'moisture, humidity,' etc. (ST V: 180)

3.17. Basque *ɦaic 'rock, stone' > (BN) *haitz,* (AN, G, L) *aitz,* (B, Z) *atx* [ač] ~ Avar *ʕuc':* 'stone', Chechen *hätt* 'avalanche', etc. < PNC *ɦə̄mVc̄ŏ* (NCED 516) ~ cf. Na-Dene: Tlingit *ʔič* 'rock, stone, pebble'

---

[213] See the discussions by Trask (1995, p. 70) and Jacobsen (1995, p. 136).

[214] NCED offers alternative reconstructions: *c̄ēnλV* or *c̄ēnxwV*. The Basque form *ziho* < *šixo allows us to choose the latter. Contra Trask (1995, p. 70), there is no evidence for a "Pre-Basque" *zino. The Zuberoan form is simply [šího], with oral vowels. There could, of course, been a nasal vowel at some (very) early stage.

[215] Some have sought to derive this word from Latin *sapere* (Spanish *saber*), but the initial prefix *e-* is characteristic of native Basque verbs, not loanwords.

3.18. Basque *behi 'cow' ~ Avar bóc':i 'cattle', etc. < PEC *bħə r̥cwV (= **1.16**)

3.19. Basque *mi(n)hi[216] > (BN, L) mihi, (Z) mihi [mĩhĩ], (G) mii, (B) min 'tongue' ~ Tindi mic:i 'tongue', Andi mic':i, Tabasaran melz, Ubykh bźa, etc. < PNC *mĕlči 'tongue' (NCED 802) ~ Burushaski -melč 'jaw'

3.20.a. Basque *śu > (c) su, (Z) sü 'fire' ~ Lak c'u, Ingush c'i, Ubykh mə-ž́á 'fire', etc. < PNC *čăjɨ 'fire' (NCED 354) ~ Burushaski śi (H,N) 'fireplace, hearth' ~ cf. Na-Dene: Haida (Swanton) č'aaʔano 'fire'

3.20.b. Basque *śoin 1 shoulder, 2 (upper) back, 3 midsection of pork (carré), 4 garment, vestment > (B) soin 1,4, soin-buru 2, (G) soin 1,4, (L) soin 1,3,4, soin-buru 2, soin-gain 1, (Z) suin 1,3, süñ-hegi 1, etc. ~ Lezgi, Rutul c'um 'shin-bone', etc. < PNC *Hcwējnə̆ (NCED 555) ~ Burushaski *-śaŋ 'limbs, body parts'

3.21. Basque *a-ćo 'old woman' > (c) atso, (BN: Salazar also) 'grandmother'[217] ~ Batsbi pst'u 'wife', Lak c:u- 'female', Ubykh b-za 'female', etc. < PNC *cwŏjV 'woman, female' (NCED 374)

3.22. Basque *oćo > (c) otso 'wolf' ~ Andi boc'o, etc. < PNC *bħĕrčĭ 'wolf' (= **1.23**)

3.23.a. Basque *huć 1 empty, 2 pure, 3 error, fault, defect, 4 lack, want, 5 vain, idle, 6 barren, sterile[218] > (B) uts 1,2,3,4,5, (L) huts 1,2,3, (Z) hüts, hütx 1,2,3, (R) uts 1,2,3,6, etc. ~ Chechen =ässa 'empty, hollow', Lak =ač'=a- 'empty', etc. < PNC *ɦə̄ćÉ (NCED 515)

3.23.b. Basque *ɦućal 1 poor, trifling, 2 dry, barren, sterile, 3 shrunken, shriveled > (AN) utsal 1, (BN) hutsal 1,3, (Z) ütsal 1,2, etc.[219] ~ PNC *=HĭcĂl 'naked, bare' > Lezgi q'ec'il, Avar ʕíc':a-b, Ubykh -p'c'ə, etc. (NCED 567)

---

[216] The "Pre-Basque" form *bini (Trask 1997, p. 174) is not tenable and cannot account for the archaic form **[mihçja]** 'the tongue' recorded by Moutard (1975). See further Appendix B.

[217] atso < *a-Bo. See Appendix A for explanation of the prefix a-.

[218] Basque (h)uts (3.23.a) and (h)utsal (3.23.b) are similar, but seem to correspond to two distinct Caucasian roots.

[219] Azkue cites examples such as lur utsala 'barren ground', etxe utsalak 'poor houses'.

3.24. Basque *ośo > (c) *oso* 'whole, complete, entire; totally, very; healthy' ~ Chechen *=üz*-na 'full', Tindi *=ec'u*-b 'full', Ubykh ⁼a-*zá,* etc. < PNC **=ñŏçV* 'full, fill' (NCED 525)

3.25. Basque **tośka* '(fine white) clay' ~ Hunzib *tac'* 'bog', etc. < PEC **tñVrçwV* (= **2.2**)

3.26. Basque **kokoć (~ *[k]okoc)*[220] 1 chin, 2 snout, 3 nape > (B) *okotz* 1,2, (AN) *kokots* 1,3, (BN,L) *kokots, kokotz* 1, (Z) *kokots* 1 ~ PEC **q̇ăçɨ* > Lak *q'ac* 'bite; mouth', Rutul, Tsakhur *q'ac* 'chin', etc. (NCED 907) ~ cf. Na-Dene: Tlingit *χ'ás* 'jaw', Eyak l-*q'aʔc* 'jaw, angle of jaw'

PDC **ʒ:* In all positions the Basque reflexes are dorso-alveolar /s̄/ (orth. *z*), /c̄/ in the cluster /nc̄/ (orth. *ntz*).

3.27. Basque **susen* 1 right, correct, 2 right(s), justice > (B, G, R) *zuzen* 1, (AN, BN, L) 1,2, (Z) *züzen* 1,2 ~ PNC **HăʒEm* > Chechen *c'ena* 'clean, pure', Godoberi *c'in*-k'i 'clean, pure', Abaza b-*zi* 'good', etc. (NCED 552) ~ Burushaski *sisín*- to be clear (of wine, water)', *sisín*-um 'clear (water); slender (person); soft (voice)' ~ cf. ST: PST **chiaŋ* > Tibetan *chaŋ*-s 'purified, clean', etc. (ST IV: 26)

3.28. Basque **i-sar̄* > (c) *izar* 'star'[221] ~ Tindi *c:aru,* Dargwa (Chirag) *zure,* Abaza ja-*č'ʷa*, etc. < PNC **ʒwăhrī* 'star' (NCED 1098)

3.29. Basque **sikiro* > (BN, L) *zikhiro,* (AN, G) *zikiro* 'castrated ram' ~ PNC **ʒĭkV̆* 'goat, kid' > Karata *c':ik'er* 'kid', Lak *c'uku* 'goat', etc. (NCED 1094) ~ Burushaski *cigír* (Y), *chigír* (N), *chiír* (H) '(she-)goat'

3.30. Basque **sinagur̄i* 'ant'[222] > (L) *zinaurri,* (BN) *xinaurri* [šinaur̄i], (G) *txingurri* [čiŋgur̄i], etc. ~ PNC **ʒHĔmVḳÃ* 'ant' > Chechen *zingat,* Ubykh *źəngʷá,* etc. (NCED 1093)

---

[220] We expect final *-ć here – variation with *-c caused by contamination with another root?

[221] See Appendix A for explanation of the fossilized prefix *i-.*

[222] Trask (1997: 296) has **zinagurri. xinaurri* and *txingurri* are diminutive palatalized forms of the original. Words such as (B) *iñurri,* (Z) *üñhürri* 'ant' are clearly of separate origin – at least as to the first element. Possibly several words have contaminated each other and merged. Cf. also (B, G) *txindurri* 'ant'.

3.31. Basque *selHai 1 meadow, 2 field, 3 ground > (B) *zelai* 1,3, (AN) *zelai* 1,2, (BN, L) *zelhai* 1 ~ PEC *ʒəlV > Avar *c':or* 'plain', Rutul *dál* 'plain, plateau', etc. (NCED 1092)

3.32. Basque *simi(n)c 'bedbug' > (AN, BN) *zimitz*, (L) *zimintza*[223] ~ Dargwa (Chirag) *zimizal* 'ant', Archi *c'imic'əla* 'butterfly', Abkhaz a-*mác'a* 'locust', etc. < PNC *miʒǍ / *ʒimiʒǍ (NCED 823)

3.33. Basque *sori 1 luck, fortune, 2 (propitious) moment, 3 omen > (B) *zori* 1,2,3, (G, AN, BN, Z) *zori* 1,2, etc. ~ PNC *ʒōɫV 'healthy, whole' > Lak *c'ullu-* 'healthy, whole', Dargwa (Tsudakhar) *zara*-se 'healthy, whole', Abkhaz a-b-*zá* 'alive, living', Hurrian *šawlə* 'health, prosperity', etc. (NCED 1095)

3.34. Basque *onci 'vessel, container; boat, ship' ~ PEC *bōnʒ(w)V 'vessel' (= **1.22**)

3.35. Basque *(H)ainc- 'hard frost' > (B) *aintzigar, antzigar*, (G) *aintzigar, antzigar, intziar*[224] ~ PNC *jămʒǍ 'snow' > Andi *anži*, Khwarshi *ĩsa*, Rutul *jiz*, etc. (NCED 674) ~ cf. Na-Dene: PAth *yəχs 'snow' > Chipewyan *yàθ*, Navajo *yàs*, etc.

PDC *ć: In most positions the reflex is dorso-alveolar /ś/ (orth. *z*), but apico alveolar in the cluster /śk/ (*esku*). In final position there is both the usual /ś/ (*laz*) and /ć/ (*amets*). The difference is as yet unexplained.

3.36. Basque *sirsu- / *sincu-r̄ 1 throat, 2 nape > (G, AN, BN, L) *zintzur* 1, (Z) *züntzür* 1, (R) *tzuntzur, txuntxur* 1, (AN) *zurzulo, zurzuil* 2 ~ Dargwa (Akushi) *surs* 'neck', Godoberi *čors:a* 'gullet', etc. < PEC *ćw̌irsV (NCED 337)

3.37. Basque *an-his-ba 'sister (of a woman)' > (BN) *ahizpa*, (Z) [ãhĩspa][225], (R) *ãizpa*, (G, AN, L) *aizpa*, (B) *aizta* ~ PNC *=ičĩ 'sister, brother' > Bezhta *is* 'brother', *isi* 'sister', Dargwa

---

[223] Vasco-Caucasian insect words are very similar between the languages, expressive, and cross-contaminating. Cf. also *zinaurri, tximitxa, koko, kukuso*.

[224] The Basque word seems to be a compound, with *igar* 'dry' (q.v.) as the second component, thus 'dry frost'.

[225] There is a mysterious nasalization in Zuberoan, which Trask (1995, p. 14), following Michelena, reconstructs as *anizpa*. In any case, the element *-(h)iz-* is compared with Caucasian *=ičĩ, etc. The element *-pa* is probably related to West Caucasian **pa* (as in Abkhaz a-*pá*, Abaza *pa* 'son' (CWC, p. 63).

(Akushi) *uzi* 'brother', *ruzi* 'sister', Adyge *šə* 'brother', etc. (NCED 669) ~ Burushaski (H, N) -*ço*, (Y) -*çu* 'sister (of a woman); brother (of a man); husband of a sister of a man'

3.38. Basque **asa-l* 'skin, bark, peel' > (B, G) *azal*, (AN, BN, L) *azal, axal*, (Z) *axal* [ášal], (R) *kaxal*[226] ~ Abaza *čʷa* 'skin, bark', Budukh *ʕič* 'skin (of cattle)', Hurrian *ašχi* 'skin', etc. < PNC **ʔw̄ārc̄wə̆* 'skin, color' (NCED 228)

3.39. Basque **ise-* 'aunt' > (c) *izeba*, (BN-Aldude) *izea*, (B) *izeko* 'aunt'[227] ~ PEC **=īlc̣wī* 'girl, woman' > Chechen d-*ēca* 'paternal aunt', Lak *duš* 'daughter', Tsakhur *iči* 'girl', etc. (NCED 952)

3.40. Basque **(ema-)ste* 1 (married) woman, wife, 2 woman (married or widowed)[228] > (B, G, AN, BN, L, R) *emazte* 1, (Z) *emazte* 1,2 ~ Chechen *stē* 'woman, female', *stē*-n 'female', *steš, stij* 'women, females', Ingush *se* 'woman, female', *istij* 'women, wives'; Dargwa (Chirag) *cade* 'female' < PEC **c̄VjdV* (NCED 375)

3.41. Basque **eśku* 'hand' > (c) *esku*, (Z) *eskü*[229] ~ PEC **gw˄c̣V* 'arm' > Tsakhur *guč*'arm', Khinalug *čigin* 'shoulder' (< **c̣˄gwV*), etc. (NCED 448)

3.42. Basque **las* > (L) *laz* 'beam, rafter' ~ PEC **ƛ̣Vc̣V* 'log, pole' > Akhwakh *ƛ':eč'a* 'log', Bezhta *ƛ'eša* 'board, step', etc. (NCED 781)

3.43. Basque **a-menć* 1 dream, 2 sleep > (G, AN, L, R) *amets* 1, (BN) *amens* 2, (B) *ames* 1[230] ~ Hunzib *niše* 'night', Lak *šana* 'sleep', etc. < PNC **finic̣wV̆* 'night, evening' (NCED 524)

---

[226] This comparison assumes that -*l* is a suffix. Cf. similar endings in Basque *magal* 'lap' (*q.v.*), *sabel* 'belly' (*q.v.*). Roncalese has the mysterious form *kaxal*, with unexplained *k*-.

[227] For the element -*ba*, see the note to *ahizpa*. For the fossilized prefix *i*-, see Appendix A.

[228] According to Trask (1997: 271) *emazte* means 'woman' in three dialects (Ronc., Aezk., Sal.), and means 'wife' elsewhere. The element *ema*- means 'female', and I regard it as native Basque, *not* a loan from Romance as commonly supposed. The supposed derivation from **ema-gazte* 'young woman' does not gibe with the common meanings.

[229] See Appendix A for the fossilized prefix *e*-.

[230] Basque /**m**/ corresponds to Caucasian **n – w*. Cf. *ametz* 'gall oak' (*q.v.*). See Appendix A for the fossilized prefix *a*-.

3.44. Basque *hauć > (BN,L) *hauts,* (Z) *hautx,* (B,G,AN,R) *auts* 'ashes, powder' ~ Ingush *jost* 'loose earth', Khinalug *inč:i* 'earth', etc. < PEC *jōmc̣V* (NCED 684)

PDC *č:* This sound corresponds consistently to Basque apico-alveolars: initial and medial /ś/ (orth. *s*); /ć/ (orth. *ts*) in the verbal root *eutsi*. In the word *lasto* it is unclear whether /śt/ is a peculiar development of *č, or *-to* is a suffix.

3.44. Basque *śolho > (AN, L, Z) *sorho* 'meadow', (G) *soro* 'field', (B) *solo* 'field (prepared for sowing)'[231] ~ PEC *čHätu > Lak *šạlu* 'earth, ground', Ingush *čil* 'ashes, dust', Tsakhur *žil* 'earth, floor', etc. (NCED 342)

3.45. Basque *śale 1 net(work), 2 grill in front of a manger, 3 manger > (B) *sale, sare* 1,2, (G, L, Z, R) *sare* 1, (BN) *sare* 1,3, etc.[232] ~ Avar *čalí* 'fence, enclosure', Rutul *čal* 'enclosure for milking sheep', etc. < PEC *čħałē (NCED 343) ~ cf. Yen: PY *čoL- > Ket *tōʎ* 'wicker hurdle' (SSEJ 287)

3.46. Basque *śoī- 'upper part of the body'in compounds: (c) *sor-balda* 'shoulder' (*q.v.*), (B, G) *sor-buru* 'shoulder' ~ PEC *čōrχV* 'body' > Chechen *čarχ* 'carcass', Avar *čerχ* 'body', etc. (NCED 346)

3.47. Basque *śabe-l 'belly' > (c) *sabel*[233] ~ Bezhta *šebo* 'liver', Chechen *žim* 'kidney', Abkhaz á-z 'gall', etc. < PNC *ǯăbV < PDC *čabV (= **1.26**)

3.48. Basque *a(r)śto 'donkey, ass' > (c) *asto,* (R) *arsto* ~ Ubykh *čədə,* Proto-Abkhazian *čada 'donkey' (CWC, p. 314) ~ Burushaski (H, N) *ćhardá,* (Y) *ćardé* 'stallion'

3.49. Basque *laśto 1 straw (of wheat, barley, rye), 2 straw (of maize), 3 straw (of oats) > (B) *lasto* 1,2, (G, AN, Z) *lasto* 1, (R) *lasto* 1,3 ~ PEC *ɬačă 'leaf; a kind of plant' > Akhwakh *ƛ'ača* 'a kind of edible plant', Budukh *q'əč* 'straw', etc. (NCED 773)

---

[231] I consider the form *sorho* (with the cluster *-rh-*) to be native Basque, in contrast to *zoru* 'ground, floor' < Latin *solu(m)*.

[232] Azkue defines Bizkaian *sale* more precisely as "Estacada puesto delante de pesebre para que los animales solo pueden asomar el morro."

[233] Assuming a suffix *-l:* cf. *azal, magal* (*q.v.*). Cf. Yeniseian: PY *tVpV· / *tVbV· 'spleen' (SSEJ 292).

3.50. Basque *moś́u > (G) *musu* 'nose, face, kiss, point', *musu-zulo* 'nostrils', (B) *mosu* 'kiss', (AN,L) *musu* 'face, kiss', (BN) *musu* 'face'[234] ~ PEC *mHărčwV > Chamalal *maš* 'snot', etc. (NCED 816) ~ Burushaski *muś́ > (H,N,Y) *–múś* 'snot' (also 'nose' in Y), (Y) *–múś-puś-i-* 'nostrils', (H,N) *muś́* 'edge, end', *-múś-kane* 'on one's face, face down', etc.

3.51. Basque *e-ući > *eutsi* (B) 'to take', (AN, B, G) 'to take hold, seize, grasp' ~ Dargwa =*uč-* 'to gather, collect', Avar =*ač:-* 'to carry', Kabardian *ša-*n 'to take, carry', etc. < PNC *=ăc̣wV̆ (NCED 253)

PDC *ć', *č': There seems to be no difference in Basque reflexes of these sounds, so they are conflated here. Initial /č/ (orth. *tx*), varying with /š/ (orth. *x*) in some (eastern) dialects; medial /ś/ (orth. *z*); /ś/ in the clusters /śk/ and /št/ (orth. *-sk-, -st-*); final /c̄/ (orth. *-tz*).

3.52. Basque *čiki > (AN, B, BN, G) *txiki* [čiki] 'little'[235] ~ Dargwa (Chirag) *c'iq'ʷaj* 'few', Agul *č'uq'* 'few', etc. < PEC *ç_wăqV (NCED 379)[236] ~ Burushaski *ćíki > (Y) *ćíki* 'small'

3.53. Basque *čimiča > (B, BN, G, R) *tximitxa* 'bedbug'[237] ~ Tabasaran *č'amč'* 'fly', Lak *č'imuč'ali* 'butterfly', etc. PEC *ç'imVçV (NCED 379) ~ Burushaski (N) *ćhumúuso* 'a maggot that eats wool'

3.54. Basque *čahal 'calf (young bovine)' > (Z) *txahal* [čahal], (BN, L, Z) *xahal* [šahal], (B) *txaal* [čaal], (B, G) *txal* [čal], (BN) *xal* [šal], (R) *xãl* [šãl] ~ Cauc: Andi *č'ora* 'heifer', Agul *luč'* 'heifer', Chechen *ēsa* 'calf', etc. < PEC *Hc̣wīlV̆ / *Hlīc̣wV̆ (NCED 556)

---

[234] The Dene-Caucasian etymology accounts for the Romance words listed by Trask (1997: 261). Cf. also PNC *mñăc̣ĕ 'edge' > Ingush *mʕiz-arg* 'snout', etc. (NCED 813), which could instead be cognate with the Basque and/or Burushaski words.

[235] Vasconic is the source of Spanish *chico, chica,* etc. See other words in this section > Spanish. Initial /č/ did not exist in Latin.

[236] Cf. also PNC *ǯiḳwĀ 'short' > Chamalal *č'ik'u-b* 'small, short', etc. (NCED 1108).

[237] Vasconic > Spanish *chinche* 'bedbug', etc. See the note to *zimitz* (3.32).

3.55. Basque *čoṝu > (B) txorru 'root of hair' ~ PEC *čʰwərV 'hair' > Hunzib č'ur 'women's hair', Archi č'> ri 'hair', etc. (NCED 378)

3.56.a. Basque *čori / *čol- > (B, G, AN, R) txori [čori], (AN, BN, L, Z) xori [šori] 'bird',[238] txol-arre 'sparrow'[239] (lit. 'bird-gray'), (G, AN) txoloma 'pigeon'[240] ~ PEC *čHwīlV > Chamalal č'or 'bird', Avar č'orólo 'quail', Lak č'įl-mu '(small) bird', etc. (NCED 388) ~ cf. ST: Tibetan m-čhil-pa 'sparrow' ~ PY *ʔVčilV 'bird' > Kott nena-šili, etc. (SSEJ 204)

3.56.b. Basque *čonta > (B) txonta 'chaffinch' (Fringilla coelebs, a small European songbird) ~ Kryz č'ülüt' 'sparrow', Chechen č'ēʁardig 'swallow', etc. < PEC *č·VƁVlit·V (NCED 391)

3.57. Basque *čainku > (BN, Z) txainku, (BN, L) xanku [šaŋku], (G) txanket 'lame' ~ PEC *čãnḳV > Rutul, Tsakhur č'anḳ' 'trap'[241] (NCED 384) ~ Burushaski (H, N) ćhaŋgú, (Y) ćaŋgú 'lame, crippled'

3.58. Basque *čehume > (R) txeme [čeme], xeme [šeme], (BN) xehume, (Z) xehüne 'jeme / demi-empan (half-span, distance between thumb and index finger)'[242] ~ Dargwa (Chirag) č'im 'span', Lezgi č'ib 'span', etc. < PNC *čwimħV (NCED 391)[243]

3.59. Basque *i-särdi > (c) izerdi, (B) izardi 'sweat', (AN, BN, R also) 'sap' ~ PEC *c̄āɫwV > Chechen c'ij 'blood', Avar č'ágo-b

---

[238] We find this straightforward etymology more plausible than the convoluted derivation proposed by Michelena and promoted by Trask (e.g., 1995, p. 46; 1997, p. 296).

[239] Cited by Trask (1997: 302) without any dialect attribution. Not found in Azkue.

[240] Apparently a blend of Basque *čol- + Romance (Span.) paloma 'pigeon'.

[241] A trap cripples that which it catches.

[242] The Spanish word is jeme, usually attributed to Latin semi- 'half', though semi- always occurs in composition with another word, and semi- obviously cannot account for the three-syllable form *čehume (with internal laryngeal) required by the northern Basque forms. Azkue's derivation from zehe 'palmo' + me [mehe] 'delgado, reducido' is also fanciful, in my opinion. The equation of Basque *čehume = PNC *čwimħV is comparatively straightforward.

[243] NCED 392 notes: "The original meaning ... was probably 'span between the thumb and the small finger' ... Outside the Andian area ... *čwimħV obtained first the meaning 'span (in general)', and sometimes ... the meaning 'span between the thumb and the fore-finger'."

'alive', etc. (NCED 376) ~ cf. Yen: PY *sur 'red, blood' > Ket śūʎ 'blood', etc. (SSEJ 278)[244]

3.60. Basque *(H)isu > (B, G) izu 'fright, horror'[245] (G) 'fierce, bad-tempered' ~ Bezhta (Khoshar) hic'o 'fright', Lak ħuč' 'fright', Abkhaz á-mc 'lie', etc. < PNC *ħVmc̣V (NCED 504) ~ Burushaski úś (gán-) 'to be wild, frightful; to fear, be afraid'

3.61. Basque *ɦauso 1 neighbor, 2 neighborhood > (BN) hauzo 1,2, (L) hauzo 2, (B, G) auzo 1,2, (Z, R) áizo 1,2 ~ Chechen ħāša 'guest', Ubykh p-č'a 'guest', etc. < PNC   *HVc̣wĖ (NCED 612)

3.62. Basque *a(r)śka 1 trough, 2 manger > (BN, Z, R) aska 1, (Z) arska 1, (B, G, AN, L) aska 2 ~ Ubykh čaq ʷə 'basin, tureen', Bezhta (Khoshar) čüχrö 'wooden gutter, kennel (on roof)', etc. < PNC *c̣ā̆q̇wă / c̣ā̆qwă (NCED 332) ~ Burushaski (Y) ćiq 'sifting tray; a measure of grain' ~ cf. ST: PSY *[Ce]kʷ 'ladle' (ST IV: 70) ~ Ket síʔk 'trough for dough' etc. (SSEJ 275) ~ Na-Dene: Eyak c'aak-ł 'dipper', Navajo c'aaʔ 'basket, plate', etc.

3.63. Basque *eśtu 'narrow, cramped, exhausted' ~ Dargwa č̣ạrṭa 'narrow', etc. < PEC *č̣HVrdV (= **2.26**)

3.64. Basque *aśko, *aśki > (c) asko 'many, much', aski 'enough' ~ Kabardian -šxʷa 'big', Lak č'ạ-u- 'many', etc. < PNC *čHəqwV (NCED 386) ~ Burushaski *śóq-um 'wide, broad' ~ cf. ST: PST *cŏk 'enough' > Tibetan čhog, etc. (ST IV: 52)

3.65. Basque *harc 'bear' > (BN, L, Z) hartz, (B, G, AN, R) artz;[246] Basque *hars-koin 'badger'[247] > (Z) harzkű, hazkű, (R) azkoĩ, (L) azkuin, (BN) azkoin, (AN, L) azkona, (AN, B, G) azkonar ~ PEC *χHVr[c̣]V > Chechen χešt 'otter', Dargwa χ:arc' 'marten, squirrel', etc. (NCED 1073) ~ cf. Yen: PY *χas > Kott hāš 'badger' (SSEJ 299) ~ Na-Dene: Haida xúuc 'brown

---

[244] For the semantic match of 'sweat ~ sap ~ blood', cf. Old English swǣtan 'to sweat' and also 'to bleed'.

[245] Since this word is found only in h-less dialects we do not know whether Proto-Basque had an initial laryngeal or not.

[246] There is clearly a resemblance to Indo-European words for 'bear' (Pokorny's *r̥kp̂o-s > Avestan arša-, Welsh arth, Latin ursus, etc.), though borrowing (by Basque) seems unlikely. Chance resemblance, borrowing between Dene-Caucasian and Nostratic, or a deep Borean etymology?

[247] This word seems to be a compound of *harc + *koin, the latter of which may be cognate with Yeniseian *kūñ 'wolverine' (SSEJ 242, Bengtson 1998b).

bear'; Tlingit *xúc* 'brown bear'; PAth **xVc'* ~ **xVs* 'brown bear' > Tsetsaut *xɔ*, etc.²⁴⁸

3.66. Basque **hac, *be-hac* > *hatz, atz* 'finger, thumb, track; inch', etc., *behatz, beatz* 'thumb, toe', etc.²⁴⁹ ~ Avar *kʷač'* 'paw', Dargwa *kač'a, kʷač'(a)* 'paw', etc. < PNC **kwăn Vč̄ě* (NCED 704) ~ Burushaski *qaṣ* 'cubit (from elbow to fingertips)'²⁵⁰ ~ cf. Na-Dene: PAth **-keč'* 'claw' > Hupa *-ḵec'*, Mattole *-č'eʔx*, etc.

3.67. Basque **hoc* 'cold' (adj.) > (BN, L, Z) *hotz*, (B, G, AN, R) *otz* ~ Hinukh =*oč'č'u* 'cold', Chechen *ša* 'ice', Ubykh *č̆ə* 'cold', etc. < PNC **(r)HEčwV / *čwE(r)HV* 'cold' (NCED 393)²⁵¹

3.68. Basque **a-menc* 'a kind of oak'²⁵² > (c) *ametz, amentx*²⁵³, (Z) [ǎmẽc] 'chêne-tauzin'²⁵⁴ ~ PNC **nVč̄ē* > Chechen *naž*, Lak *maža* 'oak tree', etc. (NCED 857) ~ Burushaski (H,N) *meṣ*, (Y) *noṣ* 'sapling, bush'

PDC **ʒ, *ʒ̂:* As with **c', *c̄'*, there is no difference between the Basque reflexes of **ʒ* and **ʒ̂*. The reflexes are consistently dorso-alveolar: initial /s̄/ (orth. *z*); medial /s̄/ (orth. *z*) or /c̄/ (orth. *-tz*); final /c̄/ (orth. *-tz*).

3.69.a. Basque **sumhV* 1 a kind of elm tree,²⁵⁵ 2 grove, 3 a kind of willow, 4 rod, switch > (B) *zumar* 1, *zumetz* 3, *zumitz* 4, (G) *zumar* 1, *zumaldi* 2, *zumitz* 4, (Z) *zünhar* 1, etc. ~ PEC **ʒ̂ĥŭmV* >

---

²⁴⁸ Na-Dene **x* for expected **χ*: influenced by cultural factors (taboo, etc.)?

²⁴⁹ The meanings of these words vary greatly depending on dialect, *e.g.,* (B) *atz* 'finger, inch', *behatz* 'toe', (L) *hatz* 'paw, track', *behatz* 'thumb, fingernail'. *Be-* is a fossilized class prefix, more fully explained in Appendix A.

²⁵⁰ In Burushaski only the semantic specialization as a unit of measurement has survived. Cf. Hunzib *k'ɔč'u* 'half-span, distance between thumb and forefinger', Basque *hatz* 'inch'.

²⁵¹ PNC reconstruction slightly modified (*r* in parentheses): "It is not quite clear whether r- ... should be treated as a former class prefix or as part of the root." (NCED, p. 394) There is no /r/ in the Basque word, so I would favor the former option.

²⁵² Azkue has 'carballo, melojo, quejigo , rebollo / rouvre, espèce de chêne'; Trask (1997: 307) has 'gall oak' ('muricated oak'); the latter also in Aulestia & White. For Basque /m/, see the note to *amets* 'dream, sleep'.

²⁵³ Cited by Trask (1997: 307), without dialectal attribution.

²⁵⁴ Larrasquet (1939).

²⁵⁵ Aulestia & White define *zumar* as 'English elm (Ulmus procera)'.

Hunzib *šumal* 'bushes', Lezgi *žum* 'quince', etc. (NCED 1107) ~ Burushaski **śumulū* 'eine ~ cf. Yen: PY **[ǯ]am-* 'berry' > Kott *čamar* šulpi 'cranberries', etc. (SSEJ 308)

3.69.b. Bsq **sil-(haga)* 'stake, post, picket'[256] > (B) *zilaga* ~ Ingush *žel* 'sheep-fold', Tsez *želi* 'wattle fence', etc. < PEC **ǯīlV* 'wattle, pen' (NCED 1108)

3.70. Basque **sul* > **sur* 'wood, timber, lumber' > (c) *zur*, (B-Arratia, Orozko) *zul* ~ Andi *žala* 'branch, rod', Avar *žul* 'broom, besom', Tsakhur *ǯol* 'sheaf', etc. < PEC **ǯw[ẽ]łī* (NCED 1103)

3.71. Basque **haice* > (BN, L) zu-*haitz*,[257] (R) *atze* 'tree', (BN, Z) -*tze* (suffix in tree names) ~ PNC **Hă(r)ǯwī* > Karata *ežela* 'pine tree', Khwarshi *aža* 'tree', etc. (NCED 549) ~ cf. Yen: Ket *ǯiʔe, diʔe* 'tree trunk', Kott *či*

3.72. Basque **hasi* 'to grow, swell; to grow, cultivate, bring up; seed; semen' > (BN, L, Z) *hazi*, (B,G,AN,R) *azi* ~ Avar =*iž-* 'to grow', Dargwa (Akushi) =*uz-* 'to grow', etc. < PEC **=Vǯ́V* (NCED 1038) ~ Burushaski **-úśa-* 'to nourish, grow' > (H,N) -*úśa-*

3.73. Basque **bisa-r̄* > (c) *bizar* 'beard' ~ Bezhta *bizal-ba* 'mustache', etc. < PEC **bilǯ́V* (= 1.14)

3.74. Basque **horc* 'tooth' > (BN, L, Z) *hortz*, (L, Z) *hortx*, (R) *ortx*, (AN) *ortz*; (G) *ortz* 'set of teeth'[258] ~ Lak *k:arč:i* 'tooth', Avar *gožó* 'fang, canine tooth', Tsez *gožu* 'molar', etc. < PEC **g ˄[r]ǯwē* (NCED 435) < PDC [**kərǯwē*] 'fang, tooth', molar'[259]

3.75. Basque **olaic* 'beestings, colostrum' > (B, G) *oreitz*, (B) *oratz*, (AN, BN, L, Z, R) *oritz*, (BN-Hasparren) *olitz* ~ Andi =*erč'-* 'to milk', Khinalug *loži* 'to pour', etc. < PNC **=HoǯĂl* (NCED 600)

---

[256] A compound of **sil-* + **haga* (q.v.).

[257] A compound beginning with *zu-* = **sur* 'wood' (3.70).

[258] Bizkaian uses the synonym *agin* 'tooth' < **hagin*.

[259] Nikolayev & Starostin reconstruct PEC **g ˄ lǯwē*, while noting (NCED, p. 436) that "[w]e must reconstruct some medial liquid, and it is most probably **-l- ...*," though all attestations with a liquid have /r/ (Lak *k:arč:i*, Akhwakh *goržo*, Agul *gʷarǯ*), and Basque /r/ is consistent with PDC **r*, but not **l*. Further, the PEC initial **g-* appears to reflect assimilation to the voiced cluster **-rǯ-*, and initial **k-* is consistent with Basque initial /h/.

4. Lateral Affricates

It is clear that lateral affricates existed in PDC, and indeed are some of the most characteristic sounds of Dene-Caucasian. They are definitely reconstructed for Proto-Caucasian (where some languages retain them to the present) and for Proto-Na-Dene (where almost all languages retain them).[260] The original pattern, which is still found in many or most Na-Dene languages,[261] was a contrast of voiceless or fortis *ƛ [tɬ] with glottalized *ƛ' [tɬ'] and voiced or lenis *λ [dl]. In Basque the reflexes of all three fall together, though patterned in an interesting way:

In initial position all lateral affricates *ƛ,*ƛ',*λ > Basque *l-

In medial position all lateral affricates *ƛ,*ƛ',*λ > **Basque *-rd-** [r̄ð][262]
In final position all lateral affricates *ƛ,*ƛ',*λ > Basque *-l

This pattern is structurally similar to that of Basque reflexes of PDC *ɬ, q.v., where the contrast between *l and *lh only occurs between vowels. It is also structurally similar to the pattern of reflexes in Burushaski:[263]

In initial position all lateral affricates *ƛ,*ƛ',*λ > Burushaski *t-, *d-

In medial position all lateral affricates *ƛ,*ƛ',*λ > Burushaski *-lt-, *-ld-
In final position all lateral affricates *ƛ,*ƛ',*λ > Burushaski *-l

PDC *ƛ,*ƛ',*λ > Basque initial *l-:

---

[260] Peiros & Starostin (1996) also reconstruct a lateral affricate *ƛ for Proto-Sino-Tibetan.

[261] In some Caucasian (mainly Avar-Andi-Tsezian) languages lateral affricates are retained, but not in the original *ƛ ~*ƛ' ~*λ [pattern. Akhwakh, for example, has a fourfold contrast based on the features ± tense [:] and ± glottalized [']: [ƛ ~ ƛ: ~ ƛ' ~ ƛ':].

[262] As discussed below, there are some cases of *-rt- rather than *-rd-.

[263] See Bengtson 1997a.

4.1. Basque *lisun* 1 moldy, musty, mustiness, 2 dirty, untidy > (BN, L, Z, R) *lizun* 1, (B, G, AN) *lizun* 1,2 ~ PEC **ƛwilc̣wV* 'dirt; bog, marsh' > Andi *ɬenc':u* 'bog, marsh', etc. (NCED 770) ~ cf. Na-Dene: Eyak *X̣'ic'k , X̣'ac'k* 'dirt, dust'; Sarsi *-X̣'i·z* '(be) swampy', Chipewyan *-X̣'és* 'mud', Navajo *-X̣'iš* 'mud, clay', etc.

4.2.a. Basque **limuri* 1 moist, humid, 2 slippery, 3 smooth, soft, 4 lewd, 5 changeable (weather) > (G) *limuri* 3,4, (BN) *limuri* 2,5, (Z) *limuri* 1,2,5, etc. ~ PEC **ƛHwemV* 'liquid' > Avar *X̣:amí*-ja-b 'liquid', Dargwa (Chirag) *šam̄-ze* 'wet, liquid', etc. (NCED 768) ~ cf. ST: PST **ƛŭm* > Lushai *tlum* 'to draw in, go in, sink', etc. (ST III: 79) ~ Na-Dene: PEA **ƛeʔχ* > Navajo *-ƛèèh, ƛééʔ* 'wet object moves', etc.

4.2.b. Basque **lerā* 'slipping, sliding; to slip, slide' > (BN, L, Z) *lerra* ~ Avar (Chadakolob) *X̣ur-s-* 'to glide', Hunzib *ɬaɬa-X̣-* 'to crawl', etc. < PEC **ʔVƛV(r)* (NCED 224)

4.2.c. Basque **lega-* 'small stone, pebble, gravel' > (B, G, BN, L) *legar;* (AN, L) *legatx* 'gravelly land' ~ Hinukh *X̣'iχʷin* 'cobblestone', Akhwakh *X̣'aχa* 'ruins', etc. < PDC **ƛãnχwV* 'a kind of stone' (NCED 774)

4.2.d. Basque **lo* 'to sleep' > (c) *lo* 'sleep', *lo egin* 'to sleep' ~ Akhwakh *X̣':unu-,* Khwarshi *ƛes-* 'to sleep', etc. < PNC **=HVwƛĀn* (NCED 619)

4.3.a. Basque **lainho* 1 cloud, 2 mist, fog, 3 vapor[264] > (AN) *lano* 1, (B, G) *laiño* 2, (BN, L) *lanho* 3, (Z) [lãnhū̃] 2, etc. ~ Chamalal *hãla* 'fog', Karata *hanX̣'u* 'fog, cloud', Godoberi *hanlu* id., Dargwa (Akushi) *hank'* 'sleep', etc. < PNC **ɦemƛ'A* 'dream' ~ Burushaski **-wélʒ́i* 'dream'[265]

4.3.b. Basque **lanbro* 1 fog, mist, 2 drizzle[266] > (B, G) *lanbro* 1,2, (AN, BN, L) *lanbro* 1 ~ PEC **rĕ̃n⫽wV̆* 'cloud, fog' >

---

[264] I first treated 4.3.a. and 4.3.b. as the same etymon, but it later became clear that **lainho* and **lanbro* must be of separate and distinct origin, though both etyma originally contained lateral affricates. Aulestia & White (1992), for example, have separate entries for *laino* 'fog, mist' and *lanbro* 'dense fog'.

[265] "Andian languages demonstrate a non-trivial semantic development 'dream' > '*vision' > 'cloud'" (NCED 513). Even if we decline to accept this semantic equation, the Andian forms clearly fit the Basque forms, semantically and phonetically, only allowing for metathesis: Proto-Andian **honƛ'V* 'fog, cloud'.

[266] Assuming metathesis: Basque **lanbro* matches well with a metathesized PEC **⫽ĕ̄nwrV̆*.

Chechen *doχk* 'fog', Khinalug *unk'* 'cloud', etc. (NCED 947) ~ Burushaski *harált* 'rain, cloud'

4.4. Basque **lok-* 1 temple (side of head), 2 middle of forehead > (B,G) *loki* 1, (R) *lokun, lokune* 1, (B-Ubidea) *loki* 2 ~ PEC *√arq̇wē* > Khwarshi *ƛ'oq'o* 'forehead', Avar *t'aʁúr = t'aɣúr* 'cap', etc. (NCED 775) ~ cf. ST: PST **[λ]ĕkʷ* > Tibetan *ltag* 'back part of the neck, nape; back', etc. (ST III: 62) ~ Na-Dene: PAth **ƛ'aχ* > Navajo *ƛ'àh* 'temples', etc.

4.5. Basque **lasto* 'straw' ~ PEC **ƛačă* 'leaf; a kind of plant' (= **3.49**)

4.6.a. Basque **lirain* > (B, G, L) *lirain* 'slender, svelte, lithe' ('esbelto [de personas y animales]') ~ PNC **=i √ɨlV* 'thin' > Avar *t'eréna-b*, Khinalug *k'ɨr* 'thin', etc. (NCED 639) ~ Burushaski (H, N) *tharén-um* 'narrow, tight (of clothes)' ~ cf. Na-Dene: Haida *ƛ'a-* 'thin, flat object'

4.6.b. Basque **lerō* > (c) *lerro* 'line, file, row' ~ PEC **√wăr(ɦ)ˉ* 'boundary' > Avar *ƛ':er* 'garden bed, terrace, row, rank', Dargwa *jara* 'furrow', etc. (NCED 782)

4.7. Bsq **lai* 'two-pronged fork for loosening soil' > (B,G, AN, L, R) *laia*[267] ~ Avar *ƛ':oχ:órχ:o* 'rake', Bezhta *ƛaχ-dami* 'rake', etc. < PEC **ƛVχwV* (NCED 781)

4.8. Basque **lape* 'shelter under the eaves of a shed' ~ PEC **ƛĕpV̆* 'stone plate or shed' (= **1.11**)

4.9. Basque **las* 'beam, rafter' ~ PEC **ƛVćV* 'log, pole' > Akhwakh *ƛ':eč'a* 'log', etc. (= **3.42**)

4.10. Basque **lema* 'rudder' (< **board, plank*') > (AN, B, G, L) *lema* ~ PEC **ƛəm?V̆* 'roof' > Karata *ƛ'ame* 'roof', etc. (NCED 777) ~ cf. PST **ƛam* 'a kind of stick' > Tibetan *lčam* 'lath, pole, rafter', etc. (ST III:58) ~ Na-Dene: Haida *ƛamat* 'cross-pieces in canoe'[268]

4.11. Basque **lahaṝ* 'bramble, creeping plant' > (BN, L) *lahar*, (AN, B, G) *laar*, (AN, G) *lar*, (Z) *nahar*, (Sal) *naar*, (R) *nar* ~

---

[267] Azkue cites the form *lai*, while Aulestia & White cite *laia* 'two-handed double-ponted spade used for turning over earth'. The latter seems to be the definite form = **lai + -a* 'the'.

[268] Starostin (2000, p. 231, #5) compares instead PST **ƛɔ̆ŋ* 'to lift, raise' with PEC **√‹m?V̆*, which is not implausible. In LDC (#145) Ket *lam*, Yug *ʌ́aʔm* 'board', etc. are also compared, but see SSEJ (p. 267), where PY **rem* is reconstructed, and no external cognates are proposed.

PNC *ʏ wĭrʔV 'leaf' > Andi X̌'oli, Dargwa k'a 'leaf', etc. (NCED 784) ~ PST *X̌ā(k) 'leaf' > Mikir lo, Magari hla, etc. (ST III:57)

4.12. Basque *laŕu 'skin, hide, leather' > (c) larru, (B) narru ~ Dargwa (Akushi) guli 'skin, sheepskin', Avar X̌':er 'color' (< '*skin') < PNC *Ł̌ŏli (NCED 789) ~ Burushaski *tar- > (H,N,Y) tar-íŋ 'skin bag'[269]

4.13.a. Basque *laŕi 1 sadness, anguish, 2 anxiety, worry > (B) larri 1,2, (G, L) larri 2 ~ Chechen lüra 'severe, dangerous', Bezhta =iX̌aro 'hard', etc. < PNC *Ł̌wĕrV 'hard, severe, stern' (NCED 792)

4.13.b. Basque *laŕe 'meadow, pasture' > (c) larre, (B) larra ~ Archi X̌oli 'yard, place in front of the house', etc. < PEC *Ł̌wĕtV 'enclosure, fence' ~ Burushaski *ter 'mountain pasture, summer pasture'

4.13.c. *laŕain 'threshing floor' > (G, AN, L, Z) larrain, (R) larren, llarne ~ Avar lol, Archi X̌orom 'threshing board' < PEC *=VrŁV 'to thresh' (NCED 1031) ~ Burushaski daltán- 'to thresh' < *rVŁVn-.

4.14.a. Basque *lehia 1 wish, desire, zeal, 2 haste, hurry, 3 persistence, longing > (BN, L, Z) lehia 1,2,3, (B, G, AN) leia 1,2,3 ~ PEC *=inŁwV 'to love, want' > Chechen laʔ- 'to want, wish', Avar =oX̌':- 'to love, want, wish', Archi X̌':an 'to love, want', etc. (NCED 644)

4.14.b. Basque *luŕ 'earth' > (c) lur, (Z) lür ~ Avar raX̌': 'earth, ground', Lak luχči 'earth, land', etc. < PNC *lhĕmŁwĭ (NCED 747)[270]

PDC *X̌,*X̌',*λ > Basque medial *-rd- [r̄ð]:

4.15.a. Basque *VrdV 'come/go' > (B) erdu 'come!, come ye!' (2nd person pl.), (Z) orde-zü 'go!' (2nd person sg.) ~ PNC *=ə̄rλŬ

---

[269] See Chapter 11 for assimilation and dissimilation, both of which are probably at play in this etymology. (? PDC *λori ~ *λeru > Bsq *laŕu, PNC *Ł̌ŏli, Bur *tar-.)

[270] This etymology requires metathesis and dissimilation. (See section 11.)

'to go, walk, enter' > Archi a=λ̃i- 'to come', Lak *ulu* 'let's go!', etc. (NCED 422)

4.15.b. Bsq **b-ardin* 'the same, equal; even, smooth, flat' > (B, BN, L, Z) *bardin,* (G, AN) *berdin* ~ Avar *r-éλ':in* 'to be similar, resemble', Tsez =*iła-si* 'similar, alike', etc. < PEC **=ăʌ̯wVn* 'to resemble, similar' (NCED 261)[271]

4.15.c. Bsq **b-arda* 'last night' > (BN, L, Z, R) *barda,* (B, G, AN) *bart* ~ Chechen *selχana* (se-*lχa*-na) 'yesterday', Avar *noλ':* 'yesterday evening, yesterday night', etc. < PNC **r-Vmʌ̯Ă* 'night, evening' (NCED 955) ~ cf. Burushaski **khú-ulto* 'today', **b-ultú* 'day', etc.

4.16. Basque **e-rdoil* 1 rust (of plants), 2 rust (of iron) > (AN) *erdoil* 1,2, (BN, L, Z, R) *erdoil* 2, (G) *erdoi* 1, (B) *ordei* 1,2 ~ PEC **ʌ̱wĕł?ĕ* 'mould' > Akhwakh *xali* 'mould (fungus)', Lezgi *xʷel* 'boil, furuncle', etc. (NCED 770) ~ cf. Na-Dene: Sarsi -*λ̃'ú·,* -*λ̃'ù·* 'to be moldy', *gí-λ̃'ùwí* 'mold'[272]

4.17. Basque **a-rdaī* > **adaī* > (c) *adar* 'horn'[273] ~ Avar *λ̃:ar,* Chechen *kur* 'horn', etc. < PEC **ʌ̯wɨrV* (NCED 771) ~ Burushaski **ltur* > (H) -*ltúr,* (Y) *tur* 'horn'

4.18.a. Basque **erdi* > (c) *erdi* 'half, middle' ~ PNC **=ĕ⁄Ĕ* 'half, middle' > Bezhta =*aλo* 'middle', =*aλo*-kos 'half', Lak =*ač'i* 'half', etc. (NCED 412) ~ cf. ST: PST **λăj* 'navel, center' > Tibetan *lte* 'navel, center', etc. (ST III: 56) ~ PY **?a(?)l* 'half' > Ket d-*aʕa,* etc. (SSEJ 178)

4.18.b. Basque **ürten* 'to go out, leave'[274] > (B) *urten,* (G) *irten* ~ Avar (Chadakolob) *tʷén-* 'to go away', Bezhta =*eλ'-* 'to go, walk', etc. < PEC **=Vmʌ̯V* 'to come, go' (NCED 1026)

4.18.c. Basque **ardac* 'axle' > (c) *ardatz,* (B) burt-*ardatz* 'axle of a wagon', etc. ~ Bezhta, Hunzib *aλ* 'spindle', Agul *hark'-il* 'pivot

---

[271] Note the probable presence of fossilized class prefixes (*b-, r-, j-*) in several of these comparisons.

[272] The Basque word presupposes the development **erdoLi* < **e-λołi,* or the like. See Appendix A for the fossilized prefix *e-*.

[273] See **12.4** for the homonym *adar* 'branch'. In both words the dissimilation of **ardar* > *adar* is similar to that in the loanword *adore* 'courage' < Latin *ardor, ardore-* (Trask 1997, p. 145). See Appendix A for the fossilized prefix *a-*.

[274] This is one of the exceptions exhibiting *–rt-* rather than *–rd-,* for reasons as yet unknown (a prosodic difference?).

of a spindle', etc. < PEC *ʕănλV 'spindle, pivot' (NCED 236) cf. also PEC *ƒül∕wɨ 'handle' (NCED 238)

4.19. Basque *ɦardo 'tinder (made from a kind of dried fungus)' > (L) hardo, (Z) ardai, (G) arda-gai,[275] (Alava) erdai, etc. ~ PEC *ʔwē ∕ V 'a kind of grass' > Chechen jol 'hay', Lezgi weq' 'grass', etc. (NCED 230) ~ cf. ST: PST *lūH 'weed' > Old Chinese *luʔ 'weeds', etc. (ST III:43) ~ Na-Dene: PND *λ'uʔχʷ > Tlingit λ'έχ 'brown fungus (usnea)'; Eyak λ'iχ 'grass, green'; Navajo λ'òh 'grass', Sarsi -λ'ò-, etc.[276]

4.20. Basque *ɦerde / *ɦelde-r̄ > (AN, BN, L) herde, erde, (B, BN, L, R, Z) helder, elder 'drivel, drool' ~ PNC *ɦămλă 'sweat' > Tindi hanla, Lezgi heq' etc. (NCED 509)[277]

4.21. Basque *i-särdi 'sweat, sap' ~ PEC *c̩āɬwV > Chechen c'ij 'blood', etc. (= **3.59**)

4.22. Basque *urdail 1 stomach', 2 abomasum, 3 womb, uterus[278] > (B) urdail 1,2,3, (AN, L) urdail 1, (Z) urdai 1 ~ PEC *=īraɬ V 'stomach, abomasum, rennet' > Tindi b-eλ':u, Archi b-a\, etc. (NCED 670) ~ Burushaski -úl 'abdomen, bowels' ~ cf. Na-Dene: Haida s-λáan 'intestines'

4.23. Basque *erdala > 1 foreign (manner, fashion), 2 foreign (language) > (B, G) erdera, erdel- 1,2, (Z, R) erdara, erdel- 2 (as in erdel-dun, erdal-dun 'non-Basque-speaker, foreigner' ~ Khwarshi λar 'guest', Chechen lūla-χō 'neighbor', etc. < PEC *ɬōlV (NCED 790)

4.24.a. Basque *mardo, *mardul 1 strong, vigorous, 2 robust, plump, 3 smooth, soft > (B) mardul 1, mardo 2, (BN, Z, R) mardo 2,3, (G) mardul 1, etc. ~ PEC *mōrɬV > Chechen mar

---

[275] A compound with the second element *gai / *e-kai 'material, thing', etc. (6.30).

[276] Note meaning 'fungus' in widely-separated Basque and Tlingit. Basque (h)ardo is contaminated in some dialects with words derived from Latin cardu(u)s 'thistle'.

[277] The Basque word (h)elder above is easily confused and contaminated with Basque lerde, lirdi 'drivel, saliva', q.v., of a quite separate origin ~ PEC *ɬwirdi (LDC #19). Note also Basque (G) bilder (bi-lder) 'drivel', which apparently incorporates an old class marker (*bi-/be-) + helder. See Appendix A for the fossilized ending -r.

[278] Caucasian has *=īraɬ V, so assimilation or dissimilation is assumed. Lak D:arlu 'kidney' requires metathesis (< PEC *=ɬarV), and assimilation would produce PEC *=ɬalV, close to the Basque form. The Basque word also has the fossilized class prefix u- (see Appendix A).

'husband', Kryz *miɣil* 'male', Archi *meƛle* 'male', etc. (NCED 830)

4.24.b. Basque **irdoř* > **idoř* 'dry'[279] > (G, AN, L, Z, R) *idor* ~ PEC **=iḻ Vr* '(be) hot, bitter' > Avar *ƛ':er-* 'to burn (oneself)', Kryz *ɣɨr* 'warm', etc. (NCED 640)

PDC **ƛ,*ƛ',*λ* > Basque final *-l.* At the present there are only three examples:

4.25. Basque **oihal* > (BN, L, Z) *oihal,* (AN, B, G, R) *oial* 'cloth, fabric'[280] ~ Bezhta *χiƛo* 'trousers, breeches', Lak *harč:ala* 'cuff, trouser leg', etc. < PEC **χwĭlḻ V* (NCED 1081)

4.26. Basque **hil* > (c) *hil, il* 'dead, death, die' ~ PNC **=iwƛĚ* 'to die, kill' > Chechen *=al-* 'to die', Bezhta *-iƛ'-* 'to kill', etc. (NCED 661) ~ cf. ST: Old Chinese **ƛij* 'corpse' ~ Na-Dene: Haida (A) *ƛ'a-*dáa 'to kill (several things)'

4.27. Basque **b-il-* 'to gather, amass, collect, unite'[281] > (BN, L, Z) *bil,* (AN, G, L, Z) *bil-*du ~ PNC **=V́nƛ·V* 'all' > Andi *hilu-,* Chechen *–errig,* etc. (not in NCED: see SSEJ 211) ~ PYen **bɨ́l-* 'all' > Ket *bild*^5, etc. (SSEJ 211)

5. Velar Occlusives and Nasal

PDC **k:* There is substantial evidence that PDC **k* was phonetically a strongly aspirated [kʰ] that is consistently reflected as Basque **h,* most likely through an intermediary stage of a velar fricative **x:*

---

[279] Basque has several words for dry, depending on the referent. In Zuberoan *agor* applies only to sources and streams of water, *ütsal (q.v.)* to aliments and terrain, *eihar* to the human body, animals, and vegetation, and *idor* to dryness in general (Larrasquet 1939). In Bizkaian *legor* or *idor* apply to vegetation, *igar* to animals and bones (Azkue 1905). See also Trask 1995, p. 13.

[280] See Appendix A for the fossilized prefix *o-*. Cf. Basque *oihan, q.v.*

[281] Both Basque **b-il-* and Yeniseian **b-íl-* exhibit a prefixed class marker, now fossilized (see Appendix A).

5.1. Basque **hac*, **be-hac* 'finger, paw, thumb, toe', etc. ~ Avar *kʷač'* 'paw', Dargwa *kač'a,* *kʷač'(a)* 'paw', etc. < PNC **kwănVčĕ* (= **3.66**)

5.2. Basque **haundi* > (BN, L, Z) *handi,* (BN, L) *haundi,* (AN, R) *andi,* (B,G) *aundi* 'great, big, large' ~ Proto-Circassian **kʰʷa(n)də* 'much, many' > Adyge *kʰʷandə* , Kabardian *kʷad* (Kuipers 1975)

5.3. Basque **hüri* > (BN, L, Z) *hiri,* (BN, R) *iri,* (B, G) *uri* 'village, town, city' ~ PNC **kiłū* > Avar *kuli* 'farmstead' Abkhaz a-*kála* 'hut', etc. (NCED 692) ~ cf. ST: PST **g(h)ual* > Tibetan *khul* 'domain, province, district', etc. (ST V: 24)

5.4. Basque **har-* > (BN, L, Z) *har-*tu, (AN, B, G) *ar-*tu 'to take, receive' ~ Archi *kar-* 'to take with, provide, deliver', Abkhaz a-*ga-*rá 'to bring, carry', etc. < PNC **=ikĀr* (NCED 632)

5.5. Basque **horc* 'tooth' ~ Lak *k:arč:i* 'tooth', etc. < PEC **g˄[r]ǯwē* (NCED 435) < PDC [**kərǯwē*] 'fang, tooth, molar'

5.6. Basque **biha-r̄* 'tomorrow' ~ Rutul *biga* 'tomorrow', etc. < PEC **bəgə* 'morning, evening' (= **1.12**)

5.7. Basque **a-hur̄* > (BN, L) *ahur,* (Z) *áhür,* (AN-Baztan) *aur* 'hollow of hand, palm'[282] ~ PEC **kHwərV* > Dargwa *kur* 'pit', Hunzib *kuro* 'brook, ravine', etc. (NCED 691) ~ cf. ST: PST **ghʷăr* > Tibetan s-*kyor, khyor* 'hollow of the hand filled with a fluid', etc. (ST V: 106)

5.8.a. Basque **a-huin-* > (BN, Z) *ahuña,* (Z) *ahüñe,* (Sal) *auña* 'kid'; (c) *ahuntz, auntz* 'goat'[283] ~ Cauc: Andi *kun* 'ram', Tsakhur *kuwar* 'young goat', Lak *ku* 'ram', etc. < PEC **kwī?nī* (NCED 710)

5.8.b. Basque **hon* 'good' > (c) *on,* (BN,Z) *hun* ~ PEC **=ĭkwVn* /**=ĭnkwV* > Urartian *gunə* 'right (not left), true', Avar *kʷarána*-b 'right' (< **kʷVnV-r-*), Chechen *dika* 'good', etc. (NCED 643)

PDC **k':* The Basque reflex is consistently **k.* So while evidence for Proto-Basque initial **p-* and **t-* is quite meager, there is abundant evidence for initial **k-* (see also under PDC **q* and **q'*). The reconstruction of Michelena and Trask, in this regard, must be amended.

---

[282] See Appendix A for the fossilized prefix *a-*.

[283] With a fossilized prefix **a-* (see Appendix A).

5.9. Basque **kako* > (AN, B, G, R) *kako,* (Z) *khako* 'hook', (B) 'clothes hanger, clothes hook', etc.[284] ~ Tabasaran *k'ak'* 'top, edge; point, tip', Abkhaz a-*k'ʷák'* 'corner', etc. < PNC **ḵwĕḵĕ* (NCED 733)

5.10. Basque **kankano* > (B) *kankano* 'large fruitstone, kernel, almond' ~ PNC **ḵV̆rḵV̆(-nV)* > Avar *k'ork'ónu* 'grape, berry', Abkhaz a-*k'ak'án* 'nut', etc. (NCED 730) ~ Burushaski (N) *khakháayo* 'walnut (in the shell)' ~ cf. Na-Dene: Haida *k'áank'aay, k'áank'aan* 'unripe berries', Navajo -*k'ǫ́ǫ́ʔ* 'seed, pit'

5.11. Basque **kain* > (B) *kain* 'fog, mist, large storm clouds' ~ PNC **ḵwĭnħV* > Khwarshi *qema* 'clouds', Rutul *gibɨl* 'cloud, rheumatism', etc. (NCED 737) ~ cf. Yen: PY **qo(ʔ)ŋ* 'fog, mist' > Yug *χoaŋ* (SSEJ 261) ~ Na-Dene: Eyak *q'əmaʔ* 'fog'

5.12. Basque **kuko* > (B) *koko* 'insect (in general), bug', (AN) *kokoso* 'flea', (AN, BN, G, L) *kukuso*, (Z) *küküso* 'flea' ~ Dargwa *k'ak'ari* 'tick', Hunzib *kaki* 'small louse', Chamalal *k'ak'uma* 'butterfly', etc. < PEC **ḵăḵV* (NCED 715)

5.13. Basque **ke, *e-ke, *kino* > (c) *ke* 'smoke', (BN,L,Z) *khe,* (AN,R) *eke,* (B) *ke / kei-* 'smoke'; (BN, L) *k(h)ino* 'bad odor', (Z) *khíño* 'bad taste' ~ PNC **ḵwĭnħV* 'smoke' > Andi *k':ʷoj* 'smoke', Bezhta *qo,* Udi *k:uin* 'smoke', Lak *k'uw* 'soot', etc. (NCED 738)

5.14. Basque **miko* > (BN, L) *miko* 'a little, a little bit' ~ Chamalal *mik'u*-b 'small', Rutul *muk'*-dɨ 'young', etc. < PEC **miḵwV* (NCED 821)

5.15. Basque **beko* 'forehead' ~ PEC **bĕḵwo* 'part of face, mouth' mouth' (= **1.17**)

5.16. Basque **toki* 'place, location' ~ Proto-Circassian **t'ak'ʷə* 'place' > Adyge *t'ak'ʷ*, etc. (= **2.6.a**)

5.17. Basque **bi-rik-* 'lung' > (AN, Sal, G, R) *birika,* (B, L) *biri* 'lung'[285] ~ PNC
*jĕrḵwĭ 'heart' > Avar *rak',* Lezgi *rik'*, etc. (NCED 678) ~ cf. ST: PST **ʔrăŋ // *ʔrăk*
'breast' (ST IV: 6)

---

[284] The relationship of this word to (BN, L, Z) *gak(h)o* 'key' is uncertain. The latter could represent dissimilation of *k(h)ako,* or an original unassimilated form (if PNC **ḵwĕḵĕ* is < **gwĕḵĕ*).

[285] Basque does not permit final /k/, except in inflectional suffixes (Trask 1997: 135). For the fossilized prefix *bi-* see Appendix A.

5.18. Basque *leka 1 pod, husk, 2 sheath (for knife)[286] ~ Chechen *lag* 'fruit-stone' Khinalug *li* 'grain' (pl. *lik'e*-bir), etc. < PNC *lĕḳV (NCED 744)

In a few cases PNC *ḳ(w) corresponds to Basque *g. The conditions for this are still unclear. See the parallel situation of PNC *q̇ = Basque *g, below (under PDC **G**):

5.19. Basque *magal* 'lap' ~ Abkhaz á-*mgʷa* 'belly', Avar *bakʷáli* 'belly', etc. < PNC *bVnḳwẴ (= **1.21**)
5.20. Basque *haga 'long pole, stick, rod (measure)' > (BN, L, Z) *haga*, (B, G, AN) *aga* ~ PEC *hăḳwV > Karata *hak'ʷa* 'branch', etc. (NCED 485) ~ cf. Yen: PY
*ʔəqe 'branch' > Kott *ogé*, etc. (SSEJ 192)

PDC *g: The usual correspondence is Basque *g, *k in the cluster *śk (*esku*). Under certain conditions (before high vowels?) PDC *gw corresponds to Basque *b (*biribil, *erbi). In the case of *gurdi/burdi* there is dialectal variation between the two types of reflex:

5.21. Basque *gal- > (c) *gal-du*, (Z) *gal-dü*, (R) *gal-tu* 'to lose, corrupt, spoil', etc. ~ PEC *=igwVɬ 'to lose, get lost; steal' > Tsakhur a=*gʷal*- 'to get lost', Tindi *'ala* 'thief', etc. (NCED 630)
5.22. Basque *gośe 1 hunger, 2 hungry, 3 ambitious > (B) *gose* 1,3, (AN, BN) *gose* 1,2,3, (Z) *gose* 1,2, etc. ~ PNC *gašē 'hunger' > Lak *k:aši,* Rutul *gaš,* etc. (NCED 431) ~ cf. Na-Dene: Galice *gas* 'become hungry'
5.23. Basque *gʷurdi > (B, G) *gurdi,* (AN, B) *burdi* 'cart, wagon', (G) *gurpil* 'wheel' < *gʷurt-bil ~ Avar *gor* 'circle', Karata *guri* 'wheel', Abaza *gʷərgʷər* 'ring', etc. < PNC *gwērV (NCED 447)
5.24.a. Basque *e-guŕ > (c) *egur* 'firewood'[287] ~ PEC *gōrV > Tsez *giri* 'pole', Udi *gor, gorgor* 'pole', etc. (NCED 440)

---

[286] Any attempt to derive *leka* from Latin *thēca* 'case, envelope' (Trask 1997: 136) seems implausible. There is no precedent for Latin *t* > Basque *l* (though there is for Latin *d* > Basque *l*. See Trask, *ibid.*). There is in fact Basque (BN, Z) *theka,* (B) *teka* 'pod (of legumes)', that could come from Latin *thēca*, or possibly an unknown Dene-Caucasian source.

[287] See Appendix A for the fossilized prefix *e-*.

5.24.b. Basque **śagu* ' ~ PNC **cārgwī* > Adyge *cəɣʷa* 'mouse', etc. (=**3.1.a.**)

5.25. Basque **eśku* 'hand' ~ PEC **gwəćV* 'arm' > Khinalug *čigin* 'shoulder'

(= **3.41**)

5.26. Basque **biribil, *boro(n)bil* > (c) *biribil,* 'round', (AN, BN) *borobil,* (B, G) *boronbil* 'round thing, sphere' ~ Avar *gʷangʷára* 'skull', Hunzib *gogor* 'cheek', Agul *gurga*-ħ 'skull', etc. < PEC **gwɨ[l]gwə* 'round object; skull' (NCED 450)

5.27. Basque **erbi* 1 hare, 2 weasel > (c) *erbi* 1, (B, G) *erbi*-nude, *erbi*-ñude 2, (G) *erbi*-ñure 'weasel' ~ PNC **r̃gwĂ* 'weasel, mouse' > Tindi *reX':u* 'weasel', Ubykh *dəɣʷə́* 'mouse', etc. (NCED 951) ~ cf. ST: PST [**ruak*] 'rat' > Burmese k-*rwak,* etc. (ST II: 100)

PDC **ŋ:* Starostin (2005) posited PDC **ŋ* with the following basic correspondences: Caucasian **n,* Sino-Tibetan **ŋ* in all positions, Yeniseian initial **b-* (probably via **m*), **ŋ* in other positions; Burushaski **h* or 0 in initial position, **ŋ* otherwise. For the PDC cluster **ŋw* the correspondences are the same except that Caucasian and Burushaski have **m* or **n*.

In Basque the reflexes of PDC **ŋ* are as follows: In initial position PDC **ŋ* and **ŋw* become Basque **n*:

5.28. Basque **ni* 'I' (1st. person singular) > (c) *ni* 'I', *n-* (1st. person verbal prefix) ~ PEC **nĭ* 'I' (1st. person singular) > Lak *na,* Dargwa (Akushi) *nu* 'I', *nu-ša* 'we' (exclusive) ~ Burushaski **a-* '1st person singular pronominal prefix' ~ PST **ŋā-* 'I, we' ~ PY **b- / *ʔab* 'I, 1st person singular' < PDC **ŋĭ* 'I'

5.29. Basque **naka-* 1 mockery, 2 repugnance, disgust, 3 dirty, foul > (BN) *naka* 1, *nakaitz* 3, (L) *nakaitz* 2, etc. ~ Tindi *nakʷa* 'oath', Abaza *kʷ*-ra 'to swear', etc. < PNC **nĕkwĭ* (NCED 846) ~ PST **ŋi̭ăkʷ* 'to abuse, maltreat' < PDC **ŋĕkwĭ* 'abuse, swear'

5.30. Basque **nini* 1 child, baby, 2 pupil (of eye), 3 doll > (AN) *nini* 1,2,3, (L) *nini* 1, *begi-nini-ko* 2, etc. ~ Burushaski **-i* 'son, daughter' ~ PST **ŋe(j)* 'child, young' < PDC **ŋVHV* 'child'

5.31. Basque **neke* 'pain, difficulty, fatigue' > (c) *neke,* (BN, L, Z) *nekhe* ~ Burushaski **maq* 'rheumatism, pain' ~ PST **ŋăkʷ* 'ague' < PDC **ŋwVQV* 'pain, disease'

In final position PDC final *ŋ, *ŋV, *ŋwV also become Bsq *n (*m intervocalically after a labial vowel in the word for 'bile' [**5.35**]):

5.32. Basque *eihu(n) 1 to weave, 2 cloth, 3 weaving (craft), 4 to braid > (BN, L, Z) eho 1, (BN, L) ehun 2, (Z) ehün 1,2,3, (B) eio 4, eun 1,2,3, etc. ~ PEC *=irχwVn 'to knit, weave, spin' > Chamalal χ:in- 'to spin', Dargwa =imχ-/=umχ- 'to plait, weave', Agul ruχ- 'to knit', etc. (NCED 655) ~ PST *γʷĕŋ 'to wind, coil' < PDC *=irχwVŋ 'to wind, spin'

5.33. Basque *śoin 1 shoulder, 2 (upper) back, 3 midsection of pork (carré), 4 garment, vestment ~ Lezgi, Rutul c'um 'shin-bone', etc. < PNC *Hçwējnə̆ ~ Burushaski *-śán 'limbs, body parts' < PDC *Hçwḗjŋə̆ 'limb, bone' (= **3.20.b**)

5.34. Basque *susen 1 right, correct, 2 right(s), justice > (B, G, R) zuzen 1, (AN, BN, L) 1,2, (Z) züzen 1,2 ~ PNC *HăʒĔm > Chechen c'ena 'clean, pure', Godoberi c'in-k'i 'clean, pure', Abaza b-zi 'good', etc. ~ Burushaski sisín- to be clear (of wine, water)', sisín-um 'clear (water); slender (person); soft (voice)' ~ PST *chiaŋ > Tibetan chaŋ-s 'purified, clean', etc. < PDC *HăʒĔŋwV 'clean' (= **3.27**)

5.35. Basque *beHa-sum(a) in (L, Z) beazuma, (BN) behazun, (G) beazun, (B) beaztun 'bile, gall' ~ PNC *cwắjmĕ > Dargwa (Chirag) sume, Avar c:in 'gall, anger', Archi s:am 'gall', etc. (NCED 329) ~ Burushaski -sán 'spleen' ~ cf. ST: PST *sĭn 'liver' > Tibetan m-čhin, etc. (ST IV: 103) ~ PY *seŋ 'liver' > Ket śē̆ŋ, etc. < PDC *cwắŋwĕ 'gall' (= **3.6**)

Where there is a medial PDC cluster of *ŋ + laryngeal the nasal disappears completely in Basque:

5.36. Basque *ke, *e-ke > (c) ke 'smoke', (BN,L,Z) khe, (AN,R) eke, (B) ke / kei- 'smoke'[288] ~ PNC *k̲wĭnħV 'smoke' > Andi k':ʷoj 'smoke', Bezhta qo, Udi k:uin 'smoke', Lak k'uw 'soot', etc. ~ PST *ghiw 'smoke, smell' ~ PY *gi(ʔ)ŋ > Kott kiŋ 'smell' < PDC *k̲wĭŋħV 'smell, smoke' (= **5.13**)

---

[288] There is retention of the nasal in Basque words that seem to be related: (BN, L) k(h)ino 'bad odor', (Z) khiño 'bad taste' (see **5.13**). Caused by a suffix?

5.37. Basque *erhi 'finger' > (BN, L, Z) erhi, (AN, R) eri, etc. ~ Burushaski *-reŋ 'hand' ~ PY *rɔ́ŋ 'hand'[289] > Ket íoŋ, íaʔŋ, Yug íɔŋ, etc. < PDC *rVŋHV 'hand, bone'

6. Uvular Occlusives

PDC *q: The Basque reflex is predominantly *k, but also *g under certain conditions:

6.1. Basque *ken- > (c) ken-du, (Z) khen-t, (AN-Aezk.) eken, (AN, BN) eken-du 'to take away, remove; go away, leave' ~ Tindi q:an- 'to snatch, take away', Khinalug =aq:in- 'to hold, keep, catch', etc. < PEC *HVqVn- (NCED 615)

6.2. Basque *khola 'nape' > (BN) gar-kola, (BN, Sal) gar-khora 'nape' ~ PEC *qHwŏɫwV > Tindi χolu 'back of the head', Lezgi χew 'collar', etc. (NCED 894) ~ cf. PST [*Kal] > Tibetan m-gal 'jaw', Magari gal 'cheek', etc. (ST V: 111) ~ PY *χol 'cheek' > Ket qɔʎet, Kott hōl, etc. (SSEJ 302) ~ Na-Dene: Haida qúl 'forehead', Eyak l-quhɫ 'cheek'[290]

6.3. Basque *kaiku > (AN, B, G, L) kaiku 'wooden bowl (used for milking sheep)'[291] ~ PEC *qwăqwV > Avar heh 'basket', Lezgi χʷaχ 'trough', etc. (NCED 899) ~ cf. ST: PST *guăk > Garo khok 'basket', etc. (ST V: 16) ~ PY *q ʌ k- 'spoon' > Ket qə̄kt(ə), etc. (SSEJ 259) ~ Na-Dene: Haida qikw 'basket', Tlingit qákw 'basket'[292]

6.4. Basque *e-kaī- > (c) ekarri, (Z) ekhar 'to bring' ~ Archi χa- 'to drag, carry', Andi q:ur-d- 'to pull, drag', etc. < PNC *=Hī qV(r) (NCED 575)

---

[289] Not in SSEJ: see Tower of Babel site.

[290] Metonymy (semantic "migration") is common in body-part words. Cf. the etymology of Basque loki 'temple' (q.v.). An accepted Indo-European etymology includes Sanskrit kakṣa- 'armpit', Latin coxa 'hip', Irish coss 'foot'(!).

[291] Contra the supposition that kaiku comes from Latin caucu-, a very obscure word for 'drinking vessel' (Trask 1995: 48). More likely this is an old Dene-Caucasian word preserved by the Basque shepherds for this lowly but basic use.

[292] The Yeniseian and Na-Dene words suggest original *qVk-, with progressive assimilation in Caucasian and regressive assimilation in Sino-Tibetan.

6.5. Basque *muku-r̄* > (B) *mukur* 'trunk, base of tree', (Z) *mũkhür* 'très grosse bûche'[293] ~ PEC *mħŏqwe* 'oak-tree' > Tsakhur *moq̇*, Avar *mik:*, etc. (NCED 811) ~ cf. ST: Old Chinese *muk* 'tree, wood'

6.6. Basque *burki* > (c) *urki* 'birch tree', (BN) *burkhi*, (Z) *bürkhi*[294] ~ Lezgi *werχ* 'birch', Karata *berχo-ƛ:* roša 'birch' (*roša* 'tree'), etc. < PEC *wēqwV* (NCED 1043) ? + contamination with PEC *mħĕrqwĕ* 'birch; wood, timber' (NCED 810)

6.7. Basque *ankio* > (B) *angio* '(fenced in) pasture' ~ Khinalug *inqa* 'field', Bezhta *öγä* 'small plot of land', etc. < PEC *HēnqwV* (NCED 561)

6.8. Basque *muga* 1 boundary, linit, 2 occasion, moment, 3 season > (B, BN, Z, R) *muga* 1, (L) *muga* 1,2,3, etc. ~ Chechen *moγa* 'line, row', Avar *muq:* 'line', etc. < PEC *mŏrqwV̆* (NCED 831)

6.9. Basque *agurV* > (B,G,AN,L) *agure* 'old man', (B) *agura* 'old woman' ~ Andi =*oχor* 'old (of a person)', Archi *χala-*t:u-id., etc. < PEC *=ŏnqV(lV)* (NCED 862)

PDC *q̇':* The Basque reflex is consistently *k:*

6.9. Basque *kirać* 1 bitter, 2 sour, 3 stench, 4 to stink > (B) *kirats* 3, (L) *kirats* 1,2,3,4, (Z) *kharats, kharatx* 1,2, etc. ~ PNC *q̇ēfilV* > Archi *q'ala* 'bitter', Ubykh *q'aq'ə̂* 'sweet', etc. (NCED 912) ~ Burushaski (Y) *qaqá*-m, (H,N) *γaqáγ̇(-um)* 'bitter' ~ cf. PST *ghāH* 'bitter' > Burmese *khah*, etc. (ST V: 18) ~ PY *qVqVr* > Ket *qōliŋ* 'bitter', etc. (SSEJ 266)

6.10. Basque *keda-r̄* 'soot' ~ Akhwakh *q':ēt'a* 'soot', < PEC *q̇idV* (= **2.20**)

6.11. Basque *kokoć* (~ *[k]okoc)* 1 chin, 2 snout, 3 nape ~ PEC *q̇ăčĭ* > Rutul, Tsakhur *q'ac'* 'chin', etc (= **3.26**)

---

[293] See Appendix A for the fossilized ending -r.

[294] The Basque word for 'birch' of course resembles the Indo-European word, but is probably not borrowed from it. The closest neighbor with the IE word was probably Old High German *birihha*, which would not render *burki*.

6.12. Basque **e-kuśi* 'to see'[295] > (B, G, AN) *ikusi,* (BN,L,Z) *ikhusi,* (G,R) *ekusi* ~ Bezhta *=ĩq-* 'to find', Budukh *irq-* 'to see', etc. < PEC **=Hārq̇V(n)* ~ **=Hirq̇V(n)* 'to see, find' (NCED 547)

6.13. Basque **u-kondo* 'elbow' > (L) *ukhondo,* (AN-Baztan, B, Sal) *ukondo,* (BN-Aldude) *ukhundo*[296] ~ PEC **q̇Hw ^ ntV* > Lezgi *q'ünt* 'elbow', Hinukh *q'ontu* 'knee', etc. (NCED 925) ~ cf. PY **g[i]d* > Ket *uʌ-git* 'elbow', etc. (SSEJ 227) ~ Na-Dene: Eyak *ɢuhd, ɢuʔd, ɢūhd* 'knee'; PAth **-ɢ(ʷ)ʊt'* > Hupa *-got',* Navajo *-gòd* 'knee'

6.14. Basque **a-kain* '(large) tick'[297] > (G) *akain, akaiñ, akaña,* (B) *akan,* (L) *lakain* ~ Cauc: Chechen *γēnig* 'louse', Dargwa *q'i* 'nit', etc. < PEC **q̱'ā̈nʔV* (NCED 911) ~ Burushaski *khin* (H,N), *khen* (Y) 'flea' ~ cf. ST: PST **kin* 'ant' (ST V: 55)

6.15. Basque **e-aki-n* > (c) *jakin* 'to know (a fact)/ = saber/savoir'[298] ~ Akhwakh *=eq'-* 'to know', Khwarshi *=iq'-* 'to know', Dargwa *=aq'- / =iq'-* 'to hear', etc. < PNC **=ĭq̇E* 'to know, hear' (NCED 646) ~ Burushaski *hákin, -ki-* 'to learn'

6.16. Basque **ośki* 'shoe' > (B-arc, BN-Amikuse, R, Z) *oski* ~ PEC **q̇Hwŏšw V (~ *šwŏq̇HwV)* > Dargwa (Akushi) *q'aš* 'foot, leg', Tabasaran *šaq'ʷ* 'heel', etc. (NCED 926) ~ Burushaski *ṣoq* 'sole of shoe' ~ cf. Na-Dene: Haida *st'a-q'usíi* 'heel'; Tlingit *q'os, χ'us* 'foot'; Eyak *-q'a·š* 'foot', *-q'e·s* 'ankle'

6.17. Basque **mak-* 'cane, stick, club, pole' ~ Bezhta *maq* 'stake', etc. < PNC **bħə̄nq̇V̆* (= **1.20**)

6.18. Basque **erēka* 'ravine, rivulet, arroyo' > (c) *erreka* ~ Tindi *rek̓:a* 'gorge, ravine', Chechen *duq'* 'mountain ridge', etc. < PNC **rĭq̇wĂ* (NCED 953)

---

[295] Bsq **ekuśi,* if it truly belongs here, has a sibilant suffix.

[296] Azkue cites an archaic Bizkaian form, *ukaondo,* which appears to be influenced by the obscure word *uk(h)o* 'forearm' (used by the 17th-century writer Oihenart). We think **u-kondo* is the continuation of the most widespread Dene-Caucasian word for 'knee/elbow'. See Appendix A for the fossilized prefix **u-*.

[297] See Appendix A for the fossilized prefix *a-*. Trask (1995) seeks to derive this word from Romance, but there is apparently no Latin antecedent, and Romance words such as Gascon *lagagno* instead more likely come from a Vasconic substratum.

[298] Michelena 1961, p. 119.

PDC *ɢ: The regular Basque reflex is *g; *ɢʷ > *b under certain conditions. (Cf. **gʷ > *b, above.)

6.19. Basque *gor̄ 'deaf', *gogor̄ 'hard, cruel'[299] > (c) gor, gogor ~ PEC *GwērV 'stone' > Khwarshi ɣur, etc. (NCED 467); cf. also PEC *GŏrGV 'stone' > Chechen ɣorɣa 'rough, coarse', etc. (NCED 463) ~ Burushaski (Y) ɣoró, (H,N) ɣuró 'stones' ~ cf. ST: PST *Kor > Tibetan gor 'stone(s), rubble', etc. (ST V: 121)

6.20. Basque *hogei '20' > (Z) hogei, (BN, L) hogoi, (B, G, AN, R) ogei ~ PEC *G̲ǎ '20' > Dargwa ɣa-, Khinalug q'a(n), etc. (NCED 456)

6.21. Basque *gali 'wheat' > (c) gari / combinatory form gal-, as in gal-buru 'ear of wheat' ~ Cauc: Tindi q':eru, Rutul ɣɨl, Archi qoqol, etc. 'wheat' < PEC *G̲ōlʔe (NCED 462)

6.22. Basque *gilc 1 key (for a lock), 2 keystone (of an arch) > (B, AN) giltz 1,2, (Z, R) giltz 1, (G, L) giltz (2)[300] ~ Bezhta ɣeso 'bar, (door-)bolt', Lak q:iča '(door-)bolt', etc. < PEC *GHwälc̓V (NCED 459)

6.23. Basque *agor̄, *egar̄i > (c) agor 'dry', egarri 'thirst'[301] ~ PNC *=iGwǍr 'dry, to dry' > Avar =aqʷara-b 'dry', Hunzib qor 'drought', etc. (NCED 631) ~ Burushaski (N) qharáo 'dried up' ~ cf. PST *kār 'dry' > Old Chinese *kār, etc. (ST V: 50) ~ PY *qɔr₁ ~ *qV[ɢ]i- 'dry' > Kott šī-gal, Arin qoja, etc. (SSEJ 265)

6.24. Basque *gʷune > (BN, L, R) gune, (Z) güne, (AN, B, G) une 'place, space, interval, point'[302] ~ PNC *GwinʔV > Bezhta qun 'farmstead', Kabardian wəna 'house', etc. (NCED 471) ~ cf.

---

[299] For the semantic relationship of 'deaf' ~ 'hard', cf. Eng. *hard of hearing,* Span. *duro de oído* (Hualde 1995).

[300] Possibly *giltz* 'joint' is a homonym, of distinct origin. If so, it is 'key' that belongs with PEC *GHwälc̓V.

[301] Basque has several words for dry, depending on the referent. In Zuberoan *agor* applies only to sources and streams of water, *ütsal (q.v.)* to aliments and terrain, *eihar* to the human body, animals, and vegetation, and *idor* to dryness in general (Larrasquet 1939). In Bizkaian *legor* or *idor* apply to vegetation, *igar* to animals and bones (Azkue 1905). See also Trask 1995, p. 13.

[302] See the discussion by Trask (1995: 36). AN, B, G *une* possibly via an intermediate form *bune.

ST: PST *qĭm 'house' > Tibetan khyim, etc. (ST V: 154) ~ Na-Dene: [*qVn] 'house' > Chipewyan kũ-ế ~ kĩ-ế, Navajo kìn, etc.

6.25. Basque *goŕi, *goŕ- 1 red, 2 raw, 3 robust, fresh, 4 rude, cruel, 5 yolk of egg, 6 meat of roasted chestnut[303] > (B) gorri 1, gordin 2,3, gorringo 5,6, (Z) gorri 1, gordin 2,3,4, gorrinko 5, etc. ~ Burushaski (N) gir 'water that flows from a wound' (< *gür < *guri ?) ~ cf. Na-Dene: Haida (S) ɢai, (A) ʕáy 'blood', sʕit (s-ʕi-t) 'to be red' (cf. Basque gorri-t 'become red'); Tlingit -ɢe / -ɢi 'bright, shining'; PAth *-ɢɑy 'white' > Navajo -gàì, etc.[304]

6.26. Basque *bełV > (c) bele, bela 'crow, raven'; belatz 'sparrow hawk' ~ Cauc: Avar γálo 'jackdaw', Adyge q:ʷaʟa-ź 'crow', etc. < PNC *ɢHwV̄łV (NCED 460) ~ Burushaski balás (H), balác (N) '(larger) bird'

6.27. Basque *bulha-r̄ > (BN, L, Z) bulhar, (AN, B, G) bular, (R) budar, burar 'chest, breast' ~ Lak q:ʷar (dial. q:ʷal) 'udder', Avar γʷári 'udder', etc. < PEC *Gwǎłħē 'udder, breast' (NCED 465)

6.28. Basque *hobi > (BN, L, Z) hobi, (B, G) oi 'gum(s) (of mouth)' ~ Akhwakh oq':o 'throat', Tsez haqu '(inside of) mouth', Circassian ʔʷə 'mouth', etc. < PNC *ħŏmG̣wĭ (NCED 526)

In several cases Basque (and sometimes Burushaski) has *g vs. Caucasian *q̇, suggesting that PDC *ɢ may under certain conditions become PNC *q̇. Note the variation in Basque gai, gei vs. ekhei **(6.30)**.

6.29. Basque *garhi > (Z) garhi, gahi, (BN, L) gari 'thin' ~ Agul q:ure-f 'thin, emaciated', Avar q':ʷarí-da-b 'narrow, cramped', etc. < PEC *q̇warHV (NCED 933)

6.30. Basque *gai / *e-kai > (AN, BN, G, L) gai, (B, R, Z) gei 'material, subject', (B-arc) 'thing', (BN, Z) ekhei 'material'[305] ~

---

[303] The relation of 'raw ~ blood' as in English raw (< hrǣw), cognate with Russian кровь 'blood', Greek κρέας 'flesh', etc.

[304] There is no *r in Proto-Na-Dene. PDC initial *r became PND *d (see under PDC *r), and in other positions it became a nasal (n) or glide (j). Here we posit PDC *ɢVr(i) 'blood, red' > PND *ɢaj.

[305] One of the Basque words that appears with or without a fossilized prefix: see Appendix A.

Lak *q'aj* 'thing(s), ware(s)', Akhwakh *q':e* 'thing(s), possession(s)', etc. < PEC **q̇wǎjē* (NCED 930)

6.31. Basque **nega-* > (AN, B, G, L, Sal) *negar,* (AN-Baztan, BN-Aezk, Aldude, L, Z) *nigar* 'weeping, tears'; (AN, BN, L) *negal* 'skin rash (herpes)' ~ Dargwa *nerγ* 'tear', Chechen *not'q'a* 'pus', etc. < PEC **něwq̇ǔ* (NCED 848) ~ Burushaski (H) *nagéi,* (N) *magéi* 'boil, ulcer' ~ cf. ST: PST **nōk / *nōŋ* 'pus' > Tibetan r-*nag* ~ s-*nag,* etc. (ST II: 40) ~ PY **dɔkŋ* 'pus' > Ket *dɔʔŋ,* Kott *takŋ* (SSEJ 223)

6.32. Basque **egu-* > (c) *egun* (with stem variants *egu-, egur-*)[306] 'day' ~ Cauc: Lak *q'ini* 'day', Avar *q':o* 'day', etc. < PEC **Hwī q̇V* (NCED 622) ~ Burushaski *gon* (H,N,Y) 'dawn'; cf. *gunc* (H,N,Y) 'day'

6.33. Basque **e-gi-n* > (c) *egin* 'to do, make', also auxiliary verb ~ Agul *aq'-* 'to do, make', Khinalug *q'i* 'to be, become', etc. < PNC **=Hǒq̇E* (NCED 599)

6.34. Basque **e-augin* > (BN) *jaugin* 'to come', contracted to (BN, L, R, Z) *jin* 'to come' ~ Hinukh =*aq'-* 'to come', Dargwa (Chirag) =*uq'-* 'to go', etc. < PNC **=Huq̇Ǔn* (NCED 611)

6.35. Basque **aȓgi* > (c) *argi* 'light, bright', (L) *ilhargi* 'moon', (B) *iretargi,* (AN, B, G) *ilargi,* (R,Z) *argizagi (argi-zagi)* 'moon' ~ Lezgi *raʁ* 'sun', Lak *barʁ,* Khinalug *inq̇,* Kabardian *dəʁa,* etc. 'sun' < PNC **wirəq̇A* (NCED 1051)[307]

PDC **ʔ/ *ʔ̣ / *ʕ:* PNC had the ordinary glottal stop **ʔ*, an emphatic glottal stop **ʔ̣,* and a voiced emphatic laryngeal fricative **ʕ*. The Basque correspondences are **ɦ* or zero to the first and **h* to the second (though there is one case of **ɦ* - see **6.49**). In the words **üthe* and **ahali* there was probably loss of initial **h* because of the rule that there can only be one aspiration in a word (Trask 1997, p. 158). See below (**7.64** ff.) for more about Basque **h* and **ɦ.*

So far there is only one etymology comparing Basque with initial PDC **ʕ:* see **6.50,** in which the laryngeal disappears in Basque.

---

[306] See Trask 1997, p. 189. Basque *-r* in *egur* could be related to the Caucasian oblique stem marker **-rV-* (Starostin 2002).

[307] PDC **HVrGV ~ *rVGHV* 'heavenly body (sun, moon)'. The PNC word seems to incorporate the old class prefix **w-*.

6.36. Basque *aṟ > (c) *ar* 'male' ~ PEC *?īrλwV 'male' > Ingush *ärh* 'ungelt', etc. (NCED 210) ~ Burushaski *hir* 'man, male'

6.37. Basque *onTiko > (AN, BN, L) *ondiko* 'misery, misfortune' ~ Avar *únti* 'sickness, ailment', *únt*-ize 'to be sick', Chechen *ant* 'shortcoming, defect' < PEC *?untV (NCED 221)

6.38. Basque *apal* 'shelf' ~ PEC *?apVɬV 'pole; board, cover' (= **1.6**)

6.39. Basque *ħaran > (BN, L) *haran,* (B, G, AN, Z, R) *aran* 'valley, field' ~ Chechen *ārē* 'plain; steppe', Lak *ar* 'plain', etc. < PEC *?ārV (NCED 202) ~ Burushaski (H, N) *har* 'small ravine, nullah'

6.40. Basque *ħardo* 'tinder (made from a kind of dried fungus)' ~ PEC *?wēλV 'a kind of grass' (= **4.19**)

6.41. Basque *ħonda-ṟ* 'sand, bottom' ~ PEC *?antV > Tsez *atu* 'dirt, mud', Khinalug *ant* 'earth, ground' (= **2.4**)

6.42. Basque *e-oHa-n[308] 'to go' > (B) *joan, juan, fuan, fan,* (AN) *joan, goan, gan,* (Z) *joan, juan, jun* [žŭn], etc. ~ PNC *=V?wV- 'to go' > Karata =o?an-, etc. (NCED 1016) ~ cf. ST: PST *?ʷă 'to go' > Burmese s-*wah,* etc. (ST V: 11) ~ PY *hejVŋ > Kott *hejaŋ* 'to go, ride', etc. (SSEJ 231)

6.43. Basque *ülhe > (BN, L, Z) *ilhe,* (AN, G) *ile,* (B) *ule* 'hair' ('wool' in Z) ~ PEC *?ālχV 'wool' > Rutul *ar:* 'spring wool', etc. (NCED 242)

6.44. Basque *ahali* 'ram' > (BN, L, Z) *ahari,* (B) *aari* 'ram', (AN-Baztan) *aal*-zain 'shepherd', etc. ~ Chechen *ʕāχar* 'lamb', Andi *iχo* 'sheep, ewe', etc. < PNC *?īlχU (~-ā̃-,-ī̃-) 'sheep, lamb' (NCED 247); alternatively, cf. Chadakolob *her* 'ewe', Hunzib *χor* 'ram', etc. < PEC *χ[ə]lV (~ *χ[ə]rV)[309] (NCED 1071)

6.45. Basque *hoin > (c) *oin,* (B) *oñ,* (BN,Z) *huin,* (Z) *huñ* 'foot'[310] ~ Lak *niq:a* (< *?inq:a) 'heel', Chechen *ħaq*-olg 'ankle',

---

[308] Michelena (1961, p. 119) posits *e-oa-n. Jacobsen (1995, p. 132) notes the presence of –h- in some northern Basque variants, and proposes *e-oCa-n. Comparison with PEC *=īxwV 'to go, walk, flow' (NCED 664) or PEC =iχwV 'to go, come, enter' (NCED 666) is also thinkable.

[309] NCED has *χ[ə]rV (~ *-l-). All the languages cited have the regular change of *l > r. If this comparison is correct the variant with *-l- is correct.

[310] In some monosyllabic words the initial *h has been lost in most dialects, namely (c) *oin* 'foot', *on* 'good', *ur* 'water', *or* 'dog', and only Zuberoan has /h/: *huñ, hun, hur, hor,* respectively. I think Z is conservative in this respect, *contra* Trask (1997, p. 162-163) who claims Z has "extended the aspiration."

etc. < PEC *ʔinGwV̆ (NCED 248) ~ Burushaski *-γā́n 'heel' > (H,N) -γā́n, (Y) -γán.

6.46. Basque *heri > (BN, L, Z) herri, (B, G, AN, R) erri 'country, town, inhabited place, people' ~ PNC *ʔw ˇhri > Lak a̰ ra-l 'army, troops', Abaza rə 'army, troops', Hurrian χūr-adə 'warrior', etc. (NCED 249) ~ cf. ST: PST *rāH > Old Chinese *r̥āʔ 'captive', Tibetan dgra (d-g-ra) 'enemy, foe', etc. (ST II: 52) ~ PY *har- > Kott ari n-git 'slave', Assan xáran-get 'servant', Arin ar, ara 'Arin (ethnonym)', etc. (SSEJ 230)

6.47. Basque *alha > (BN, L, Z) alha, (AN, BN, G, R, Sal) ala 'grazing, pasture'; (BN, L, Z) alha-tu 'to graze, to feed' ~ Hinukh hil 'to bite', Kryz ʕül- 'to eat', Archi lah-bos 'to get hungry', etc. < PEC *=iʔwVl (NCED 625)

6.48. Basque *lahaī 'bramble, creeping plant' ~ PNC *ⱴ wĭrʔV 'leaf' > Andi ƛ'oli, etc. (= 4.11)

6.49. Basque *ḟaise 'wind' (ventus) > (L) haize, (B, G, AN, BN, Z, R) aize ~ Bezhta, Hunzib has 'sky, cloud, fog', Akhwakh as:i 'breath, etc. < PNC *ʔămsa (~ -^,-i) 'sky, cloud, soul, breath, god' (NCED 243)

6.50. Basque *ardac 'axle' ~ Bezhta, Hunzib aƛ 'spindle', etc. < PEC *ʄ ăn ⱴ V 'spindle, pivot'; cf. PEC *ʄ ül ⱴ wĭ 'handle' (= **4.18.c**)

7. Fricatives

Proto-Dene-Caucasian probably had several fricatives corresponding to most of the positions of the occlusives: *f (?), *s, *š, *ɬ, *x, *χ, *h. There are some indications that some of these fricatives may have had voiced allophones.

PDC *f: Basque *h is the consistent correspondence to Caucasian *f, though it is uncertain whether *f can be projected to PDC:

7.1. Basque *hobi 'grave, tomb' > (BN, L, Z) hobi, (B, G, AN, R) obi[311] ~ PEC *fiwi 'grave' > Avar χob, Tindi hoba, Lak haw, etc. (NCED 428)

---

[311] There is a remarkably similar Latin word, fovea 'pit, pitfall', which is often cited (e.g., Meyer-Lübke 1935, no. 3463) as the origin of Basque hobi. The Basque and Caucasian words mean specifically 'grave', while the Romance words mean 'pit' in general (Spanish hoya, etc.).

7.2. Basque *hu(n)ki > (BN, L, Z) *hunki* 'touch, feel', *hunki*-tu 'to touch, feel', (G, AN) *uki*-tu id. ~ Bagwali *hunk'a* 'fist', Dargwa *χ:unk'* 'fist', etc. < PEC *fimḳwV* (NCED 428)

7.3. Basque *oihan 1 forest, 2 desert > (BN, L, Z) *oihan* 1, (AN, G) *oian* 1, (B-arc) *oian* 2 ~ PNC *fãnV* > Chechen *ħun* 'forest', Lak *han* 'shady slope', Abaza *χwa* 'mountain, hill', etc. (NCED 425) ~ Burushaski (H, N) *hun* 'wood; timber, beam, hewn log', (Y) *hun* 'wood, firewood'

7.4. Basque *behoī 'mare' > (BN, L) *behor,* (B, G, AN, R) *beor,* (Z) *bohor,* (R) *beor, beur*[312] ~ Lezgi *χʷar* 'mare', Adyge *fãra* 'thoroughbred horse', etc. < PNC *farnē* (NCED 425)

7.5. Basque *bahe > (BN, L, Z) *bahe,* (B, G, R) *bae* 'sieve'[313] ~ Tsakhur *wex:ʷa* 'sieve', Lak *=ihi-* 'to filter', etc. < PNC *=ifV* 'to sift' (NCED 630)

PDC *s / *z:* The Basque reflex is consistently *s (realized as dorso-alveolar /s̄/ = orthographic *z*):

7.6. Basque *sain 1 vein, 2 root, 3 nerve, 4 root (of hair) > (B) *zan* 1, (G) *zain, zaiñ* 1,2,4, (BN, R) *zain* 1,2,3, (Z) *zañ* [s̄ãñ] 1,2,3, etc. ~ PEC *s̲ēħmV* > Chamalal *s:ē* 'sinew, muscle', Chechen *sam-g* 'sausage', Dargwa *ʕems* 'muscle', etc. (NCED 959) ~ cf. ST: PST *(r-)sǎ* > Old Chinese *sə* 'silk, thread', Jingpo lə-*sa* 'tendon, sinew', etc. (ST IV: 96)

7.7. Basque *sahaī 'old' > (BN, L, Z) *zahar,* (AN-Baztan) *zagar,* (B) *zaar, zar,* (G, AN, R) *zar* ~ Lezgi *sur* 'old', *jis* 'year', Chechen *šira* 'old', *šo / šera-* 'year', Ubykh *žʷə* 'old', etc. < PNC *swĕrho* 'old, year' (NCED 968)

7.8. Basque *seden 1 weevil (of wheat, maize), 2 wood borer, 3 lard worm > (B) *zeden* 1,2, ((G, L) *zeden* 1,3, etc. ~ Tsez *zedo* 'moth', Akhwakh *šide-ƛ:u* 'tick', etc. < PEC *sindV* (NCED 962)

---

[312] Initial *be-* may be a fossilized prefix (see Appendix A). Otherwise, the segment *-hor* matches well with PNC *far-*.

[313] Attempts to derive this word from Latin *vannu(s)* 'winnowing fan' (e.g., Trask 1997, p. 141) are totally amiss. The result in Basque, according to accepted phonological changes, would have been *banu. There is no nasal vowel in the Zuberoan form, simply /báhe/, and final /e/ never comes from Latin *–u*.

7.9. Basque **susun* 'poplar, aspen (tree)' > (B) *zuzun* ~ PNC **sw ĭnē* > Karata *seni* 'barberry', Kabardian *sāna* 'currants', etc. (NCED 971) ~ cf. Yen: Kott *såńef* 'mountain ash' (Castrén)

7.10. Basque **se-* (interrogative stem) in (c) *zer* 'what?', *zein* 'which?', *ze-la* 'how', etc. ~ PNC **sāj* > Ingush *se* 'what?', Ubykh *sa* 'what?', etc. (NCED 958) ~ Burushaski *bé-sa-*n 'what, which?', *bé-se* 'why?' ~ cf. ST: PST **su* 'who?' (ST IV: 108); Lepcha *să-re* 'which, what?', *să-ba* 'where?', etc. ~ PY **ʔas- / *sV-* (interrogative stem) > Ket *aśeś* 'what?', etc. (SSEJ 182) ~ Na-Dene: Haida *gú·-su* 'what?', *us* (yes-or-no question marker); Tlingit *dà·-sa* 'what?', *sa* (interrogative particle), etc.

7.11. Basque **luse* 'long (of time or things), tall' > (c) *luze* ~ Burushaski *γusán-*um 'long, far, tall'[314] ~ cf. PST **lu* 'long, far' > Old Chinese **lhu* 'far away', Burmese *lu* 'disproportionately tall', etc. (ST III: 144)

7.12. Basque **e-sa-n* 'to be' > (c) *izan* ~ Chechen =*is-* 'to stay', Ubykh *-s-* 'to sit, lie', etc. < PNC **=ä̃sV* (NCED 281) ~ Burushaski *óos- / -š-* 'to lay, put, hold', etc.

7.13. Basque **bi-si* 'life, alive, lively' > (c) *bizi*[315] ~ Lak *s:iħ* 'breath, vapor', Chechen *sa* 'soul', etc. < PNC **sĭHwV* (NCED 961) ~ cf. ST: PST **sĭj(H)* > Old Chinese **sijʔ* 'to die; death', etc. (ST IV: 102) ~ Na-Dene: Tlingit *sa, sen* 'to breathe, blow'; Eyak *sĩh* 'to die'[316]

7.14. Basque **üsen* > (c) *izen*, (B) *uzen* 'name'[317] ~ Burushaski (H,N) *sén-, séi-,* nu-*sé(n)* 'to say, name, read', *sén-*as 'named, by the name of'; (Y) *sén-, sí-* 'to say, name' ~ cf. ST: Old Chinese **sĕŋ* 'name' ~ Na-Dene: Haida (A) *su* 'to say'; Tlingit *-sà, -sá, -sén* 'to name', *sà* 'name, voice'

7.15. Basque **ɦänsūr* 'bone' > (BN, L) *hezur*, (B) *azur*, (G, AN) *ezur*, (Z) *ézür*, (R) *enzur, ẽzur*[318] ~ PEC **rīmswe* (~ **mswīre*) 'rib

---

[314] Burushaski /γ/ is the regular correspondence to PDC **ɬ, q.v.

[315] An instance of the fossilized prefix *bi-/be-* (see Appendix A).

[316] "The semantic developments 'to breathe' > 'get tired' ... > 'die' are quite usual." (NCED 961). Cf. Russian душа *dušá* 'mind, soul, spirit' : душить *dušít'* 'to smother'.

[317] See Appendix A for the fossilized prefixes *i-, u-*.

[318] Michelena (1961) posited Pre-Basque **enazur.* However, we must posit initial **ɦ*, since BN and L have *h* and Z does not.

> side' > Lak *niws* rib', Proto-Lezgian **s:ʷira* > Rutul *sur* 'part, side', etc. (NCED 954) ~ cf. ST: PST **rə̄(-t, -s)* 'bone' > Tibetan *rus,* Chepang *hrus,* etc. (ST II: 69)

7.16. Basque **-s* (orthographic *–z*) (instrumental suffix) ~ PNC **=s̱* (instrumental suffix: Starostin 2002)

PDC **ś:* The few examples indicate Basque **s* = dorso-alveolar /š/ (orthographic *z*):

7.17. Basque **sülβo* 1 hole, 2 cave, 3 nostril, 4 anus[319] > (L) *zulho, zilo* 1, (B, G, AN) *zulo* 1, (Z) *zilo, xilo* 1, (AN, BN, L, Z) *ziloka* 2, (AN, BN, L, R, Z) sudur-*zilo* 3, (G) musu-*zulo* 'nostril', ipurt-*zulo* 4, etc. ~ PEC **s̱wōɫV* > Avar *šulu* 'pipe', Andi tom-*š:il* '(tubular) bone',[320] Bezhta *šelo* 'horn' (< '*tube'), etc. (NCED 978)

7.18.a. Basque **sirin* 1 excrement of birds, 2 diarrhea > (AN, B, G) *zirin* 1, (AN, BN, L, Z, R) *zirin* 2 ~ Akhwakh *šili* 'sheep's dung', Tabasaran ur-*sil* 'dung', etc. < PEC **siɬ̄* (NCED 973)

7.18.b. Basque **ihas* last year' > (Z) *ihaz,* (B, G, AN) *igaz,* (BN, L) *iaz* ~ Chamalal *sas:* 'last year', Lezgi *šaz,* etc. < PEC **s̱wǎjV* 'last year'[321] (NCED 975)

PDC **š / *ž:* The Basque reflex is predominantly apico-alveolar **ś* (orthographic *s*). In the word for 'milk' the dialects vary between the internal cluster /śn/ and /sn/:

7.19. Basque **śić* 'moth' > (B, G) *sits*[322] ~ PEC **s̱wĕʒV* 'a kind of biting insect' > Lak *suc'* 'tick', Rutul *šʷät* 'midge, mosquito', etc. (NCED 988)

7.20. Basque **gośe* 'hunger, hungry' ~ PNC **gašē* 'hunger' > Lak *k:aši,* Rutul *gaš,* etc. (= **5.22**)

---

[319] This is the origin of the word *silhouette,* from the French official Étienne de Silhouette, who had roots in Lapurdi. *Silhouette* = (L) *zilhoeta* = (Southern Basque) *zuloeta* 'place of caves'.

[320] Lit. 'marrow-pipe', per NCED.

[321] "The root may have also contained a laryngeal," based on pharyngealization in Lezgian (NCED). This is in accord with the laryngeal **γ* in Basque.

[322] Probably by sibilant harmony (Trask 1997, p. 88) from **sitz* = **sic.*

7.21. Basque *puś- / *puš- 'bubble, bladder' ~ Batsbi *puš* 'bump, lump', Dargwa (Kaitag) *puš*-lik' 'bladder' < PNC *pärṣ̌wA (= **1.3**)

7.22. Basque *beśo 1 arm, 2 humerus > (B, G, L, Z) *beso* 1, *besondo* 2, etc. ~ Chechen *biši* 'hand (of a child)', Tsez *baša* 'finger' < PEC *wũ̄śV ~ *bũ̄śV (NCED 315)

7.23. Basque *e-Sne 'milk' > (B, BN, G, R, Z) *ezne,* (B, BN, G, L) *esne*[323] ~ PEC *šãmʔV > Tindi *š:ū* 'milk', Chechen *šin* 'udder', etc. (NCED 982) ~ Burushaski *ṣiŋ* 'milk, proceeds of milk'[324]

7.24. Basque *-śa- / *-śo (elements denoting kinship) 1 uncle, father-in-law, 3 parent(s), 4 great-grandparent, 5 granddaughter, 6 grandson, etc. > (B) *osaba* 1, *guraso* 3, (L) *osaba* 1,2, *burhaso* 3, (BN) *osaba* 1, *buraso* 4, *ilobaso* 6, (Z) *osaba* 1, *alhabaso* 5, *semeso* 6, etc. ~ PNC *=ı̄šwĔ > Andi w-*ošo* 'son', j-*oši* 'daughter', etc. (NCED 671) ~ Burushaski (Y) -*ís* 'young (of animals); child (of humans)', (H,N) -*s*-k(o) 'young (of animals); (jokingly) human child' ~ cf. ST: PST *sū 'grandchild' > Old Chinese *sūn,* Dimasa *su,* etc. (ST IV: 121) Na-Dene: Eyak *yahš* '(woman's) child'; PAth *-ya·ž^wə 'little; (woman's) child' > Navajo -*yází* 'child, little one', -*yááž* 'baby', *yáás̆* 'little one'

PDC *ł: The PDC voiceless lateral fricative *ł (NCED *λ) becomes ordinary /l/ in initial position, but the distinction between PDC *ł and *l is maintained in intervocalic position in the northern Basque dialects (BN, L, Z), where the former is reflected as /lh/:

7.25. Basque *lance-r̄ > (BN, Z) *lantzer* 'drizzle, fine and minute rain' ~ PEC *λä̃[m]ċV 'to sift, filter' > Chechen *litt* 'to filter', Bezhta *ɬacari* 'sieve', etc. (NCED 758)

7.26. Basque *lor̄ 1 track, trace, footprint, 2 hauling, cartage > (B, G) *lorratz* 1, *lor* 2 ~ Chechen *lar* 'track, footprint', Chamalal *ɬal* 'hoof, horseshoe', etc. < PNC *λĕɬV (NCED 759)

---

[323] See Appendix A for the fossilized prefix *e-*.

[324] With secondary retroflex [ṣ] conditioned by following velar nasal.

7.27. Basque **lirdi* 'drivel, saliva'[325] > (G) *lirdi, lerde,* (B, AN) *lerde* ~ PEC **ƛwirdɨ* > Agul *furd* 'manure', Avar *xʷerd* 'pus', etc. ~ Burushaski *γiṭ* slime' ~ cf. PST **lV̆t* > Tibetan *lud* 'phlegm, mucus; manure, dung', etc. (ST III: 51) ~ Na-Dene: PAth **ɬuˑt'* > Kutchin *ɬid* 'scar', Navajo *ɬóód* 'sore', etc. [326]

7.28. Basque **leher̄* 'pine tree' > (BN, Z) *leher,* (R) *ler* ~ Avar *ɬːalú* 'yew tree', Lak *ħalu* 'grove' < PEC **ƛħwaɬū* (NCED 761)

7.29. Basque **lur̄ün* 1 steam, vapor, 2 odor, smell > (B) *lurrun* 1, (G) *lurrin* 1, (AN, BN, L) *urrin* 2, (Z) *ürrin* 2[327] ~ PNC **λwə̄tʔV* > Akhwakh *ɬʷē / ɬoji* 'wind, breeze', etc. (NCED 762) ~ cf. ST: PST **lij* > Burmese *lij* = *liy* 'wind', etc. (ST III: 24) ~ PY **ʔuʎ-* > Imbat *úlit* 'whirlwind'

7.30. Basque **luse* 'long, tall' ~ Burushaski *γusán*-um 'long, far, tall', etc. (= **7.11**)

7.31. Basque **olho* 1 oats, 2 wild oats > (B) *olo* 1, *alo* 2, (BN) *olho* 1, *olha* 2, (Z) *olho* 1, *olha, alho* 2, etc. ~ Cauc: PNC **λwi̯wV* 'millet' > Rutul *xɨw* 'bread', Lak *šʷa* 'mown crops', etc. (NCED 763)

7.32. Basque **a-lhon- / *a-lhe(n)- / *a-lhor̄* > (G-Zarauz) *alontza* 'mixture of grain', (G) *ale* 'seed', (G,AN,L) *alor* 'field (destined for sowing)', (BN,Z) *alhor* id.[328] ~ PEC **λwĩnʔɨ̄* 'seed' > Avar *xon,* Archi *ɬːʷin,* Rutul *xin,* etc. (NCED 1021) ~ Burushaski **γunó* > (H,N) *γunó,* (Y) *γonó* 'seed, sperm'

7.33. Basque **i-lhinti* 'firebrand, ember' > (B) *ilinti, illenti, illeti, ilindi,* (Z) *ilhinti,* etc.[329] ~ PEC **λwɨndV* > Andi *ɬudi* 'firewood', etc. (NCED 764) ~ cf. Na-Dene: Eyak *ɬid, ɬəd* 'dead wood, dry

---

[325] The opposition of *lirdi : lerde* suggests that the latter was reshaped by the influence of the synonym **fierde* (see 4.20). Only G has *lirdi,* and it appears to lack **fierde*.

[326] This etymology (together with **7.30, 7.32**) confirm the unusual development of PDC **ɬ* > Burushaski *γ* = [ɣ] (voiced uvular fricative). For typology, cf. Old Armenian *astɬ* > Modern Armenian *astγ* 'star', etc. (Old Armenian *ɬ* was a "dark" [velar] *l.*)

[327] The disappearance of *l-* in some of the words remains unexplained.

[328] See Appendix A for the fossilized prefix *a-*.

[329] See Appendix A for the fossilized prefix *i-*.

wood'; Chipewyan -łìr, -łə̀r, -łìr, -łìy 'to dry (leaves, bark, grass, etc. in the sun or by fire)'[330]

7.34. Basque *e-lhu-r̄ 'snow' > (BN, L) elhur, (Z) élhür, (AN, G, R) elur, (B) erur, edur[331] ~ PEC *λ̃iwV 'snow' > Chechen lō, etc. (NCED 684) ~ cf. Na-Dene: PAth *łuˑ > Kato loo 'frost', Navajo ń-ló 'hail'; Eyak ła· 'glacier'

PDC *x / *γ: There is some evidence that *x and *γ were originally allophonic variants of the same phoneme, since in some cases PNC *x matches Basque *g or *γ (*ergi), while in others PNC *γ matches Basque *h (*si(n)ho, *arhan, *belhar̄). In some Basque dialects (especially Baztan) g corresponds to BN, L, Z h. It appears that the Basque reflexes of the velar fricatives *x / *γ fall together with those of the uvular fricatives *χ / *ү (see below).

7.35. Basque *i-hinc 'dew' ~ PEC *xwĩmc̣wī > Lak xunc̣a 'bog', etc. (= **3.16**)

7.36. Basque *u-hain 'wave' (ridge of water) > (Z) ühaiñ, ühañ, (L) uhin[332] ~ PEC *x̱ãnfĩ 'water' > Chechen χi, Andi ł:en, Tsakhur x́an, etc. (NCED 1060) ~ cf. Na-Dene: Haida (A) ʕán-ƛ 'water, river', (S) ɢan-λ 'fresh water'; Tlingit hín 'water, river'; Eyak χã 'to melt'; PAth *-ɣeˑn > Navajo ɣî́h, ɣî́ʔ, ɣî́h 'melt (snow, ice)', etc.

7.37. Basque *her̄o 1 root (tree, plant, tooth), 2 nipple (of udder) > (Z) herro 1, (B, G, AN, L) erro 1,2, (BN, R) erro 1 ~ Avar rix 'vein, blood vessel', Chamalal hĩhʷã 'string', Lak x:ʷa 'sinew, tendon, string', etc. < PNC *x̱wɨʔrV (NCED 1064)

7.38. Basque *si(n)ho 'fat, tallow' ~ Tindi c'inłu-, Dargwa c'erx:- 'fat' (adj) < PEC *c̣ēnx̱wV 'fat' (adj) (= **3.12**)

7.39. Basque *arhan 1 plum, 2 sloe > (BN, Z) arhan 1, (Z) ahan 1, (B) aran 1,2, etc. ~ Avar géni 'pear', Hunzib hĩ, etc. < PEC

---
[330] These words are all associated with fire making and its attendant materials. Cf. the note by Trask (1995: 41)
[331] For the fossilized prefix e-, and the fossilized ending -r, see Appendix A. For the dialectal variation of lh ~ l ~ r ~ d, see the discussion under PDC *ł.
[332] The analysis as *hur 'water' + *gain 'top' (Trask 1995) seems semantically and phonetically improbable. There is no attested *ugain, only uhin or üha(i)ñ.

*γōn?V 'pear' (NCED 475) ~ Burushaski γaíŋ 'grapes' ~ cf. ST: Tibetan r-gun 'vine, grape', etc. (ST V: 153)

7.40. Basque *belha-r̄ 1 grass, hay, 2 first mowing of hay > (BN, L, Z) belhar 2, (AN, G) belar 1, (B, G) berar 1, (B) bedar 1 ~ Lezgi werg 'nettle', Archi urk:i 'burdock', etc. < PEC *u̯ely̌V (NCED 1013)

7.41. Basque *ergi 'steer, young ox, bull calf' > (c) ergi ~ Avar rexé-d 'cattle, herd', Chechen dāχni 'cattle', Abkhaz á-raχʷ 'cattle', etc. < PNC *rVxwV 'cattle' (NCED 956)

PDC *χ / *γ : These are the uvular counterparts to *x / *γ, and the probable allophonic variation is similar in both sets, which appear to merge in Basque as *h and *g. The older stage of *h, [x], was recorded by Moutard (1975) in BN dialects, e.g., **[a(x)hwa]** 'the mouth' (see **7.47**), **[oxhja]** 'the bed' (see **7.48**). The voiced "softening" > [γ] appears in some dialects, e.g. ago [aγo] 'mouth', oge [oγe] 'bed', etc. A peculiar development > /f/ is found in a few dialects (**7.48a**). *χʷ > *b (**7.54, 7.55**) is parallel with *gʷ, *ɢʷ > *b (see above, sections **5** and **6**).

7.42. Basque *hor 'dog' > (Z) hor, ho, (c) or[333] ~ PNC *χHwěje, PEC *χHwějrV- 'dog' > Kabardian ħa, Avar hoj, Budukh χor, Dargwa (Chirag) χ:wa, etc. (NCED 1073)

7.43. Basque *hali 'thread'[334] > (BN, L, Z) hari / hal-, (B, B, AN, R) ari / al- ~ PEC *χāłV > Tsez χero 'sinew', Chechen χal 'thread', etc. (NCED 1067) ~ Burushaski γay̓ 'thread, strand (in weaving)' ~ cf. Na-Dene: Eyak χehł 'rope, cord, twine, string; to tie'

7.44. Basque *hari 'stone' > (BN, L, Z) harri, (B, G, AN, R) arri ~ PEC *χHěrχV 'small stone, gravel' > Akhwakh χaχi 'road metal', Lezgi χirχem 'road gravel', etc. (NCED 1073)

7.45. Basque *hama- 'ten' > (BN, L, Z) hamar, hama- (AN, B, G, R) amar, ama- ~ Proto-Lezgian *χ:am: 'hand(ful), arm(ful)' >

---

[333] See the note to oin 'foot' (**6.45**).

[334] This is one of several Basque words that have -r- in free form, but -l- in combinatory form as first element in a compound (Trask 1997: 188ff.). See the discussion under PDC *l.

Tabasaran χab 'armful', Udi maχa 'handful, palm', etc. < PEC *mHŏχi (NCED 819)

7.46. Basque *harc 'bear', *hars-koin 'badger' ~ PEC *χHVr[ç]V > Chechen χešt 'otter', Dargwa χ:arc' 'marten, squirrel', etc. (= **3.65**)

7.47. Basque *a-h(ʷ)o 'mouth' > (BN, L, Z) aho, (AN, B, G, R) ago, ao, (B) abo[335] ~ PNC *χwɨ- in *χwɨm(V)ṗV 'mouthful' > Khinalug χob, etc. (NCED 1082) ~ cf. ST: PST *khʷə(H) > Old Chinese *khō? 'mouth' (ST V: 107) ~ PY *χowe 'mouth' > Yug xo, etc. (SSEJ 302) ~ Na-Dene: *χU? 'tooth' > Tlingit ʔúχ, Eyak χu·ɬ, Navajo -γòò? 'tooth'

7.48.a. Basque *oh(ʷ)e 'bed' > (BN, L, Z) ohe, (BN-Aldude, Baigorri) ofe, (B, G, L) oge, etc. ~ Tabasaran aχin 'bed' (cf. aχ- 'to sleep'), Agul aχun 'mattress' (cf. aχa- 'to sleep'), etc. < PNC *=aχVr 'to fall, lie' (NCED 273)

7.48.b. Basque *(H)ori 'leaf'[336] > (B) orri 'leaf (of a tree)', (G) orri 'leaf (of maize, cabbage, lettuce)' ~ Avar χ:oró 'tops (of plants)', Agul χar 'meadow', etc. < PEC *χērə̆ (NCED 1070)

7.49. Basque *ahali 'ram' ~ Chechen ʕāχar 'lamb', etc. < PNC *ʔīlχU (= **6.44**)

7.50. Basque *oihal 'cloth, fabric' ~ Bezhta χiλo 'trousers, breeches', etc. < PEC *χwĭlƚ V (= **4.25**)

7.51. Basque *eiho 1 to grind (grain), 2 (grain) mill > (B) eio 1, (G, AN, R) eo 1, (BN) eho 1, eihara 2, (L, Z) eho 1, eihera 2 ~ Ingush aħ- 'to grind', ħajra 'mill', Andi ʔiχʷo-qi- 'to grind', etc. < PNC *HĕmχwV 'to grind' (NCED 559)

7.52. Basque *eiho 1 to beat, 2 to kill, 3 put lights out, 4 to be tired out, fatigued[337] > (BN, L, Z) eho 1,4, (G, AN, R) eo 1, (B) eio 4 ~ Avar =uχ- 'to beat, hit', Rutul =iχa- 'to beat, hit', etc. < PNC *HīrχA (NCED 581)

7.53. Basque *eihu(n) 1 to weave, 2 cloth, 3 weaving (craft), 4 to braid > (BN, L, Z) eho 1, (BN, L) ehun 2, (Z) ehün 1,2,3, (B) eio

---

[335] See Appendix A for the fossilized prefix a-.

[336] The word is attested only in non-aspirating dialects, so we do not know whether it comes from *ori or *hori or *ħori. External comparison suggests *hori.

[337] For meaning 4, cf. colloquial English "I'm beat" = "very tired."

4, *eun* 1,2,3, etc. ~ PEC **=irχwVn* 'to knit, weave, spin' > Chamalal *χ:in-* 'to spin', etc. (= **5.32**)

7.54. Basque **hobe* 'better' > (BN, L, Z) *hobe,* (B, G, AN, R) *obe* ~ Rutul *hɨχ-dɨ* 'good', Lak *χ:uj-* 'good', etc. < PEC **HVχwV* 'good' (NCED 620) ~ Burushaski (Y) *xa* 'good (of persons and fairies)'

7.55. Basque **ɦibai* > (BN, L) *hibai,* (B, G, AN, Z, R) *ibai* 'river' ~ Godoberi *inχ:i* 'river, brook', Kabardian psə-*χʷa* 'river', etc. < PNC **jimχwǍ* (NCED 683)

7.56. Basque **gau* > (c) *gau,* (Z, R-Uztarroz) *gai* 'night' ~ Proto-Lezgian **χ:am: / *χ:an:* > Tsakhur *χam* 'night', Tabasaran *χab-aq* 'evening', Agul *χaw-aq* 'evening'[338] ~ Burushaski (Y) *γuhá, γuhá-sa* 'time of waning moon', (H) *γuá* 'new moon, time without moon' ~ cf. ST: PST **γVm(H)* 'dark, shade' > Old Chinese **ʔə̄mh* 'dark', etc. (ST V: 40)

7.57. Basque **gurhi* 1 fat, grease, 2 butter, 3 juice (veg. or meat), 4 custard > (Z) *gurhi, gorhi* 1,2, (B-arc, BN, Sal) *guri,* (AN, G) *gurin* 2,3,4 ~ Lezgi *ʁeri* = *ẏeri* 'butter', Tsez *χuri* 'piece of dry cheese', etc. < PEC **χərHV (~ *χHərV)* (NCED 1071)[339]

7.58. Basque **negu* 'winter' > (c) *negu* [neγu], (Z) *negü* ~ PNC **ʕwĭnʔV = *γwĭnʔV* > Chechen *ʕa / ʕäna-* 'winter', Lak *γʷi- / γin-* 'summer', etc. (NCED 482) ~ cf. ST: PST **G(h)ŭn* > Tibetan d-*gun* 'winter', etc. (ST V: 34)

7.59. Basque **e-sagu-* 'to know (a person)' ~ Avar *c'eχ:é-* 'to search, ask', etc. < PNC **c̣EnχV(n)* 'to search, ask' (= **3.13**)

7.60. Basque **ugali* > (AN, B, G) *ugari* 'abundant' / (B, G) *ugal-du* 'to increase, multiply' ~ Dargwa (Akushi) *χala-l* 'big', Tindi =*eχ:ala-b* 'long', etc. < PNC **HāχutV / *HālχV* (NCED 550)

7.61. Basque **hega-* > (Z) *hegaxti,* (AN, B, BN, G, L) *egazti(n)* 'flying creature, fowl', (AN, B) *egaz* 'flying', etc.[340] ~ Tsakhur *al-*

---

[338] Lezgian forms from the Starling Caucasian Database (companion disk to NCED). **χ:* represents a tense voiceless pharyngealized uvular fricative (NCED).

[339] Alternatively, cf. PEC **χwɨlʔi* > Bezhta *χo* 'meat', Dargwa (Akushi) *ħali* 'fat', etc. (NCED 1081) ~ cf. Na-Dene: Navajo -*γòl* 'marrow'

[340] There appears to have been contamination between this root and the word **hegal* 'wing', q.v.

iχas, Dargwa (Chirag) *iχ-,* etc. 'to fly' < PEC **HiχV* (NCED 582)

7.62. Basque **ülhe* > (N) *ilhe,* (S) *ile,* (B) *ule* 'hair' ('wool' in Z) ~ PEC **ʔālχV* 'wool' > Rutul *ar*: 'spring wool', etc. (= **6.43**)

7.63. Basque **harhe* > **arhe* 'harrow' > (BN,L,Z) *arhe,* (AN,B,G,L) *are* ~ Avar *ɣár-ize* 'to harrow', *ɣári* 'wooden ladder', Lezgi, Tabasaran *ɣar* 'harrow', etc. < PEC **ɓarhV* = **ɣarhV* (NCED 477)

PDC **h / *ɦ / *ħ:* It is still uncertain how many laryngeals to reconstruct for PDC. In Basque we must reconstruct two laryngeals: **h,* which remains as [h] in all three of the aspirating dialects (Basse Navarre, Lapurdi, and Zuberoa = BN, L, Z), and **ɦ,* which remains as [h] in BN and L but is lost in Z. Both **h* and **ɦ* are lost in the non-aspirating dialects (B, G, AN, R), except in some early records (see **7.70**). In any case, PNC **h, *ɦ,* and **ħ* almost always correspond to a Basque laryngeal, either **h* or **ɦ*. In the twenty-nine cases below the patterns are as follows:

Out of nine cases where PNC/PEC has **h,* Basque also has **h* in seven of them (except **7.79.** Basque **belɦa-r̄* 'forehead' and **7.94.** Basque **ɦaseli* 'fox').

Of ten cases where PNC/PEC has **ɦ,* Basque has **h* in eight of the ten. The exceptions, where Basque also has **ɦ,* are **7.71** and **7.72.**

Of two cases where PNC/PEC has **ħ,* Basque has **h* in **7.91.** (Basque **čehume* 'half-span' ~ PNC **čwimħV* 'span'), and in **7.75.** (Basque **(H)isu* 'fright, horror, fierce, bad-tempered' ~ PNC **ħVmć̩V*) the Basque laryngeal is indeterminate (because the word only occurs in non-aspirating dialects). So there are not enough examples of **ħ* to discern any pattern in its Basque reflexes.

In ten other cases the PNC/PEC laryngeal is indeterminate (i.e., there is insufficient evidence within Caucasian to decide between **h, *ɦ,* or **ħ*.) In such cases the cover symbol is **H*.

See also above (**6.36**, ff.) for the PDC laryngeals **ʔ/ *ʡ / *ʕ*.

7.64. Basque **huin* 1 marrow, 2 pith, 3 brain > (Z) *hün* 1,3, (L) *huiñ, fuiñ* 1,2, (B, Sal, R) *un* 1,2, (Sal, R) *un* 3 ~ PEC **hwẽʔnV* > Akhwakh *hini* 'blood', Avar *han* 'meat', etc. (NCED 496) ~

Burushaski (Y) *huní* 'stone (of fruit)' ~ cf. ST: PST **ʔʷīj* 'blood' > Magari *hyu*, Mikir *vi* (ST V: 12)[341]

7.65. Basque **haga* 'long pole' ~ PEC **hăḵwV* > Karata *hak'ʷa* 'branch', etc. (= **5.20**)

7.66. Basque **habe* 'pillar, beam' ~ PEC **hwĕbē* > Avar *ħubí* 'post, pole, stem', etc. (= **1.24**)

7.67. Basque **nahi* 'will, willingness, desire, wish' > (BN, L, Z) *nahi*, (B,G, AN, R) *nai* ~ PEC **ʔnVhV̄* > Lak *nih* 'fright', Lezgi *neh* 'vicious, sinful', etc. (NCED 216) ~ cf. Na-Dene: PAth **-ne·* 'mind' > Navajo *-nìʔ* 'mind', *-ní* (in *ʔóó-ní* 'jealousy, grudge', *yí-ní* 'worry, lonesomeness')

7.68. Basque **arhe* 'harrow' ~ Avar *γár-ize* 'to harrow', etc. < PEC **ɓarhV = *γarhV* (= **7.63**)

7.69. Basque **ilha-r̄* 1 bean(s), 2 pea(s), 3 vetch, 4 heather > (Z) *ilhar* 1, (L) *ilhar* 1,3, (G) *ilar, illar* 3, (B) *irar, idar* 2,3,4, etc.[342] ~ Cauc: Avar *holó* 'bean(s)', Botlikh, Godoberi *hali* 'pea(s)', Tsez *hil* 'pea(s)', Lak *hulū* 'lentil', etc. < PEC **hōwɬ[ā]* (NCED 493)

7.70. Basque **ha[n]ar̄* 'worm'[343] > (R) *ār*, Old Bizkaian (1596) *haar*, Modern Bizkaian *aar, ar*, (BN, L, Z) *har* ~ PEC **ɦabarV* 'worm' > Avar *ħapára*, etc. (NCED 508) ~ Burushaski (H,N) *har* 'Kornwurm'

7.71. Basque **ɦaic* 'rock, stone' ~ Avar *ʕuc'*: 'stone', etc. < PNC **ɦə̄mVc̣ŏ* (= **3.17**)

7.72. Basque **ɦerde / *ɦelde-r̄* 'drivel, drool' ~ PNC **ɦăm⋋ ă* 'sweat' > Tindi *hanla*, etc. (= **4.20**)

7.73. Basque **hobi* 'gum(s) (of mouth)' ~ Akhwakh *oq':o* 'throat', Circassian *ʔʷə* 'mouth', etc. < PNC **ɦŏmG̣wĭ* (= **6.28**)

---

[341] Basque words of the type **muin* 'marrow, brain' (*q.v.*) are of separate origin (PEC **mắhnū* 'brain, head'), but in Basque have been associated and contaminated with this word. The semantic series 'blood ~ flesh ~ marrow ~ brain ~ kernel' is well documented. Cf., in Dravidian, Malayalam *niṇam* 'coagulated blood', Tamil *ñīṇam* 'fat, flesh, serum', and Kannada *neṇa* 'fat, marrow'.

[342] Zuberoan has, for example: *ilhar* 'bean(s)', *ilhar-biribil* 'peas', *ilhar-xuri* 'peas', etc. The comparison supposes a phonetic change of the type **hila-r > ilhar*. Cf. Basque (L) *ilhargi* 'moon' < **hil- + argi* (Trask 1997: 161).

[343] The only evidence for a nasal is the Roncalese form *ār* (with nasal *ā*). The Old Bizkaian *haar* and modern Bizkaian *aar* bear witness to an original disyllabic form compatible with PEC **ɦabarV*. V. Blažek has suggested the progression **Habr(a) > *HaMr(a) >hār(a)*.

7.74. Basque **hur* 'water' > (Z) *hur,*[344] (c) *ur* ~ PEC **ħwĭlV* > Avar ʕ*or* 'river', Lezgi *hül* 'sea, liquid', etc. (NCED 537) ~ Burushaski *hur* 'wooden water conduit, gutter'

7.75. Basque **(H)isu* 'fright, horror, fierce, bad-tempered' ~ Bezhta *hic'o*, Lak *ħuč'* 'fright', etc. < PNC **ħVmć̣V* (= **3.60**)

7.76. Basque **ɦauso* 'neighbor' ~ Chechen *ħāša* 'guest', etc. < PNC **HVc̣wĔ* (= **3.61**)

7.77. Basque **ɦodäi* 'cloud, thunder' ~ Dargwa (Akushi) *dạʕ* 'wind', etc., < PEC **dwiHV* 'wind' (=**2.21**)

7.78. Basque **hoc* 'cold' ~ Hinukh =*oč'č'u* 'cold', etc. < PNC **(r)HEc̣wV / *c̣wE(r)HV* 'cold' (= **3.67**)

7.79. Basque **belɦa-r̄* 'forehead' ~ Rutul *bäl* 'forehead', Tindi *bala* 'edge, end, corner', etc. < PEC **bʕātħŏ* (= **1.13**)

7.80. Basque **huć* 'empty, pure', etc. ~ Chechen =*ässa* 'empty, hollow', Lak =*ač'* =*a-* 'empty', etc. < PNC **ɦə̣c̣Ĕ* (= **3.23.a**)

7.81. Basque **ɦućal* 'poor, trifling, dry, barren,' etc. ~ PNC **=HĭcĂl* 'naked, bare' > Avar ʕ*íc':a*-b, Ubykh -*p'c'ə*, etc. (= **3.23.b**)

7.82. Basque **hega-* 'flying', etc. ~ Tsakhur al-*iχas*, Dargwa (Chirag) *iχ-,* etc. 'to fly' < PEC **HiχV* (= **7.61**)

7.83. Basque **gurhi* 'fat, grease, butter', etc. ~ Lezgi *ʁeri* = *ġeri* 'butter', Tsez *χuri* 'piece of dry cheese', etc. < PEC **χərHV (~ *χHərV)* (= **7.57**)

7.84. Basque **hobe* 'better' ~ Lak *χ:uj-* 'good', etc. < PEC **HVχwV* 'good' (= **7.54**)

7.85. Basque **leher̄* 'pine tree' > (BN, Z) *leher,* (R) *ler* ~ Avar *ɬ:alú* 'yew tree', Lak *ħalu* 'grove' < PEC **ɬħwaɬū* (= **7.28**)

7.86. Basque **sahar̄* 'old' ~ Lezgi *sur* 'old', etc. < PNC **swĕrho* 'old, year' (= **7.7.**)

7.87. Basque **garhi* 'thin' ~ Avar *q':ʷarí*-da-b 'narrow, cramped', etc. < PEC **q̇warHV* (= **6.29.**)

7.88. Basque **bulha-r̄* 'chest, breast' ~ Avar *ɣʷári* 'udder', etc. < PEC **Gwălɦē* 'udder, breast' (= **6.27**)

---

[344] For *ur,* see the note to *oin* 'foot' (**6.45**)

7.89. Basque *śolho 'meadow, field', (B) solo 'field (prepared for sowing)' ~ PEC *čHäłu > Lak šạlu 'earth, ground', etc. (= **3.44**)

7.90. Basque *čahal 'calf (young bovine) ~ Andi č'ora 'heifer', etc. < PEC *Hc̣ẃīlV̆ / *Hlīc̣wV̆ (= **3.54**)

7.91. Basque *čehume 'half-span' ~ Dargwa (Chirag) č'im 'span', etc. < PNC *čwimħV (= **3.58**)

7.92. Basque *sumhV 'a kind of elm tree', etc. ~ PEC *ǯ̌ĥŭmV > Hunzib šumal 'bushes', Lezgi žum 'quince', etc. (= **3.69.a**)

7.93. Basque *hegi 1 crest, ridge, 2 small plateau overhanging a cliff, 3 border, edge, corner > (BN, L) hegi 1,2, (Z) hegi 1,3, (B, G, AN, R) egi 1 ~ Dargwa (h)urqi 'mountains', Avar ʕorq:í 'boundary', etc. < PEC *ĥwərqē 'mountain ridge' (NCED 536) ~ Burushaski (H, N) hurgó, (Y) horgó 'up(hill), ascent'

7.94. Basque *ħaseli ~ *aseħali > (B) azegari, (BN, L) hazeri, (Z, R) axeri, etc. 'fox' ~ Tindi sari, Akhwakh šari, Tsez ziru, Archi s:ol 'fox', etc. < PNC *chwōlĕ̆ < *cEhwōlĕ̆ 'fox, jackal' ~ Burushaski hal 'fox' (= **3.5**)

8. Resonants

Proto-Dene-Caucasian had the usual resonants and glides, e.g. *m, *n, *r, *l, *w, *j. Some examples of reflexes are as follows:

PDC ***m:*** There is substantial evidence that PDC ***m*** is retained as Basque /**m**/, initially and medially. No Basque dialects permit final /**m**/: all final nasals become /**n**/ or /**ñ**/, e.g., behazun (**3.6**), zain, zañ (**7.6**). The following etymologies require us to re-examine the proposal by Michelena (and Trask) that Pre-Basque had no phoneme *m. PDC clusters of the type *-mG̱w-, *-mχw- become Basque *b (*hobi, *ħibai).

8.1. Basque *muku-r > (B) mukur 'trunk, base of tree', (Z) mũkhür 'très grosse bûche' ~ PEC *mĥŏqwe 'oak-tree' > Tsakhur moq, etc. (= **6.5**)

8.2. Basque *muśu 'nose, snout, face, mouth, lip, kiss' ~ PEC *mHărčwV > Chamalal maš 'snot', etc. ~ Burushaski –muś 'snot', etc. (= **3.50**)

8.3. Basque *muga 'border, limit, frontier' ~ Avar muq: 'line', etc. < PEC *mŏrqwV̆ (= **6.8**)

8.4. Basque **mi(n)hi* 'tongue' ~ Tindi *mic:i* 'tongue', Andi *mic':i,*Tabasaran *melz,* Ubykh *bźa,* etc. < PNC **mĕlči* 'tongue' (= **3.19**)

8.5. Basque **miko* 'a little, a little bit' ~ Chamalal *mik'u*-b 'small', Rutul *muk'-dɨ* 'young', etc. < PEC **miḳwV* (= **5.14**)

8.6. Basque **mulho* > (L) *mulho, mulo* 'small heap, montoncito', (Z) *mulho* 'petite colline, eminence, butte'[345] ~ Hinukh *malu* 'mountain', Tsez *mali* 'hillock, knoll', Archi *mul* 'mountain', etc. < PEC **muɦalV* (NCED 834)

8.7. Basque **muin* 1 marrow, 2 brain, 3 sap, 4 germ, sprout > (B) *muin, muiñ* 4, (G) *muin, muiñ, mun* 1,3, (AN) *muin, muiñ* 1,2,3, (L) *muin, mun* 1,3, etc.[346] ~ Akhwakh *mina* 'head', Udi *ma* 'brain, marrow', etc. < PEC **mãhnū* 'brain, head' (NCED 797)

8.8. Basque **mardo* 'robust, plump', etc., **mardul* 'vigorous, strong', etc. ~ PEC **mōrɫV* > Chechen *mar* 'husband', Kryz *miɣil* 'male', Archi *meƛle* 'male', etc. (= **4.24**)

8.9. Basque **moko* 1 beak, 2 extremity, point, 3 face, 4 façade > (G, AN) *moko* 1,2, (BN, L) *mokho* 1,2,3,4, *mokhoz-mokho* 'face to face' ~ Proto-Andian **muqV* > *nuqV* > Avar *nuʕ* 'witness', Chechen *baq'* 'true', etc. < PEC **wĭmq̇V* '*(eye-)witness, true'[347] (NCED1050) ~ Burushaski **moq-* > (Y) *-móqot* 'cheek', *-móqis̨* 'face', (H, N) *-móqis̨* 'cheek' ~ cf. PST **mjV̆k* 'eye' > Old Chinese **muk* 'eye'; Tib. *mig* 'eye', etc. ~ Na-Dene: Tlingit *wàq (wàG)* 'eye', PAth **-we·G-* 'eye', etc.

8.10. Basque **sama-ŕ* 'fleece', etc. ~ PEC **čḧwĕme* 'eyebrow' > Lezgi r-*c'am,* etc. (= **3.11**)

8.11. Basque **sumhV* 'elm, grove', etc. ~ PEC **ǯɦŭmV* > Hunzib *šumal* 'bushes', Lezgi *žum* 'quince', etc. (– **3.69.a**)

8.12. Basque **hama-* 'ten' ~ Proto-Lezgian **χ:am:* 'hand(ful), arm(ful)', etc. < PEC **mHŏχi* (= **7.45**)

---

[345] Despite Trask's (1997, p. 261) attempt to derive this word from Romance, it is clearly native (note the cluster *-lh-*), there is no Latin antecedent, and it has a clear DC etymology.

[346] This word is often confused by vasconists (and apparently by Basque speakers) with the semantically similar word **huin (q.v.),* though external comparison shows that **muin* and **huin* come from distinct origins.

[347] The Caucasian forms, if they indeed belong here, are quite divergent semantically, requiring a hypothetical change 'eye' > 'eye-witness' > 'true'. However, PEC **wĭmq̇V* is a good phonetic match for the ST and Na-Dene words for 'eye'.

8.13. Basque **lam-* > (AN, BN, R) *lamika-*tu, (BN) *lamizka-*tu 'to lick' ~ Andi *lam-* 'to lick', Dargwa (Akushi) *limc'i-k'*es 'to lick', etc. < PEC **ɬamV* (NCED 754)

8.14. Basque **čehume* 'half-span' ~ Dargwa (Chirag) *č'im* 'span', etc. < PNC **čwimħV* (= **3.58**)

8.15. Basque **limuri* 'humid, slippery', etc. ~ PEC **ɬHwemV* 'liquid' > Avar *ɬ:amí-*ja-b, etc. (= **4.2.a**)

8.16. Basque **lema* 'rudder' (< '*board') ~ PEC **ɬəmʔV̆* 'roof' > Karata *ɬ'ame,* etc. (= **4.10**)

8.17. Basque **čimiča* 'bedbug' ~ Tabasaran *č'amč'* 'fly', etc. < PEC **c̣imV́c̣V*, Burushaski *ćhumúuso* 'maggot', etc. (= **3.53**)

8.18. Basque **hobi* 'gum(s) (of mouth)' ~ Akhwakh *oq':o* 'throat', etc. < PNC **ɦŏmG̣wĭ* (= **6.28, 7.73**)

8.19. Basque **ɦibai* 'river' ~ Godoberi *inχ:i* 'river, brook', etc. < PNC **jimχwǍ* (= **7.55**)

PDC **n:* Only a few examples are needed for this trivial correspondence of **n* = **n*:

8.20. Basque **negu* 'winter' ~ PNC **ʁwĭnʔV* = **γwĭnʔV* > Chechen *ʕa / ʕäna-* 'winter', Lak *γʷi- / γin-* 'summer', etc. (= **7.58**)

8.21. Basque **nahi* 'will, willingness, desire' ~ PEC **ʔnVhV̆* > Lak *nih* 'fright', Lezgi *neh* 'vicious, sinful', etc. (= **7.67**)

8.22. Basque **niga-* 'weeping, tears; herpes' ~ Dargwa *nerγ* 'tear', Chechen *not'q'a* 'pus', etc. < PEC **něwq̇ŭ* ~ Burushaski (H) *nagéi,* (N) *magéi* 'boil, ulcer', etc. (= **6.31**)

8.23. Basque **thini* 'summit, top' ~ Burushaski *-thán* 'point, summit, peak', etc. (= **2.3**)

8.24. Basque **i-tain* 'tick' ~ PNC **ṭaHnā* 'nit' > Akhwakh *t'ani,* etc. (= **2.7**)

8.25. Basque **arhan* 'plum, sloe' ~ Avar *géni* 'pear', Hunzib *hĩ,* etc. < PEC **γōnʔV* 'pear' ~ Burushaski *γaíŋ* 'grapes' (= **7.39**)

PDC *r, *rː In numerous cases PDC *r corresponds to Basque /r̄/.[348] To save space, only a few examples are cited here:

8.26. Basque *ēreka 'ravine, rivulet, arroyo' ~ Tindi reḱ:a 'gorge, ravine', etc. < PNC *r̄ịgwÃ (= **6.18**)

8.27. Basque *erbi 'hare, weasel' ~ PNC *r̄ịgwĂ 'weasel, mouse' > Tindi reƛ':u 'weasel', etc. (= **5.27**)

8.28. Basque *herī 'country, town, inhabited place, people' ~ PNC *ʔwˇhri > Lak ara-l 'army, troops', etc. (= **6.46**)

8.29. Basque *harī 'stone' ~ PEC *χHĕrχV 'small stone, gravel' > Akhwakh χaχi 'road metal', Lezgi χirχem 'road gravel', etc. (= **7.44**)

8.30. Basque *čoru 'root of hair' ~ PEC *c̣ħwə̄rV 'hair' > Avar č'or, etc. (= **3.55**)

8.31.a. Basque *larī 'sadness, anguish', etc. ~ PNC *ɬwĕrV 'hard, severe, stern' (= **4.13.a**)

8.31.b. Basque *e-arī 'to sit; set, put' > (B, G, AN, Z) jarri ~ Tsakhur ġ-i-ʔar- 'to sit, sit down', Abkhaz a-ja-rá 'to lie', etc. < PNC *=eʔ(w)Vr (NCED 409) ~ Burushaski *hur- 'to sit' > (Y) hurúṭ-, (H,N) hurúṭ-, hurú-

8.32. Basque *e-gur̄ 'firewood' ~ PEC *gō̄rV > Tsez giri 'pole', Udi gor, gorgor 'pole', etc. (= **5.24.a**)

8.33. Basque *agōr, *egarī > (c) agor 'dry', egarri 'thirst' ~ PNC *=iGwĂr 'dry, to dry' > Avar =aq̇ːʷarab, etc. ~ Burushaski (N) qharáo 'dried up' (= **6.23**)

8.34. Basque *ha[n]ar̄ 'worm' ~ PEC *ħabarV 'worm' > Avar ħapára, etc. ~ Burushaski (H,N) har 'Kornwurm' (= **7.70**)

8.35. Basque *gogōr 'hard', *gor̄ 'deaf' ~ PEC *GwēRV 'stone' > Khwarshi γur, etc. ~ Burushaski (Y) γoró, (H,N) γuró 'stones' (= **6.19**)

8.36. Basque *adar̄ 'horn' ~ Avar ƛ:ar 'horn', etc. < PEC *ɬ̣wi̊rV ~ Burushaski (H) -ltúr, (Y) tur 'horn' (= **4.17**)

---

[348] With a few exceptions (zur 'wood', (h)ur 'water', zer 'what', etc.) final Basque -r is sounded as a trill /r̄/, e.g. egur [eɣur̄] 'firewood', egurra [eɣur̄a] 'the firewood'. In L and BN the trill /r̄/ is realized as a voiced uvular fricative [ʁ], "somewhat resembling French /r/ but noticeably scrapier." See Trask (1997, p. 144ff.).

In PDC clusters of *r* + a dental, Basque has /r̄d/ (merging with the /r̄d/ < lateral affricates: see section **4**). Note that Burushaski in the same situation has the retroflex /ṭ/:

8.37. Basque **e-purdi* 'rump, buttocks' ~ Archi *pạrt'i* 'large intestine', Bezhta *pirt'i* 'bladder, lung', etc. < PEC **pHVrṭwV* ~ Burushaski (Y) *phaṭ* 'stomach (of fowl)', (H,N) *-pháṭ* 'viscera (of fowl)', etc. (= **1.5, 2.15**)

8.38. Basque **lirdi* 'drivel, saliva' ~ PEC **λwirdɨ* > Agul *furd* 'manure', Avar *xʷerd* 'pus', etc. ~ Burushaski *γiṭ* slime' (= **2.25, 7.27**)

In combination with a following velar or post-velar obstruent (**-rg-, *-rq-, *-rq'-, *-rχ-*) PDC **r* is lost in Basque:

8.39. Basque **śagu* 'mouse' ~ PNC **cārgwɨ* > Adyge *cəɣʷa* 'mouse', Tsakhur *sok* 'weasel', etc. ~ Burushaski (Y) *čargé* 'flying squirrel' (= **3.1.a**)

8.40. Basque **hegi* 'crest, ridge, plateau, border, edge, corner' ~ Dargwa *(h)urqi* 'mountains', Avar *ʕorq:i* 'boundary', etc. < PEC **ħwə̄rqē* 'mountain ridge' ~ Burushaski (H, N) *hurgó,* (Y) *horgó* 'up(hill), ascent' (= **7.93**)

8.41. Basque **muga* 'border, limit, frontier' ~ Chechen *moγa* 'line, row', Avar *muq:* 'line', etc. < PEC **mŏrgwV̆* (= **6.8, 8.3**)

8.42. Basque **loki* 'temple (of head), forehead' ~ PEC **ʲarq̇wĕ* > Khwarshi *λ'oq'o* 'forehead', etc. (= **4.4**)

8.43. Basque **e-kuśi* 'to see' ~ Bezhta *=ĩq-* 'to find', Budukh *irq-* 'to see', etc. < PEC **=Hārq̇V(n)* ~ **=Hirq̇V(n)* 'to see, find' (= **6.12**)

8.44. Basque **ehun* 'to weave; cloth' ~ PEC **=irχwVn* 'to knit, weave, spin' (= **7.53**)

8.45. Basque **eho* 'to beat' ~ Avar *=uχ-* 'to beat, hit', Rutul *=iχa-* 'to beat, hit', etc. < PNC **HīrχA* (= **7.52**)

There are also a few cases of PDC *r > Basque /r/ (single tap), possibly reflecting an allophonic variation [r ~ r̄] in PDC, or a phonemic distinction /r/ ~ /r̄/ that was lost in Caucasian. S.A. Starostin (2005a) posited a "[Proto-Sino-Caucasian] *r´ is preserved only in Yenisseian; in other languages it has the same reflex as normal *r." Of nine examples of *r´ there are tentative Basque cognates for two with "soft" [r] corresponding to Yeniseian *r̄ (see **8.50.b, 8.50.c**). The other examples below *could* represent reflexes of PDC but there is no confirmation from Yeniseian. **8.48** has a Yeniseian cognate, but with *r* in final position, where the distinction was neutralized.

8.46. Basque *fiaran 'valley, field' ~ Chechen ārē 'plain; steppe', Lak ar 'plain', etc. < PEC *ʔārV (= **6.39**)

8.47. Basque *bi-rik- 'lung' ~ PNC *jĕrkwĩ 'heart' > Avar rak', Lezgi rik', etc. (= **5.17**)

8.48. Basque *u-dagara 'otter' ~ PEC *darq̇wV > Andi darGʷa 'weasel, marten', Lak t:arq'a 'weasel, ermine' ~ PY *täχVr 'otter' (= **2.20**)

8.49. Basque *garhi 'thin' ~ Agul q:ure-f 'thin, emaciated', Avar q':ʷarí-da-b 'narrow, cramped', etc. < PEC *q̇warHV (= **6.29**)

8.50.a. Basque *arhe 'harrow' ~ Avar γár-ize 'to harrow', γári 'wooden ladder', Lezgi, Tabasaran γar 'harrow', etc. < PEC *ɓarhV = *γarhV (= 7.63, 7.68)

8.50.b. Basque *suri 'white' > (c) zuri ~ Chechen siri, sira 'gray', Ingush sira, Tsez zira, Khwarshi zara id. < PEC *sV̄rV (NCED 966) ~ PY *su(ʔ)r̄- 'yellow' > Ket sul-emam, Kott šui, etc. (SSEJ 278)

8.50.c. Basque *erhi 'finger' > (BN, L, Z) erhi, (AN, R) eri id.; (B, G) er-puru 'thumb' (lit. 'finger-head'), etc. ~ Burushaski *-reŋ 'hand' ~ PY *r̄ɔŋ 'hand'[349] > Ket lóŋ, laʔŋ, Yug lɔŋ, etc. (= **5.37**)

PDC *l, *ḷ: Starostin (2005a) posited two lateral resonants for PDC, ordinary (front) *l and a back or velarized *ḷ. However, they are distinguished only in Caucasian and Sino-Tibetan. Basque also has a distinction between *l and *ḷ (= Michelena's *l and *L), but it does not

---

[349] Not in SSEJ: see Tower of Babel site.

seem to correspond to the PDC distinction (i.e., some words with PDC *ɫ correspond to Basque *l), and there are in fact very few clear-cut cases of Basque *ɫ (see **8.77.** ff.). At any rate, all PDC laterals are realized as Basque *l /l/ in initial and stem-final position, and after a fossilized prefix. See below (**8.61**, *et seq.*) for the reflexes in medial position:

8.51. Basque *leka 'bean pod, husk' ~ Chechen *lag* 'fruit-stone' Khinalug *li / lik'i* 'grain', etc. < PNC *lĕk̮V (= **5.18**)

8.52. Basque *lūr 'earth' ~ PNC *lhĕmL̥wĭ > Avar *raƛ':*, etc. (= **4.14.b.**)

8.53. Basque *lam- 'to lick' ~ Andi *lam-* 'to lick', Dargwa (Akushi) *limc'i-k'es* 'to lick', etc. < PEC *ɫamV (= **8.13**)

8.54. Basque *lotu 'to tie' ~ Lezgi *ilit'-iz* 'to bind around', Kryz *ju-t'ul-* 'to tie, bind', etc. < PNC *jeṭal- 'to tie, bind; untie', etc. (= **2.12**)

8.55. Basque *be-lāri 'ear' > (B,G,AN) *belarri*, (BN,L,Z) *beharri*, (AN) *bearri*, (R) *biárri*[350] ~ Proto-Nakh *-lari 'ear' (oblique base > Chechen *lerg,* Batsbi *lark',* etc.), Dargwa *laħi, liħi* 'ear', etc. < PNC *ɫĕHɫe 'ear' (NCED 756)

8.56. Basque *gal- 'to lose' ~ PEC *=igwVɫ 'to lose, get lost; steal' > Tsakhur a=gʷal- 'to get lost', Tindi *'ala* 'thief', etc. (= **5.21**)

8.57. Basque *čahal 'calf' ~ Cauc: Andi *č'ora* 'heifer', Agul *luč'* 'heifer', etc. < PEC *Hc̣wɨlV / *Hlɨc̣wV (= **3.54**)

8.58. Basque *maga-l 'lap' ~ Abkhaz á-mgʷa 'belly', Avar *bakʷáli* 'belly', etc. < PNC *bVnḳwÃ (= **1.20**)

8.59. Basque *ñućal 'trifling, barren', etc. ~ PNC *=Hɨc̣Ãl 'naked, bare' (= **3.23**)

8.60. Basque *apal 'shelf' ~ Avar *epel* 'lid, cover', Inkhokhwari *apar* 'pole (for planking the ceiling)' < PEC *ʔapVɫV 'pole; board, cover' (= **1.6**)

In intervocalic position (and at the end of a few monosyllables) PDC *l and *ɫ become Basque /r/ (single tap). Bizkaian dialects sometimes retain /l/:

---

[350] The variant *beharri is secondary, influenced by the verb *be(h)a-tu* 'to listen, look'.

8.61. Basque *hur 'water' ~ PEC *ƕwɨlV > Avar ʕor 'river', Lezgi hül 'sea, liquid', etc. ~ Burushaski hur 'wooden water conduit, gutter' (= **7.74**)

8.62. Basque *sul > *sur 'wood, timber, lumber' ~ Andi žala 'branch, rod', Avar žul 'broom, besom', Tsakhur ǯol 'sheaf', etc. < PEC *ǯw[ĕ]ɬ̄ (= **3.70**)

8.63. Basque *sori 'fortune, luck', etc. ~ PNC *ʒōɬV > Lak c'ullu- 'healthy, whole'; Hurrian šawlə 'health, prosperity', etc. (= **3.33**)

8.64. Basque *bero 'hot' ~ Cauc: PWC *bla/ə 'to burn'; Tsez boboru, Khwarshi bobolu 'hot' ~ Burushaski babárum (babár- um) (Y) 'hot, pungent' (of food), (H,N) 'pungent (taste); burning (pain); hot-tempered, irascible (person)' (= **1.19**)

8.65.a. Basque *kirać 'bitter, sour', etc. ~ PNC *q̇ĕfilV > Archi q'ala 'bitter', Ubykh q'aq'ə́ 'sweet', etc. (= **6.9**)

8.65.b. Basque *sirin 'excrement of birds, diarrhea' > zirin ~ Akhwakh šili 'sheep's dung', Tabasaran ur-sil 'dung', etc. < PEC *siɬ̄ (= **7.18.a**)

8.66. Basque *asaro 'autumn, November', etc. ~ PNC *c̣ōjwɨlfiV > Tindi c:ibar 'winter', Khinalug cuwa-ž 'autumn', etc. (= **3.7**)

8.67. Basque *śale 'net, grill, manger' ~ Avar čalí 'fence', etc. < PEC *čfiaɬē (= **3.45**)

8.68. Basque *agurV > (B,G,AN,L) agure 'old man', (B) agura 'old woman' ~ Archi χala-t:u- 'old (person)', etc. < PEC *=ŏnqV(lV) (= **6.9**)

In a number of cases, Basque has words in which the ordinary form has /r/, while /l/ appears in combinatory forms and stem variants (allomorphs):[351]

8.69.a. Basque *a-bele > *abere 'domestic animal'/ (combinatory form) *a-bel- ~ Udi bele 'cattle', Chechen bula 'aurochs', etc. < PNC *bŭɬV (= **1.24**)

8.69.b. Basque *ahali > *ahari 'ram', *ahal- > (AN-Baztan) aal-zain 'shepherd' ~ Chadakolob her 'ewe', Hunzib χor 'ram', etc. < PEC *χ[ə]lV (= **6.44**)

---

[351] See Trask 1997: 188ff.

8.69.c. Basque *ħaseli ~ *aseħali 'fox' > (h)azeri, etc. / (combinatory form as in *azel-eme* 'vixen')³⁵² ~ Tindi *sari*, Archi *s:ol* 'fox', etc. < PNC **cEhwōl̃e* ~ Burushaski *hal* 'fox' (= **3.5**)

8.70. Basque **erdala* > **erdara* 'foreign' / (combinatory form) *erdal-,* as in *erdal-dun* 'non-Basque-speaker, foreigner' ~ Khwarshi *λar* 'guest', Chechen *lūla-χō* 'neighbor', etc. < PEC **Ł̣ōlV* (= **4.23**)

8.71. Basque **gali* > **gari* 'wheat' / (combinatory form) *gal-* ~ Cauc: Tindi *q':eru*, Rutul *γil*, Archi *qoqol*, etc. 'wheat' < PEC **ɢōlʔe* (= **6.21**)

8.72. Basque **hali* > **hari* / (combinatory form) *hal-* 'thread' ~ PEC **χātV* > Tsez *χero* 'sinew', Chechen *χal* 'thread', etc. ~ Burushaski *γaγ̇* 'thread, strand' (= **7.43**)

8.73. Basque **čoli* > **čori* / **čol-* 'bird' / *txol-arre* 'sparrow' ('bird-gray') ~ PEC **čHwīlV* > Chamalal *č'or* 'bird', etc. (= **3.56.a**)

8.74. Basque **ugali* > **ugari* 'abundant' / *ugal-*du 'to increase, multiply' ~ Dargwa (Akushi) *χala-l* 'big', Tindi =*eχ:ala-b* 'long', etc. < PNC **HāχułV / *HālχV* (= **7.60**)

PDC **ł* + post-velar fricative corresponds to Basque **rh* (preserved in northern dialects, reduced to /r/ or /l/ in southern dialects):

8.75. Basque **gurhi* 'butter, fat' ~ ? PEC **χwɨlʔi* > Bezhta *χo* 'meat', Dargwa (Akushi) *ħạli* 'fat', etc. (but see the alternative comparison in **7.57**)

8.76. Basque **sorho* 'meadow, field' ~ PEC **čHäłu* > Lak *šạlu* 'earth, ground', Tsakhur *ǯil* 'earth, floor', etc. (= **3.44**)

In the following cases, PDC **l / *ł* remains as Basque **l* in intervocalic position:³⁵³

8.77. Basque **euli* 'fly' (insect) > (B, G) *euli*, (AN, BN, L) *uli*, (G) *elbi*, (R) *éllu*, (Z) *ülü, üllü*, etc. ~ Cauc: Archi *hiliku, hilku*

---

³⁵² Not found in Azkue, but given to me by José Ignacio Hualde (p.c.).

³⁵³ Note that in **8.78** and **8.80** Basque has a cluster with laryngeal (-*lh-*, -*lħ-*), though there is no laryngeal in PNC. However, note that in each case PNC has a tense consonant (**ɟ , **ṣ*).

'fly', nisin-*hiliku* 'bug'[354] ~ Burushaski (Y) *haúlal* 'butterfly, moth', (H,N) *hoólalas* id.

8.78. Basque **sełhai* 'field, meadow' ~ PEC **ʒəlV* > Avar *c':or* 'plain', etc. (= **3.31**)

8.79. Basque **punpuła* 'tear, bubble', etc. ~ PNC **pHulq̃ɨ* 'dirt; secretion in the eye' (= **1.4**)

8.80. Basque **sülfio* 'hole, cave' ~ PEC **s̱wōłV* > Avar *šulu* 'pipe', Bezhta *šelo* 'horn' (< '*tube'), etc. (= **7.17**)

8.81. Basque **bełV* 'crow, raven' ~ Cauc: Avar *γálo* 'jackdaw', Adyge *q:ʷaʟa-ź* 'crow', etc. < PNC **ɢHwV̄łV* ~ Burushaski *balás* (H), *balác* (N) '(larger) bird' (= **6.26**)

8.82. Basque **e-cułi* 'to turn, turn over, return', etc. ~ Agul *ilcan-* 'to turn (on an axis)', Tabasaran b-*ilcun*-ag 'whirligig, hummingtop', etc. < PEC **=īrcVl* 'to twirl, turn round' (= **3.10**)

8.83. Basque **koła / *kola* 'nape' ~ PEC **qHwŏłwV* > Tindi *χolu* 'back of the head', Lezgi *χew* 'collar', etc. (= **6.2**)

PDC **l / *ł* + (velar fricative, post-velar fricative, laryngeal) is preserved as /**lh**/ in northern (N) Basque dialects, > /**l**/ in southern (S) Basque. In some southern dialects the change of **lh > l* must have been very early, resulting in the change of *-l-* to *–r-* discussed above (**8.61-8.76**), then sometimes *–r- > -d-*, by dissimilation; thus, for example, Roncalese **bulhaɾ̄ > bular > burar > budar* 'breast' (**8.91**). In every case the Caucasian cognate has a lateral, so the supposition that **r* was original (*e.g.*, Trask 1997, p. 145, following Michelena) is shown to be purely speculative.

8.84. Basque (N) *bilho,* (S) *bilo, billo* 'hair' ~ Lak *p'iħulli* 'feather', Dargwa (Akushi) *pa̱ħa̱la* 'feather', etc. < PNC **ṗVhVłV* ~ Burushaski *phulγíuẏ, pholγó* 'feather' (− **1.8**)

8.85. Basque (N) *alha,* (S) *ala* 'grazing, pasture'; (BN, L, Z) *alha*-tu 'to graze, to feed' ~ Hinukh *hil* 'to bite', Kryz *ʕül-* 'to eat', Archi *lah*-bos 'to get hungry', etc. < PEC **=iʔwVl* (= **6.47**)

8.86. Basque**elhe* > (BN, L, Z) *elhe,* (AN, R) *ele* 'speech, word' ~ PEC **lĕHwV* > Inkhokwari *loje* 'word, sound, voice', Dargwa *luʕi* 'number' (NCED 744) ~ cf. ST: PST **lă* 'speak, speech' > Lushei *hla* 'hymn, song', etc.; PST **lō* 'sing' > Old Chinese **law*

---

[354] The word is isolated in one Caucasian language, but has promising external parallels.

'sing, song', etc. (ST III: 1, 30) ~ Na-Dene: PAth *-li 'to sing' > Kato leʔ, etc. (KL 143)

8.87. Basque *belfia-r̄ > (BN) belhar, (Sal, Z) belar 'forehead' ~ Rutul bäl 'forehead', Tindi bala 'edge, end, corner', etc. < PEC *b ꝉ āthŏ (= **1.13**)

8.88. Basque *ilha-r̄ 'bean(s), pea(s), vetch, heather' > (Z) ilhar, (L) ilhar, (G) ilar, illar, (B) irar, idar, etc. ~ Avar holó 'bean(s)', etc. < PEC *hōwɫ[ā] (= **7.69**)

8.89. Basque *belha-r̄ 'grass, hay' > (BN, L, Z) belhar, (AN, G) belar, (B, G) berar, (B) bedar ~ Lezgi werg 'nettle', Archi urk:i 'burdock', etc. < PEC *u̯elɣV (= **7.40**)

8.90. Basque *mulho 'petite colline, eminence, butte' > (L, Z) mulho ~ PEC *mufialV 'mountain' > Hinukh malu, etc. (= **8.6**)

8.91. Basque *bulhaR̄ > (N) bulhar, (S) bular, (R) budar 'chest, breast' ~ Lak q:ʷar (~ dial. q:ʷal) 'udder', Avar gʷári 'udder', etc. < PEC *Gwăłfiē 'udder, breast' (= **6.27**)

8.92. Basque *ülhe > (N) ilhe, (S) ile, (B) ule 'hair' ('wool' in Z) ~ PEC *ʔālχV 'wool' > Rutul ar: 'spring wool', etc. (= **6.43, 7.62**)

PDC *w: The Basque reflex is consistently /b/. This development is convergent with that of Latin v in Castilian, which merged with Latin b (e.g., vaca [baka], etc.). Initial *wu > *bu has been reduced to /u/ (urde, urki).

8.93. Basque *baśo, *baśa 'forest, desert, wild' ~ Akhwakh beča 'mountain', Tindi besa 'mountain', Archi sob 'mountain pasture', etc. < PEC *wīce (= **3.3.a**)

8.94. Basque *bahe 'sieve' ~ Tsakhur wex:ʷa 'sieve', etc. (= **7.5**)

8.95. Basque *beśo 'arm' ~ Chechen biši 'hand (of a child)', Tsez baša 'finger' < PEC *wũ̯šV or *bũ̯šV (= **7.22**)[355]

8.96. Basque (*śor̄-)balda > (c) sor-balda 'shoulder'[356] ~ PEC (*wəŁV) 'neck' > Bezhta boło, Hunzib bolo, etc. ~ Burushaski (H,N) -wáld-as, (Y) -wáld-es 'back'

---

[355] There is not enough evidence to decide between PNC *w or *b.

[356] Assuming sor-balda dissimilated < *sor-barda, with the regular reflex of a lateral affricate (see section **4**).

8.97. Basque *be-/bi-* fossilized class prefix, as in *be-hatz* 'thumb, toe', *be-larri* 'ear', *bi-zi* 'life', etc.[357] ~ PNC *w-* (marker of II-class singular): cf. e.g. Tindi *b-eʏ:u* 'stomach', *b-aʏ:i* 'in the middle'; WC fossilized *b-* or *p-*: Ubykh *b-ɮa* 'eye', *p-č̣a* 'guest', etc. ~ cf. ST: Garo *bi-bik* 'bowels', *bi-bal* 'flower', *bi-mik* 'sprout', *bi-tši* 'egg', etc.; Tibetan *b-žin* 'face'

8.98. Basque **behe* > (c) *behe* 'floor, ground, lower part, bottom', *behean* 'below, down, under(neath)', etc. ~ Tindi *beχ:i* 'bottom, buttock', Godoberi ladi-*baχ:u* 'lower part, below', etc. < PNC *w=ˇʏA* (NCED 423)[358]

8.99. Basque **belha-r̄* 'grass, hay' ~ Lezgi *werg* 'nettle', Archi *urk:i* 'burdock', etc. < PEC *u̯elγV* (= **7.40, 8.89**)[359]

8.100. Basque **urde* > (c) *urde* 'pig'[360] ~ PNC *wH̄arʏw^* > Tsez *beλo*, Lezgi *wak* 'boar, pig', etc. (NCED 1047) ~ cf. ST: PST **wăk* 'pig' > Burmese *wak*, Lushai *vok*, etc. (ST I: 121)

8.101. Basque **burki* 'birch tree' > (BN) *burkhi*,(Z) *bürkhi*, (c) *urki* ~ Lezgi *werχ* 'birch', etc. < PEC *w̄eqwV* ? + PEC **mh̄erqwě* 'birch; wood, timber' (= **6.6**)

8.102. Basque **hobi* 'grave, tomb'[361] ~ PEC **fɨwɨ* 'grave' > Avar *χob*, Tindi *hoba*, Lak *haw*, etc. (**= 7.1**)

PDC **j:* There are very few Basque cognates that seem to indicate a laryngeal was original:[362]

8.103. Basque **hauć* > (BN,L) *hauts,* (Z) *hautx,* (B,G,AN,R) *auts* 'ashes, powder' ~ Ingush *jost* 'loose earth', etc. < PEC **jōmć̣V* (= **3.44**)

---

[357] See Appendix A.

[358] A Caucasian root with changing class prefixes. Karata *reχ:i* 'lower part, below' has the prefix **r-* rather than **w-*, as in Tindi and Godoberi.

[359] The rare Caucasian phoneme **u̯* apparently merges with **w* in Basque.

[360] With the regular change of PDC intervocalic **ʏ* > Basque *–rd-* (cf. **4.15.a-4.24.b**).

[361] There is a remarkably similar Latin word, *fovea* 'pit, pitfall', which is often cited (*e.g.,* Meyer-Lübke 1935, no. 3463) as the origin of Basque *hobi*. The Basque and Caucasian words mean specifically 'grave', while the Romance words mean 'pit' in general (Spanish *hoya*, etc.).

[362] For typology of change, cf. Germanic **xilpan* 'to help' > Old Swedish *hielpa* > Modern Swedish *hjälpa* [jɛlpa].

8.104. Basque *(H)ainc- 'hard frost' > (B) *aintzigar, antzigar*, (G) *aintzigar, antzigar, intziar* ~ PNC *jămʒĂ 'snow' > Andi *anži*, Khwarshi *ĩsa*, Rutul *jiz*, etc. (= **3.35**)

8.105. Basque *ɦibai > (BN, L) *hibai*, (B, G, AN, Z, R) *ibai* 'river' ~ Godoberi *inχːi* 'river, brook', Kabardian psə-χʷa 'river', etc. < PNC *jimχwĂ (= **7.55**)

9. Vowel Correspondences

Although some details remain to be resolved, numerous examples verify the general trends. Because most of the comparisons are repeated from the consonantal sections, they are reproduced in abbreviated form.[363]

Basque /a/ regularly corresponds to Caucasian *a (*ă, *ā):

9.1. Basque *ha-, -a (article, demonstrative) ~ PEC *hă demonstrative stem (NCED 436)

9.2. Basque *śale 'net, grate; stockade' ~ PEC *čɦałē 'enclosure, fence' (= **3.45**)

9.3. Basque *hac, *be-hac 'finger, paw', etc. ~ Avar kʷač 'paw', etc. < PNC *kwănVčě (= **3.66**)

9.4. Basque *apo 'hoof' ~ Bezhta, Hunzib *ap'a* 'paw', etc. < PNC *HapV̆ (= **1.9**)

9.5. Basque *u-dagera 'otter' ~ PEC *darq̇wV 'weasel, marten, ermine' (= **2.19**)

9.6. Basque *i-sār 'star', etc. ~ PNC *ʒwăhrī 'star' (= **3.28**)

9.7. Basque *śabel 'belly, stomach' ~ PNC *ǯăbV 'kidney, liver' (= **1.25**)

9.8. Basque *laśto 'straw' ~ PEC *λačă 'leaf; a kind of plant' (= **3.49**)

9.9. Basque *lam- 'to lick' ~ Andi *lam-* 'to lick', etc. < PEC *łamV (= **8.13**)

9.10. Basque *śagu 'mouse' ~ PNC *cārgwī 'weasel, marten, mouse' (= **3.1.a**)

9.11. Basque *apal 'shelf' ~ PEC *ʔapVłV 'pole; board, cover' (= **1.6**)

---

[363] Cross-references in this section will only be to the *first* occurrence of a comparison. For all occurrences see the index in Appendix C.

9.12. Basque **hari* / **hal-* 'thread' ~ PEC **χāłV* 'sinew, thread' (= **7.43**)

9.13. Basque **haundi* 'big, great' ~ Proto-Circassian **kʰʷa(n)də* 'much, many' (= **5.2**)

9.14. Basque **tak-hoin* 'heel (of a shoe)' ~ PNC **dHāqwĀ* 'back of head', etc. (= **2.15**)

9.15. Basque **haice* 'tree'~ PNC **Hă(r)ǯwī* 'tree' (= **3.71**)

9.16. Basque **garhi* 'thin' ~ PEC **q̇warHV* 'narrow' (= **6.29**)

9.17. Basque **ha[n]ar̄,* (R) *ãr* 'worm' ~ PEC **ɦabarV* 'worm' (= **7.70**)

9.18. Basque **gau* 'night' ~ Proto-Lezgian **χ:am:* 'night, evening' (= **7.56**)

9.19. Basque **arhe* 'harrow' ~ PEC **ɓarhV = *γarhV* 'harrow' (= **7.63**)

9.20. Basque **haga* 'long pole' ~ PEC **hăk̇wV* > Karata *hak'ʷa* 'branch', etc. (= **5.20**)

9.21. Basque **har̄-* 'to take, receive' ~ Archi *kar-* 'to take with', etc. < PNC **=ikĀr* (= **5.4**)

In several cases, Basque /a/ corresponds to Caucasian **e,* in the environment of a liquid or (original) lateral affricate:

9.22. Basque **be-lar̄i* 'ear' ~ PNC **łĕHłe* 'ear' (= **8.55**)

9.23. Basque **e-ar̄i* 'to sit; set, put' ~ PNC **=eʔ(w)Vr* (= **8.31.b**)

9.24. Basque **sahar̄* 'old' ~ PNC **swĕrho* 'old, year' (= **7.7**)

9.25. Basque **har̄i* 'stone' ~ PEC **χHĕrχV* 'small stone, gravel' (= **7.44**)

9.26. Basque **lar̄i* 'sadness, anguish' ~ PNC **ƛwĕrV* 'hard, severe, stern' (= **4.13**)

9.27. Basque **lape* 'shelter of a shed' ~ PEC **λ̇ĕpV* 'stone plate or shed' (= **1.7**)

9.28. Basque **lanbro* 'fog, mist' ~ PEC **r̆ĕnλ̇wV* 'cloud, fog' (= **4.3.b**)

9.29. Basque **ɦardo* 'tinder' ~ PEC **ʔwēλ̣V* 'a kind of grass' (= **4.19**)

Basque /e/ corresponds to Caucasian **e* and **ə:*

9.30. Basque *beko 'forehead, beak' ~ PEC *bĕḳwo 'part of face, mouth' (= **1.16**)

9.31. Basque *leka 'bean pod, husk' ~ PNC *lĕḳV 'seed, grain' (= **5.18**)

9.32. Basque *belha-r̄ 'grass, hay' ~ PEC *u̯elɣV 'nettle, burdock' (= **7.40**)

9.33. Basque *erdi 'half, middle' ~ PNC *=ĕƛĔ 'half, middle' (= **4.18**)

9.34. Basque *elhe 'speech, word' ~ PEC *lĕHwV 'word' (= **8.86**)

9.35. Basque *nega- 'tear(s), weeping; herpes' ~ PEC *nĕwq̇ŭ 'tear, pus' (= **6.31**)

9.36. Basque *gośe 'hunger, hungry' ~ PNC *gašē 'hunger' (= **5.22**)

9.37. Basque *habe 'pillar, beam' ~ PEC *hwĕbē 'post, pole, tower' (= **1.24**)

9.38. Basque *śale 'net, grate; stockade' ~ PEC *čʰatē 'enclosure, fence' (= **3.45**)

9.39. Basque *selHai 'field, meadow' ~ PEC *ʒəlV 'plain, plateau' (= **3.31**)

9.40. Basque *se > (B-arc) ze 'not'[364] ~ PEC *ʒə́ 'not' (NCED 1101)

9.41. Basque *lema 'rudder' ~ PEC *ƛəmʔV̆ 'roof' (= **4.10**)

9.42. Basque *her̄i 'inhabited place, people' ~ PNC *ʔwə̆hri 'people, troop' (= **6.46**)

9.43. Basque *behi 'cow' ~ PEC *bħərc̣'wV 'cattle' (= **1.15**)

9.44. Basque *hegi 'ridge, border' ~ PEC *ħwə̄rgē 'mountain ridge' (= **8.40**)

Basque /e/ also corresponds to the infrequent Caucasian phoneme *ü:

9.45. Basque *beśo 'arm' ~ PEC *wṹšV 'hand, finger' (= **7.22**)

9.46. Basque *a-bere / *a-bel- 'cattle' ~ PNC *bṹɫV 'horned animal' (= **1.23**)

Basque /i/ corresponds to Caucasian *i and *ɨ:

---

[364] Common Basque *ez* 'not' (negative particle).

9.47. Basque **hil* 'dead; die; kill' ~ PNC **=iwƛĔ* 'die; kill' (= **4.26**)

9.48. Basque **bizar̄* 'beard' ~ PEC **bilʒ́V* 'beard' (= **1.13**)

9.49. Basque **e-beni* 'to put'[365] ~ PEC **ʔima(n)* 'to stay, be' (NCED 210)

9.50. Basque **ise-* 'aunt' ~ PEC **=īlć̣wī* 'girl, woman' (= **3.39**)

9.51. Basque **bi-si* 'life, alive' ~ Lak *s:iħ* 'breath, vapor', etc. < PNC **s̱ĭHwV* (= **7.13**)

9.52. Basque **sikiro* 'castrated ram' ~ PNC **ǯikV̆* 'goat, kid' (= **3.29**)

9.53. Basque **hic* 'word' ~ Chechen *=ic-* 'to tell', etc. < PNC **=[ī]mcŬ* (= **3.8**)

9.54. Basque **miko* 'little (bit)' ~ PEC **miḳwV* 'small, young one' (= **5.14**)

9.55. Basque **ti-(pi)* 'little, small' ~ Avar *hit'ína-b* 'small', etc. < PNC **ṭiHV / *HiṭV* (= **2.4**)

9.56. Basque **lisun* 'moldy, musty, mustiness' ~ PEC **ƛwilc̣wV* 'dirt; bog, marsh' (= **4.1**)

9.57. Basque **iculi* 'to turn, turn over, return', etc. ~ PEC **=ī rcVl* 'to twirl, turn round' (= **3.10**)

9.58. Basque **siminc(a)* 'bedbug' ~ PNC **miʒĂ / *ʒimiʒĂ* 'stinging insect' (= **3.32**)

9.59. Basque **čimiča* 'bedbug' ~ PEC **ć̣imVć̣V* 'butterfly' (= **3.53**)

9.60. Basque **hiri* 'village, city' ~ PNC **kiłū* 'farmstead, hut' (= **5.3**)

9.61. Basque **i-lhinti* 'firebrand' - PEC **ƛwindV* 'firewood' (= **7.33**)

9.62. Basque **lirdi* 'drivel, saliva' ~ PEC **ƛ̣wirdɨ* 'manure, pus' (= **2.24**)

9.63. Basque **kino* 'bad odor' ~ PNC **ḵwɨ̆nħV* 'smoke' (= **5.13**)

9.64. Basque **i-hinc* 'dew' ~ PEC **xwɨ̆mcwī* 'dirt, bog' (= **3.16**)

9.65. Basque **lirain* 'slender' ~ PNC **=iƛ̣ɨlV* 'thin' (= **4.6**)

9.66. Basque **an-his-pa* 'sister (of a woman)' ~ PNC **=ɨ̆c̣í* 'sister, brother' (= **3.37**)

---

[365] Standard *ipini*, (AN, B, G) *ipiñi*, (B, BN, Sal) *imiñi* 'to put, place'. Cf. Burushaski *man-* 'to be, become', etc.

9.67. Basque *ḣośin 'depth of water' ~ PEC *ʔwīnc̣V̆ < *wic̣i nV 'well, spring' (= **3.2**)

9.68. Basque *ni 'I' (1st. person singular) ~ PEC *nĭ 'I' (1st. person singular) (= **8.22.b**)

Basque /o/ corresponds to Caucasian *o, also to Caucasian *e, *ə, *i, and *ɨ (in labial environments). Note the convergent developments (> o) in some Caucasian languages:

9.68. Basque *ośo 'whole, complete' ~ PNC *=ḣŏc̣V 'full, fill' (= **3.24**)

9.69. Basque *a-ćo 'old woman' ~ PNC *c̣wŏjV 'woman, female' (= **3.21**)

9.70. Basque *kola in gar-kola, gar-khora 'nape' ~ PEC *qHwŏɬwV 'neck, collar' (= **6.2**)

9.71. Basque *onci 'vessel, container; boat, ship' ~ PEC *bōnʒ(w)V 'vessel' (= **1.21**)

9.72. Basque *sori 'fortune, luck', etc. ~ PNC *ʒōɬV 'healthy, whole' (= **3.33**)

9.73. Basque *hobi 'gum(s) (of mouth)' ~ PNC *ḣŏmGwĭ 'throat, mouth' (= **6.28**)

9.74. Basque *śoī- 'body' (in compounds) ~ PEC *čōrχV 'body' (= **3.46**)

9.75. Basque *oćo 'wolf' ~ PNC *bħĕrc̣ĭ 'wolf' > Andi boc'o, etc. (=**1.22**)

9.76. Basque *hor 'dog' ~ PEC *χHwĕjrV- 'dog' > Budukh χor, etc. (= **7.42**)

9.77. Basque *erdoil 'rust' ~ PEC *λ̣wĕɬʔĕ 'mould' (= **4.16**)

9.78. Basque *gogoī 'hard' ~ PEC *GwērV 'stone' (= **6.19**)

9.79. Basque *čoru 'root of hair' ~ PEC *c̣ħwərV 'hair' > Avar č'or, etc. (= **3.55**)

9.80. Basque *a-lhon- / *a-lhoī 'seed, grain' ~ PEC *λwīnʔɨ 'seed' > Avar xon, etc. (= **7.32**)

9.81. Basque *čori / *čol- 'bird' ~ PEC *čHwīlV > Chamalal č'or 'bird', etc. (= **3.56.a**)

9.82. Basque *a-ho 'mouth' ~ PNC *χwɨ-m(V)ṗV 'mouthful' > Khinalug χob (= **7.47**)

9.83. Basque **olho* 'oats' ~ PNC **λwĭwV* 'millet' > Chechen *ho?*, etc. (= **7.31**)

9.84. Basque **hoc* 'cold' ~ Hinukh =*oč'č'u* 'cold', etc. < PNC **(r)HEčwV / *čwE(r)HV* 'cold' (= **3.67**)

Basque /u/ corresponds to Caucasian **u, *wV, *Vw*. Note the convergent developments (> *u*) in some Caucasian languages:

9.84. Basque **sumhV* 'elm, tree' ~ PEC **ǯhŭmV* 'bush, quince', etc. (= **3.69.a**)
9.85. Basque **su* 'you' (polite) ~ PNC **źwĕ* 'you' (plural) > Lak *zu*, etc. (NCED 1086)
9.86. Basque **mulho* 'petite colline, eminence, butte' ~ PEC **muɦalV* 'mountain' (= **8.6**)
9.87. Basque **punpula* 'tear', etc. ~ PNC **pHulqĭ* 'dirt; secretion in the eye' (= **1.4**)
9.88. Basque **huin* 'brain, marrow, pith' ~ PEC **hwĕʔnV* 'blood' ('meat') > Lak *y*, etc. (= **7.64**)
9.89. Basque **sul > *sur* 'wood, timber, lumber' ~ PEC **ǯw[ĕ]ħ* 'twig, rod, sheaf' (= **3.70**)
9.90. Basque **ɦänsūr* 'bone' ~ PEC **rīmswe (*mswīre)* 'rib > side' > Agul *sur*, etc. (= **7.15**)
9.91. Basque **a-hun-* 'kid' ~ PEC **kwīʔnī* 'ram' > Andi *kun*, etc. (= **5.8.a**)
9.92. Basque **hur* 'water' ~ PEC **ɦwĭlV* 'river, reservoir' > Lezgi *hül*, etc. (= **7.74**)
9.93. Basque **susun* 'poplar, aspen' ~ PNC **swĭnē* > Lak *sunū*, 'pomegranate' (= **7.9**)
9.94. Basque **gurhi* 'butter, fat' ~ PEC **χwĭlʔi* 'fat, meat' > Tabasaran :*ul*, etc. (= **7.57**)
9.95. Basque **sursu-* 'nape' ~ PEC **ćwĭrsV* 'gullet' > Dargwa (Akushi) *surs* (= **3.36**)
9.96. Basque **gʷune* 'place, space' ~ PNC **GwinʔV* 'village, house' > Tsez *qun*, etc. (= **6.24**)
9.97. Basque **tuntun* 'Basque drum' ~ PNC **dwə̆nʔV* 'drum' (= **2.17**)
9.98. Basque **lurün* 'odor' ~ PNC **λwəɬʔV* 'wind, breeze' > Lezgi *ful*, etc. (= **7.29**)

9.99. Basque **a-hūr* 'hollow of hand, palm' ~ PEC **kHwə̄rV* 'pit' > Dargwa *kur*, etc. (= **5.7**)

9.100. Basque **sülfio* 'hole, burrow' ~ PEC **s̱wōtV* > Avar *šulu* 'pipe', etc. (= **7.17**)

9.101. Basque **tutu* 'tube, pipe', etc. ~ PEC **dfiwōdwō* 'tube, pipe' > Lak *dụdu*, etc. (= **2.16**)

9.102. Basque **bulhaī* 'chest, breast' ~ PEC **Gwǎlfiē* 'udder, breast' (= **6.27**)

9.103. Basque **i-dul-ki* 'block of wood' ~ PEC **dwǎłĩ* 'stick' > Dargwa *t:ult:a* 'tree' (= **2.23**)

9.104. Basque **e-lhu-ī* 'snow' ~ PEC **λĭwV* 'snow' (= **7.34**)

10. Syllabic Structures

The syllabic structure of PDC nouns was typically CV(C)CV, and traces of this original pattern are frequent in Basque and some Caucasian (Dagestanian) languages:[366]

The following examples represent the structure with final high-front vowel **CV(C)Ci/e:**

- Basque *hiri* 'village, city' ~ Avar *kulí* 'farmstead' (= **5.3**)
- Basque *behi* 'cow' (< **bexi*) ~ Avar *bóc':i* 'cattle' (= **1.15**)
- Basque *garhi, gari* 'thin' ~ Avar *q':ʷarí*-da-b 'narrow, cramped', etc. (= **6.29**)
- Basque *azeri, azegari* 'fox' ~ Tindi *sari*, Akhwakh *šari* 'fox' (= **3.5**)
- Basque *bihi* 'grain, seed, kernel' ~ Tindi, Karata *beč'i-n* 'barley' (= **1.17**)
- Basque *txori* /čori/ 'bird' ~ Tindi *čuri*-ɓaɓa 'quail' (= **3.56**)
- Basque *erdi* 'half, middle' ~ Tindi b-*a ⁄:i* 'in the middle' (= **4.18**)
- Basque *ontzi, untzi* 'vessel, container; boat, ship' ~ Karata *muc':i* 'jar, pot' (= **1.21**)

---

[366] Note that in the cited cases Basque and Caucasian words have similar final vowels (i/e = i/e; u/o = u/o).

- Basque *herri* 'inhabited place, people' ~ PNC *ʔw ˄˘hri 'people, troop' (= **6.46**)
- Basque *hobi* 'gum(s) (of mouth)' ~ PNC *ɦŏmG̱wĭ 'throat, mouth' (= **6.28**)
- Basque *ilhinti* 'firebrand' ~ Andi V*udi*, Chamalal V*unni* 'firewood' (= **7.33**)
- Basque *ipurdi* 'rump' ~ Bezhta *pirt'i* 'bladder, lung', Archi p*art'i* 'intestine' (= **1.5**)
- Basque *lerde, lirdi* 'drivel, saliva' ~ PEC *λ̱wirdɨ 'manure, pus' (= **2.24**)
- Basque *gur(h)i(n)* 'butter, fat' ~ PEC *χwɨ̆lʔi > Dargwa ħ*a*li 'fat', etc. (= **7.57**)
- Basque *ziri-n* 'diarrhea, excrement' ~ Akhwakh *šili* 'sheep's dung' < PEC *siɫɨ (= **7.18**)
- Basque *hegi* 'ridge, edge' ~ Dargwa (Akushi) *urqi* 'mountains' (= **8.40**)
- Basque (B,G) *loki* 'temple (of head)' ~ PEC *⋎ arq̇wĕ 'forehead' (= **4.4**)
- Basque *gose* 'hunger, hungry' ~ Lak *k:aši*, Dargwa *gaši* 'hunger' (= **5.22**)
- Basque *abere* 'cattle, domestic animal(s)' ~ Udi *bele* 'cattle' (= **1.23**)
- Basque *habe* 'pillar, beam' ~ Avar ħ*ubí* 'post, pole, stem' (= **1.24**)
- Basque *sarc, sale* 'net, grate; stockade' ~ Avar *čalí* 'fence' (= **3.45**)
- Basque *ar(h)e* 'harrow, rake' ~ Avar γ*ár*-ize 'to harrow', γ*ári* 'wooden ladder' (= **7.63**)
- Basque (R) *atze* 'tree' ~ Hinukh *aže* 'tree' (= **3.71**)
- Basque *el(h)e* 'speech, word' ~ Inkhokhwari *loje* 'word, sound, voice' (= **8.86**)

Note that the designations of three major organs of the human head are of this type both in Basque and in Caucasian:

- Basque *be-larri* 'ear' ~ Dargwa (Tsudakhar) *laħi*, (Akushi, Urakhi) *liħi* 'ear' (= **8.55**)
- Basque *begi* 'eye' ~ Dargwa (Akushi, Urakhi) *ħuli* 'eye' (NCED 250)
- Basque *mihi* 'tongue' ~ Tindi *mic:i*, Akhwakh *mic':i* 'tongue' (= **3.19**)

The following examples represent the structure with final back-round vowel **CV(C)Cu/o**:

- Basque *sagu* 'mouse' ~ Avar *ca ∨́:u*, Andi *sar ∨:u* 'weasel', etc. (= **3.1.a**)
- Basque *itsu* 'blind' ~ Tindi *=ec:u*-b 'blind', etc. (= **3.4**)
- Basque *txainku* [čä́jŋkü], *xanku* [šanku] 'lame' ~ Burushaski *čhaŋgú, čaŋgú* 'lame' (= **3.57**)
- Basque *tutu* 'tube, roll, pipe', etc. ~ PEC **dħwōdwō* 'tube, pipe' > Lak *dudu*, etc. (= **2.16**)
- Basque *zulo* 'hole, burrow' ~ PEC **ṣwōɬV* > Avar *šulu* 'pipe', etc. (= **7.17**)
- Basque *mul(h)o* 'petite colline, eminence, butte' ~ Hinukh *malu* 'mountain' (= **8.6**)
- Basque *ukondo* 'elbow' ~ Hinukh, Khwarshi *q'ontu* 'knee', etc. (= **6.13**)
- Basque *ziho* 'fat, tallow' ~ Tindi *c'inɬu-* 'fat' (adj) (= **3.12**)
- Basque (L) *miko* 'a little (bit)' ~ Chamalal *mik'u*-b 'small' (= **5.14**)
- Basque (B) *kankano* 'stone, kernel, almond' ~ Avar *k'ork'ónu* 'grape, berry' (= **5.10**)
- Basque *otso* 'wolf' ~ Andi *boc'o*, Bezhta *bac'o* 'wolf', etc. (= **1.22**)
- Basque *sorho, solo* 'meadow, field' ~ Lak *šalu* 'earth, ground' (= **3.44**)

The following examples represent the structure with final /a/ **CV(C)Ca**:

- Basque *udagara* 'otter' ~ Andi *darɢʷa* 'weasel, marten' (= **2.19**)
- Basque *tximitxa* [čimiča] 'bedbug' ~ Andi *č'emerč'a* 'butterfly' (= **3.53**)
- Basque *haga* 'long pole' ~ Karata *hak'ʷa* 'branch' (= **5.20**)
- Basque *lema* 'rudder' (< '*board') ~ Bezhta *ƛama* 'roof' (= **4.10**)
- Basque *erreka* 'ravine, rivulet, arroyo' ~ Tindi *rek̓:a* 'gorge, ravine' (= **6.18**)
- Basque *leka* 'bean pod, husk' ~ Lak *lač'a* 'wheat' (= **5.18**)
- Basque *aska* 'crib, manger, trough' ~ Tabasaran *č'aq'a* 'wooden jar' < PNC *$\hat{c}\tilde{a}\dot{q}w\breve{a}$ / $\hat{c}\tilde{a}qw\breve{a}$ (= **3.62**)

In the remaining DC languages (Sino-Tibetan, Yeniseian, Na-Dene) there is a strong tendency to reduce all words to monosyllabic forms, or at least to reduce syllables by apocope or syncope. Indeed, this tendency to reduce syllables is found to varying degrees in all DC branches.

Apocope: For example, final vowels posited for PDC have frequently been lost in Basque, particularly when a root contains a nasal or rhotic. PNC/PEC reconstructions represent the earlier stage:

- Basque **sain* 'nerve, blood vessel' ~ PEC *$\underline{s}\bar{e}ħmV$ 'muscle, intestine' (= **7.6**)
- Basque **huin* 'brain, marrow, pith' ~ PEC *$hw\breve{e}ʔnV$ 'blood' ('meat') (= **7.64**)
- Basque **muin* 'marrow, brain, pith' ~ PEC *$m\breve{a}hn\bar{u}$ 'brain, head' (= **8.7**)
- Basque **hor* 'dog' ~ PEC *$\chi Hw\breve{e}jrV$- 'dog' > Budukh *χor*, etc. (= **7.42**)
- Basque **ha[n]ar̄* 'worm' ~ PEC *$ħabarV$ 'worm' ~ Burushaski *har* 'corn-worm' (= **7.70**)
- Basque **ar̄* 'male' ~ PEC *$ʔīrλwV$ 'male' ~ Burushaski *hir* 'man, husband' (= **6.36**)
- Basque **i-sar̄* 'star' ~ PNC *$ʒw\breve{a}hr\bar{\i}$ 'star' (= **3.28**)

Syncope: In a number of cases, all involving internal clusters with -ś- (-śk-, -śt-, -śn-) an original stem vowel has been eliminated in Basque. Caucasian and Burushaski forms represent the earlier stage:

- Basque *eśku 'hand' < *e-śVgu ~ PEC *ćəgwV / *gwəćV 'arm' (= **3.41**)
- Basque *a(r)śto 'donkey' < *a(r)-śVdo ~ Ubykh čədə, PAbkhazian *čada 'donkey' ~ Burushaski *ćhardV 'stallion' (= **3.48**)
- Basque *a(r)śka 'crib, manger, trough' < *a(r)-śVka ~ Ubykh čaq̇ʷə́ 'basin, tureen', etc. < PNC *c̣ä̃q̇wă / c̣ã́q̇wă ~ Burushaski (Y) ćhiq 'sifting tray' (= **3.62**)
- Basque *aśko, *aśki 'much, enough' < *a-śVko, *a-śVki ~ Kabardian -šxʷa 'big', Lak č'a̱-u- 'many', etc. < PNC *čHəqwV ~ Burushaski (Y) çik, çiq 'all, altogether' (= **3.64**)
- Basque *ośki 'shoe' < *o-śVki ~ PEC *šwŏq̇HwV > Tabasaran šaq'ʷ 'heel' ~ Burushaski ṣoq 'sole of shoe' (= **6.16**)
- Basque *eśtu 'narrow' < *e-śVdu ~ Dargwa čarṭa, Andi č:iṭir 'narrow', etc. < PEC *čHVrdV (= **2.25**)
- Basque esne, ezne 'milk' < *e-śVne ~ PEC *šä̃mʔV > Tindi š:ū 'milk', Chechen šin 'udder', etc. ~ Burushaski ṣiŋ 'milk, proceeds of milk' (= **7.23**)

A similar kind of syncope takes place with words containing rhotic + velar:

- Basque *erbi 'hare', erbi-nude 'weasel' < *e-rVgʷi ~ PNC *r̃igwӐ 'weasel, mouse' (= **5.27**)
- Basque *ergi 'steer, young ox, bull calf' < *e-rVGi ~ PNC *rVxwV 'cattle' (= **7.41**)

Verbal stems: Because of the typical structure of DC verbs, with both prefixes and suffixes surrounding the verb root, it is very common (especially in the Vasco-Caucasian subgroup) for verbal roots to become "squeezed" and truncated into very short forms, sometimes with only one consonant. The maximal form of the Proto-Caucasian verbal root was

*(H)V(R)CV(R) (NCED, p. 87), though in many cases it manifested simply as *-VCV(R) or even *-VCV. Note the following comparisons:

- Basque *e-gi-n 'to do, make', also auxiliary verb ~ Agul aq'- 'to do, make', etc. < PNC *=$H\breve{o}\dot{q}E$ (= **6.33**)
- Basque *$eiho$ 'to grind' ~ Andi $?i\chi^w o$-qi- 'to grind', etc. < PNC *$H\breve{e}m\chi wV$ 'to grind' (= **7.51**)
- Basque *$eiho$ 'to beat' ~ Rutul =$\dot{a}\chi a$- 'to beat, hit', etc. < PNC *$H\bar{\imath}r\chi A$ (= **7.52**)
- Basque *$eihu$-n 'to weave' ~ Dargwa =$im\chi$-/=$um\chi$- 'to plait, weave', etc. PEC *=$ir\chi wVn$ 'to knit, weave, spin' (= **7.53**)
- Basque *e-$ka\bar{r}i$ 'to bring' ~ Archi :a- 'to drag, carry', etc. < PNC *=$H\bar{\imath}qV(r)$ (= **6.4**)
- Basque *e-$to\bar{r}i$ 'to come' ~ Avar $t'ur$- 'to run away', etc. < PEC *=$\breve{\imath}\underset{.}{t}Vr$ (= **2.8**)
- Basque *e-te-n 'to break, cut' ~ > Hunzib =it'- 'to divide', Tsakhur =$et'a$- 'to break', etc. < PEC *=$\breve{\imath}\underset{.}{t}V$ 'to cut, divide' (= **2.9**)
- Basque *e-can 'to lie down, rest, put down' ~ Agul $c'a$- 'to give', etc. < PNC *=$i\underset{.}{c}\breve{A}$ (= **3.14**)
- Basque *e-$u\acute{c}i$ 'to take hold, seize, grasp' ~ Dargwa =$u\check{c}$- 'to gather, collect', etc. < PNC *=$\breve{a}\check{c}w\breve{V}$ (= **3.51**)
- Basque *e-$culi$ 'to turn, turn over, return', etc. ~ Agul $ilcan$- 'to turn (on an axis)', etc. < PEC *=$\bar{\imath}rcVl$ 'to twirl, turn round' (= **3.10**)
- Basque *isa-n 'to be' ~ Chechen =is- 'to stay', Ubykh -s- 'to sit, lie', etc. < PNC *=$\tilde{a}sV$ (= **7.12**)
- Basque *e-aki-n > $jakin$ 'to know (a fact)' ~ Akhwakh =$e\dot{q}$- 'to know', Khwarshi =$i\dot{q}$- 'to know', etc. < PNC *=$\breve{\imath}\dot{q}E$ 'to know, hear' ~ Burushaski $hákin$, -ki- 'to learn' (= **6.15**)
- Basque *e-$augi$-n > $jaugin, jin$ 'to come') ~ Hinukh =aq'- 'to come', Dargwa (Chirag) =$u\dot{q}'$- 'to go', etc. < PNC *=$Hu\dot{q}\breve{U}n$ (= **6.34**)

The Basque forms cited are perfective participles, which are the usual citation forms in dictionaries.

11. Irregular Changes: Metathesis, Assimilation, Dissimilation

Besides the many regular changes described above, we must acknowledge that seemingly "irregular" processes are also at work in linguistic change, namely *metathesis, assimilation*, and *dissimilation*.

Metathesis is quite frequent in Caucasian languages, apparently because their phonetic systems are so complex, that the relative *order* of phonetic segments is less important than in languages with simple systems. A single Caucasian language or dialect can have two variants of the same common word: for example, in the Akushi dialect of Dargwa, 'tongue' can be *mez* or *lezmi*, while in most other Dargwa dialects one or the other variant is preferred: Chirag *mec:*, Urakhi *miʒ*, vs. Kadar *limzi*, Kaitag *luc:umi*,etc. (see NCED 802). The phonetic system of present-day Basque is much simpler than that of any Caucasian language, but even in Basque some metathetic variants are known between the dialects. 'Liver' is *gibel* in most Basque, but also *bigel* in Alto Navarro. 'To seem, appear' varies between *iduri* and *irudi*, 'otter' is *udagara, ugadara* (and others: see **2.19**), 'butterfly' is *mitxeleta* or *tximeleta*.[367] It should not be surprising that if there are cognates between Basque and Caucasian, some would involve metathesis, thus:

- Basque **fiänsur̄* 'bone' **vs.** PEC **r̃imswe* 'side, rib', but Rutul *sur* presupposing **mswīre* (**7.15**)
- Basque **lanbro* 'fog' vs. PEC **rĕn ⊻ wV̆* 'cloud, fog'; **lanbro* fits well with metathesized PEC **⊻ĕnwrV* (4.3)
- Basque **u-dagera* 'otter' vs. PEC **darq̇wV* 'weasel, marten, ermine' (2.19)
- Basque **olaic* 'beestings, colostrum' vs. Khinalug *loži* 'to pour', etc. < PNC **=HoǯĂ̄l* (3.75)
- Basque **eśku* 'hand' vs. PEC **gwəćV* 'arm' (but Khinalug *čigin* < **ćəgwV*) (3.41)

---

[367] Trask 1997, pp. 168-169.

- Basque *lotu 'to tie' vs. PNC *jeṭal- (but Lezgi ilit'- presupposes *jelaṭ-) (**8.54**)

The following examples involve metathesis of laryngeals:

- Basque *saha̅r 'old' **vs.** PNC *swĕrho 'old, year' (**7.7**)
- Basque *laha̅r 'bramble, creeping plant' **vs.** PNC *⩘wɨrʡV 'leaf' (**4.11**)
- Basque *čahal 'calf' **vs.** PEC *Hc̕wɨ̅lV / *Hlɨ̅c̕wV̂ (**3.54**)
- Basque *čehume 'half-span' **vs.** PNC *čwimħV 'span' (**3.58**)
- Basque *leher̅ 'pine' **vs.** PEC *λ̣ħwałū 'a kind of tree' (**7.28**)
- Basque *bilho 'hair' **vs.** PNC *ṗVħVɬV 'feather, mane' (**1.8**)
- Basque *mulho 'petite colline, eminence, butte' **vs.** PEC *muħalV 'mountain'(**8.6**)
- Basque *alha 'grazing, pasture'; *alha-tu 'to graze, to feed' **vs.** Kryz ʕül- 'to eat', etc. < PEC *=iʡwVl (**6.47**)
- Basque *ilhar̅ 'vetch, peas, beans' **vs.** Avar holó 'bean(s)', etc. < PEC *hōwł[ā] (**7.69**)
- Basque *sorho 'meadow', etc. **vs.** PEC *c̣Häłu 'earth, ground' (**3.44**)
- Basque *sumhV 'elm, tree' **vs.** PEC *ǯħŭmV 'bush, grass' (**3.69**)
- Basque *ħodäi 'cloud' **vs.** PEC *dwiHV 'wind' (**2.22**)

For metathesis of vowels, cf.:

Basque *ugari 'abundant' / *ugal-du 'to increase, multiply' **vs.** PNC *HāχułV / *HālχV 'big, long' (**7.60**)

Assimilation and *dissimilation* come into play mainly in words that have two liquids (or lateral affricates) in both languages:

- Basque *lur̅ 'earth' vs. PNC *lhĕmɫwɨ̆ > Avar raλ':, etc.(**8.52**)
- Basque *erori 'to fall' vs. PNC *HraλwE 'to fall' > Budukh araxa-, etc. (NCED 602)

- Basque *loŕ 'hauling; track, trace, footprint' vs. PNC *λĕtɬV 'foot, track' (7.26)
- Basque *leheŕ 'pine' vs. Avar ɬ:alú 'yew tree', etc. < PEC **λ̰ɦwatū (7.28)
- Basque *be-lhaun, *be-lhaur- 'knee'[368] vs. PEC *λ̃wilV 'elbow' (NCED 770) [369]
- Basque *lahaŕ ~ (Z) nahar, (Sal) naar, (R) nar 'bramble, creeping thorn' vs. PNC *λ̰wɨrHV 'leaf' (4.11)
- Basque *laŕu 'skin,' etc. ~ (B) narru vs. PNC *Łoli > Avar λ̃':er (4.12)

In these examples we see the interchange of laterals and rhotics, as well as alternation of ordinary laterals /l/ with lateral fricatives /ɬ/ or lateral affricates /λ̃, Ł/.

Without external comparison, it is difficult or impossible to tell which language (if any) retains the original form. In the last two examples we find another kind of dissimilation /l/ > /n/ in some of the Basque words. For a typological parallel, cf. Icelandic *lykill*, (west) Norwegian *lykel*, vs. Swedish *nyckel*, Danish *nøgle* 'key'.

12. Some Special Cases

12.1. Basque *bi 'two' > (c) bi, (BN, L, Z) bi-ga, (AN-Baztan, BN-Aldude, Sal) bi-da ~ Udi p:a̰, Ubykh t̰q́ʷa, Khinalug ḳu, etc. < PNC *q̰Hwā̃ 'two' (NCED 924); Chirikba postulates PWC *dɢʷə (CWC 395).[370]

The longer forms *biga, bida* occur only in northern dialects as a noun phrase or in counting, beside *bi* which occurs everywhere (Trask 1997, p. 273). Despite a superficial resemblance to Latin *bi-* 'two' (as a prefix, < *dwi-*), *bis* 'twice', Basque *bi is generally regarded as a native word. The Udi form *p:a̰* 'two' shows that a labial occlusive can come from a

---

[368] (BN,L) *belhaun*, (B,G,AN) *belaun*, (Z) *belhain, belhañ*, (R) *belain*. The stem variant *bel(h)aur-* appears in words such as (BN, R) *bel(h)aurikatu*, (Z) [belhájka] 'to kneel', (AN, BN) *bel(h)auriko*, (Z) [belhájko] 'on one's knees', etc. The ordinary stem *bel(h)aun* can be derived from *be-lhaul-n*, with a fossilized suffix possibly cognate with the PNC oblique stem marker *nV (Starostin 2002).

[369] Akhwakh *eλelo*, Tsez *horu*, Agul q:ar-*xil*, etc.

[370] Contrasting with PWC *tqɪ́:ʷA (NCED 924).

labialised uvular *qHw. In Basque the derivation is very likely from something like *gʷi < PDC *ɢʷi (or sim.) The -ga, -da suffixes in northern Basque may have parallels in Avar-Andian, e.g. Avar k'i-go, Akhwakh k'e-da 'two.'

12.2. Basque *begi 'eye' ~ Chechen bʕärg, Avar ber, Hunzib hare, Lak ja, Dargwa ħuli, ʕule, ule, Tabasaran ul, Khinalug pil, Ubykh bɮa, etc. 'eye' < PNC *ʔwĭlʔi (NCED 250) ~ Burushaski -lčin, -lči 'eye', il-, -il 'eye' (in compounds such as il-gaṭ 'corner of the eye', ṣiq-il 'light-eyed, gray-eyed').

As mentioned in Chapter 10, the words for three important organs of the human head are parallel in form in Basque, East Caucasian, and West Caucasian:[371]

- Basque *mi(n)hi 'tongue' ~ PEC *mĕlči 'tongue' ~ PWC *bəźA 'tongue' (**3.19**)
- Basque *be-lari 'ear' ~ PNC *ɬĕHɬi 'ear' ~ PWC *ŁA- 'ear' (**8.55**)
- Basque *begi 'eye' ~ PEC *ʔwĭlʔi 'eye' ~ PWC *b-la 'eye'

In Basque and Caucasian, these words all end in -i. From a bewildering array of Caucasian words Nikolayev and Starostin posit *ʔwĭlʔi 'eye,' which may contain an incorporated class prefix *w (II-class sing.), and go back to something like *w-ʔĭlʔi, possibly assimilated from something like *w-ʔĭlyi. A form such as the last could be the predecessor of Basque begi, though details need to be worked out. The Burushaski forms -lči(n), il-, -il 'eye' reflect the noun root without the class prefix.

12.3. Basque *hi 'you' (familiar 'thou'); *h- second person singular agreement prefix on verbs (e.g., h-ator 'you're coming'); -k < *-ga second person singular agreement suffix (e.g., daki-k 'you know it') (Trask 1997, p. 218) ~ Chechen, Ingush, Batsbi ħo 'thou', Dargwa ħu, ʕu, ʕu̯, u̯, i, gu (in various dialects) 'thou', Tsakhur ɣu 'thou', Khinalug oχ 'thee' (dative), etc. < PEC *ɦwV

---
[371] Bengtson 1999b.

/ *?ŏƃwV = *γwV̄ / *?ŏγwV (NCED 483) ~ Burushaski *gu-* / *gú-* / *-kú-* / *gó-* / *-kó-* / *góo-* / *-kóo-* second person singular pronominal prefix (on verbs as pronominal markers, on nouns as possessive markers).

In Burushaski and Proto-East Caucasian this stem is suppletive with another stem: Burushaski *un* 'thou' ~ PEC **u̯ō-n* 'thou' > Archi *un*, Avar *mun*, etc. (NCED 1014).[372] The suppletion was lost in Basque, which retains only the first stem mentioned above.[373] Basque *hi /* *h-* /* *-ga* are derivable from PDC *χi (*χü) / **χ-* / **-γ*, though only Caucasian has unequivocal evidence of uvulars in this word. We know from familiar European languages that pronominal forms sometimes deviate from the usual correspondences observed in nouns and verbs.

12.4. Basque (c) *adar* 'branch' (< **ardaɾ̄*) ~ Avar ʕarƛ':él 'branch, bough', Tsez *aƛ'iru* 'pod', etc. < PEC **ñăl ʕ V̵V* (NCED 508) ~ Burushaski (H, N) *yáltar* 'the upper leafy branches of a tree';[374] cf. *galtár* 'kleiner Zweig'.

Common Basque *adar* means both 'horn' and 'branch', though the Caucasian and Burushaski cognates cited above (**4.17**): Avar *ƛ:ar*, Chechen *kur*, etc. < PEC *ƛwĭrV; Burushaski *-ltúr, tur* all mean 'horn' and never 'branch'. It now seems that *adar* 'horn' and *adar* 'branch' are homonyms of two distinct origins. In both cases something like **ardaɾ̄* [aɾ̄ðaɾ̄] was dissimilated to [aðaɾ̄], orthographic *adar*. Note the parallelism of:

- Basque **ardaɾ̄* 'branch'   : Avar ʕarƛ':él 'branch' : Burushaski *yáltar* 'branches'
- Basque **ardaɾ̄* 'horn'   : Avar   *ƛ:ar* 'horn'   : Burushaski *-ltúr* 'horn'

---

[372] A similar suppletion is found in Yeniseian (see Starostin 1982, 1995).

[373] Basque does have a kind of suppletion – or suffix alternation – in the second person singular of verbs, *e.g., du-k* 'you have it (masc.)' *vs. du-n* 'you have it (fem.)'. This is the sole example of grammatical sex-marking in Basque (Trask 1997, p. 218). Whether this alternation is related to the suppletion found in Caucasian and Burushaski remains to be investigated.

[374] Berger: 'die oberen belaubten Zweige des Baums, die Krone'.

The Basque and Burushaski words for 'branch' indicate that the final resonant was *r, assimilated to *ł in Caucasian. We have seen elsewhere several examples of homonyms in Basque, e.g., *hobi 'gums' (**6.28**) and *hobi 'grave' (**7.1**); (near homonyms) *belfia-r̄ 'forehead' (**1.13**) and *belha-r̄ 'grass, hay' (**7.40**); *eiho 'grind' (**7.51**), *eiho 'beat' (**7.52**), each with distinct Caucasian cognates. This is to be expected, since the Basque sound system is so much simpler than that of Caucasian.

12.5. Basque *lau, laur 'four' ~ PWC *p'X̌'ə 'four' > Ubykh p'X̌'ə, etc. (CWC 395); PEC *bū̃nłe 'eight' > Chechen barh, Tindi biX̌':i-da, Archi meX̌e, etc. (NCED 314) ~ Burushaski alto / altác / altá / altán 'two'[375], wálto / wálti / wal- 'four', altámbo / altámbi / altám 'eight' ~ cf. ST: PST *(p)-l̃ij 'four' > Old Chinese *slhij-s, Tibetan bži, Garo bri, Miri phli, etc. (ST 3: 25).

This is apparently a very old DC numeral word. Burushaski has it in several multiples: '2, 4, 8', and áltar '20', which is carried through the vigesimal system: altó-áltar '40', iskí-áltar '60', etc. The word for 'four' has a labial prefix in three families: Burushaski w-ált-, West Caucasian *p'X̌'ə, and Sino-Tibetan *(p)-l̃ij. Basque has no prefix on 'four' (nor indeed on any numerals). These can all be reconstructed (roughly) as PDC *(b)-(V)X̌V 'four'.

12.6. Basque *gison / *gisa- > (c) gizon, (Z) gizun 'man', (combinatory form giza-); Aquitanian CISON (a name) ~ Proto-Abkhazian *qać'a 'man' (CWC 389)

A proto-form such as *ɢ[i]ć'V could account for these forms, with consonant and vowel assimilation in WC. In the corpus of Basque words discussed in this paper Basque agrees with West Caucasian (as against East Caucasian) in relatively few cases: *a(r)śto 'donkey', *bi-ska-r̄ 'back', *haundi 'big', *toki 'place'. This could be an artificial bias caused by the extensive phonetic changes in West Caucasian, making it more difficult to detect cognates.

---

[375] Different forms depending on class of the referent.

13. Conclusions

Based on the etymologies and correspondences proposed above, I suggest the following tentative outline of the early Basque phonemes:

	Occlusives		Fricatives		Resonants			
	voiceless	voiced	voiceless	voiced				
labial	p	b	(f)²⁹	β			m	
dental	t	d		ð	r	r̄	n	j
dorso-alveolar	c̄		s̄					
palatal (hissing-hushing)	ć		ś					
hushing	č		š³⁰					
lateral			ł		l		ł̄	
velar	k	g	x	γ				
laryngeal			h	ɦ				

At subsequent stages:

13.1. Voiced stops and fricatives merged in a conditioned allophonic pattern of initial stop and medial fricative: /b/ [b ~ β], /d/ [d ~ ð], /g/ [g ~ γ]. Six phonemes became three. This is how, for example, some initial fricatives became stops, *e.g.* **gurhi* 'butter, fat' < **γurhi* < **χ ^ rHV* (**7.57**). A generally similar change took place in Castilian Spanish, with Latin *v* and *b* merging, e.g. *vaca* [báka], *haber* [aβér], etc. (An areal development: see Hualde 1991.)

13.2. /x/ merged with /h/, *e.g.* **xali* > *hari* 'thread' (**7.43**), etc. The phonetic realization [x] remained sporadically (before glides) in northern dialects, e.g. [oxhja] 'the bed', [baxhja] 'the sieve' (Moutard 1975, p. 40).

13.3. /h/, corresponding most firmly to Caucasian **h* and **ɦ* (**7.64-7.76**), as well as some other laryngeals, remains as /h/ in the northern dialects (BN, L, Z), but is lost in the others. For example, **nahi* > (BN, L, Z) *nahi,* (AN, B, G, R, Sal) *nai* 'will, wish' (**7.67**).

13.4. /ɦ/ remains as /h/ in Basse Navarre and Lapurdi, but is lost in Zuberoan: cf. **ɦodäi* 'cloud, thunder' (**2.22**), **ɦaic* 'rock' (**3.17**), **ɦaise* 'wind' (**6.49**), **ɦaran* 'valley' (**6.39**), **ɦardo* 'tinder' (**4.19**), **ɦauso* 'neighbor' (**3.61**), **belɦa-r̄* 'forehead'

(**1.13**) ~ Zuberoan *odei, atx, aize, aran, ardai, aizo, belar,* respectively.

13.5. Reflexes of the three laterals differ only in medial position. Medial /l/ (= *l_1) becomes flap /r/ (merging with original /r/), remaining as /l/ in some stem variants: *e.g., *gali > gari* 'wheat' / stem variant *gal-*, etc. (see **8.61-8.76**).

13.6. /ł/ = *l_2 (possibly a velar or 'dark' *l*, as in English *fall*) remains as /l/ in all positions (though we can detect its presence only in medial position): *e.g. *euli* 'fly' (see **8.77-8.92**). The correspondence of Basque /ł/ = *l_2 to Caucasian *ł is not consistent, suggesting that the 'dark' allophone developed separately in both families.

13.7. The lateral fricative /ɬ/ in medial position becomes the cluster /lh/, merging with the earlier /lh/ resulting from *l_2 + post-velar fricative (see **8.84-8.92**): *e.g.* (BN, L, Z) *elhur, elhür* 'snow'. The cluster becomes ordinary /l/ in the non-aspirating dialects. In initial position /ɬ/ merges in all dialects with the other laterals as /l/ (see **7.25-7.34**).

The table above differs in some ways from the Pre-Basque phonological system proposed by Michelena (1961) and Trask (1995, 1997), notably in that they propose that /m/ did not exist. I think the evidence presented above (**8.1-8.19**) clearly indicates that /m/ has remained intact (with a few exceptions) from Proto-Dene-Caucasian through the present time. The alternative would be to suppose that all occurrences of PDC *m* changed to something else (**nw, *nb* ?), and then changed back to /m/. A look at the index of Basque words (Appendix D) shows that there are in fact more words with initial *m-* than initial *n-*.

Another vasconist dictum that needs to be re-examined is the claim that "[w]ith just a tiny handful of possible exceptions, the Basque aspiration is not etymological – that is, *h* does not continue an earlier segment …the aspiration originated as a suprasegmental feature."[376] It is indeed true that *some* instances of aspiration came about in the latter manner, but clearly not all. We have seen above (**5.1-5.8**) that one of the sources of Basque /h/ was the Dene-Caucasian velar stop *k*, definitely segmental. Other sources were PDC *χ (**7.42-7.63**), *ʔ (**6.45-6.47**), *f (**7.1-7.5**), and *h (*ɦ) (**7.64-7.76**). Moutard's recordings of the strong fricative [x] (**13.2**) verify the segmental nature of the phoneme /h/.

---

[376] Trask 1997, p. 158.

Michelena has provided us a tremendous service in cataloguing the diverse phonetic forms of the Basque dialects, and giving us some direction in understanding the changes. Michelena did not accept the relationship between Basque and Caucasian, and thus could not apply external comparison to the problems of Basque phonology. In his defense, I would point out that in his lifetime the materials on Caucasian languages were very sparse, with no deep reconstructions. We now have a significant advantage because of new sources and reconstructions of Caucasian languages that are now available (Nikolayev & Starostin 1994, Chirikba 1996). For Burushaski we now have the definitive books by Berger (1974, 1998). With these materials we now have a solid basis of what to compare from the Caucasian and Burushaski side.

This essay is only a beginning, and I have already pointed out some unsolved problems. However, I suggest that the evidence presented here is already sufficient to demonstrate that the relationship between Basque and Caucasian is real, and can be verified by numerous recurrent phonological correspondences.

ABBREVIATIONS

AN	Alto Navarro = *Nafarroa Garaia* = High Navarrese (Basque dialect)
arc	archaic
B	*Bizkaia* = Biscayan (Basque dialect)
BN	Basse Navarre = *Nafarroa Beherea* = Low Navarrese (Basque dialect)
c	common (Basque) = *Euskara Batua*
CWC	*Common West Caucasian* = Chirikba 1996
DC	Dene-Caucasian = Sino-Caucasian
G	*Gipuzkoa* = Guipúzcoan (Basque dialect)
H	Hunza (Burushaski dialect)
L	*Lapurdi* = Labourdin (Basque dialect)
LDC	"Lexica Dene-Caucasica" = Blažek & Bengtson 1995
N	Nagiri, Nagari (Burushaski dialect); northern (Basque)
NCED	*North Caucasian Etymological Dictionary* = Nikolayev & Starostin 1994
PA	Proto-Athabaskan
PDC	Proto-Dene-Caucasian
PEA	Proto-Eyak-Athabaskan
PEC	Proto-East Caucasian (= Proto-Nakh-Daghestanian)
PNC	Proto-(North) Caucasian
PND	Proto-Na-Dene
PST	Proto-Sino-Tibetan
PWC	Proto-West Caucasian (= Proto-Abkhazo-Adygean)
PY	Proto-Yeniseian
R	Roncalese = *Erronkari* (Basque dialect)
S	southern (Basque)

Sal	Salazarese = *Saraitza* (Basque dialect)
SSEJ	"Sravnitel'nyj slovar' enisejskix jazykov" = Starostin 1995
ST	*(A Comparative Vocabulary of Five) Sino-Tibetan (Languages)* = Peiros & Starostin 1996
Y	Yasini = Werchikwar (Burushaski dialect)
Z	*Zuberoa* = Souletin (Basque dialect)

APPENDIX A:
MORPHOLOGICAL NOTES

To explain some of the etymologies proposed in this paper, it is necessary to discuss some Dene-Caucasian morphological features and how they are reflected in Basque.

There is evidence from all DC branches that there was a system of noun classification in Proto-DC. Systems of this type, more or less transformed, which persist to this day in many Caucasian languages, Burushaski, and Yeniseian (Ket). In the other languages, especially Basque and Sino-Tibetan, only fossilized vestiges remain. In the comparison of Basque with other DC languages, it has long been known that Basque frequently has "leftover" initial segments that appear to be fossilized prefixes. The most striking of these is probably *be-/bi-*, and has been noticed by linguists for decades (*e.g.,* Uhlenbeck 1927). The original separability of this and other such elements is shown by internal reconstruction in Basque words that appear with or without the prefixes:

- Basque *hatz* vs. *be-hatz:* Meanings vary widely depending on dialect, e.g. in Bizkaian, *atz* 'finger' vs. *beatz* 'toe'; in Zuberoan, *hatz* 'finger' or 'paw' vs. *behatz* 'thumb';[377]
- Basque (c) *k(h)e* vs. (AN, BN, R) *e-ke* 'smoke';
- Basque (AN, BN, L) *(h)erde,* (B, BN, L, R, Z) *(h)elder* 'drivel' vs. (G) *bilder* (< *bi- + helder);*
- Basque (c) *gai, gei* 'material, subject, topic' vs. (BN, Z) *e-khei* id.

Following are some examples of the Basque fossilized prefix *be-/bi-:*

- Basque *be-hatz* 'thumb, toe' (vs. unprefixed *hatz* 'finger, paw') ~ Avar *kʷač̣* 'paw', etc. (**3.66**)
- Basque *be-larri* 'ear' ~ Batsbi *lark̲* < **lari-k̲* 'ear', etc. (**8.55**)
- Basque *bizkar (bi-z-ka-r)*[378] 'back' ~ Caucasian: Abkhaz *azkʷa* 'back' ~ Burushaski *-sqa* 'on one's back' ~ ST: Tibetan s-*ku* 'body' ~ Na-Dene: Haida s-*ku* 'back'

---

[377] Trask's (1997, p. 287) attempt to explain *be-* as 'lower' is clearly wrong, as shown by Z 'thumb' (also in AN, BN, G).

[378] The segments *-z-* and *-r* are discussed later in this Appendix.

- Basque *bi-zi* 'life, alive' ~ Lak *s:iħ* 'breath, vapor', Chechen *sa* 'soul', etc. ~ PST **sĭj(H)* 'to die' (ST IV: 102) ~ Na-Dene: Tlingit *sa, sen* 'to breathe, blow'; Eyak *sĩh* 'to die' (**7.13**)[379]

Cf. also *be-l(h)aun* 'knee' (see Chapter **11**); *be-hazun* 'bile' (**3.6**); *bilder* 'drivel' (**4.20**); *bi-rika* 'lung' (**5.17**). Semantically, all of these words have to do with body parts, or fluids (bile, saliva), or attributes (life) of the body. In a Dene-Caucasian context, the most obvious comparison is with the East Caucasian class element that frequently appears in the form *b-*, sometimes prefixed to nouns, e.g. Tindi *b-eƛ:u* 'stomach' (NCED 670), *b-aƛ:i* 'in the middle' (NCED 412); and the prefix appearing as *b-* or *p-* in some West Caucasian words: Ubykh *b-ɮa* 'eye' (NCED 250), *p-č̣a* 'guest' (NCED 612). This element is reconstructed as PNC **w-* 'marker of III class singular' (Diakonoff & Starostin 1986; Starostin 2002). On the possible connection with Sino-Tibetan **b-* (and/or **m-*), see below.

Basque has several other fossilized prefixes in addition to *be-/bi-*. Because of the patterning of *be-/bi-* (with an alternation between two similar vowels), I have posited that the *e-* and *i-* prefixes be conflated as *e-/i-*, for example:

- Basque *elhur, elur (< *e-ɬu-r)* 'snow'[380] ~ PEC **λĭwV* 'snow' > Chechen *lō*, etc. (**7.34**)
- Basque *egur (e-gur)* 'firewood' ~ Udi *gor, gorgor* 'pole', etc. (**5.24**)
- Basque *izar (i-zar)* 'star', etc. ~ Tindi *c:aru* 'star', etc. (**3.28**)
- Basque *ihintz (i-hintz < *i-xinc)* 'dew' ~ Lak *xunc̣a* 'bog', etc. (**3.16**)

Cf. also (Z) *e-khei* 'material' (**6.30**); *e-sne* 'milk' (**7.23**); *e-sku* 'hand' (**3.41**); *e-rdoil* 'rust' (**4.16**); *e-l(h)e* 'word' (**8.86**); *i-lhinti* 'firebrand' (**7.33**); *i-dulki* 'block of wood' (**2.23**); *i-t(h)ain* 'tick' (**2.7**); *i-zen* 'name' (**7.14**); *i-zerdi* 'sweat, sap' (**4.21**); *i-purdi* 'rump' (**1.5**); *i-zter* 'thigh' (**2.12**). This noun class putatively included liquids and other mass nouns (milk, dew, snow, wood), as well as some body parts. This *e-/i-* prefix can be connected with the East Caucasian class marker reconstructed as **j-* 'II-

---

[379] "The semantic developments 'to breathe' > 'get tired' ... > 'die' are quite usual." (NCED 961). Cf. Russian *dušá* 'mind, soul, spirit' : *dušít'* 'to smother'.

[380] Basque *-r* is a relic of the DC plural ending (see below).

class singular' (Diakonoff & Starostin 1986; Starostin 2002). For example, in the Avar-Andian languages this prefix appears in words for 'sister' (e.g. Avar *j-ac*) and 'daughter' (Avar *j-as*), as opposed to words for 'brother' (Avar *w-ac*) and 'son' (Avar *w-as*), which have reflexes of the I-class prefix *ṵ-* (see below). Elsewhere, the word for 'snow' in Lezgian languages (Lezgi *žiw*, Tabasaran *jif*, Agul *ibx̌* < **jiwλ*) seems to reflect an incorporated **j-* prefix equivalent to *e-* in the Basque word (*elhur ~ elur* < **e-ɬu-r* 'snow').

Parallel with *be-/bi-* and *e-/i-*, I have proposed to conflate the *o-* and *u-* prefixes as *o-/u-*, for example:

- Basque *ol(h)o* 'oats' (< **o-ɬo*) ~ PNC **λwĭwV* 'millet' (**7.31**)
- Basque *oihal*, 'cloth, fabric' (< **o(i)-xal*) ~ PEC **χwĭlƚ V* 'clothing' (**4.25**)
- Basque *urdail (u-rdail)* 'stomach' ~ Karata m-*eλu* 'stomach', etc. (**4.22**)
- Basque *ukondo (u-kondo)* 'elbow' ~ Hinukh *q̇ontu* 'knee', etc. (**6.13**)

Cf. also *o-dol* 'blood' (**2.22**); *o-he* 'bed' (**7.48**); *oi-han* 'forest' (**7.3**); *o-ski* 'shoe' (**6.16**); (B) *u-zen* 'name' (**7.14**); *u-dagara* 'otter' (**2.19**); *u-hin* 'wave' (**7.36**). Contra Trask (1995: 74), body part words in more than one class is typologically usual. (Even in Indo-European such words may be masculine, feminine, or neuter.) This *o-/u-* prefix is likely to be cognate with PEC **ṵ-* 'I-class singular' (Diakonoff & Starostin 1986; Starostin 2002). Caucasian **ṵ-* and **j-* are opposed as masculine and feminine, respectively. There may be a trace of the original DC opposition in Basque *o-saba* 'uncle' (**7.24**) *vs.* *i-zeba* 'aunt' (**3.39**).

Another fossilized prefix takes the form of *ar-*, for example:

- Basque (BN,Z) *arhan (ar-han)* 'plum' ~ Avar *géni* 'pear', etc. ~ Burushaski *γaíŋ* 'grapes' ~ Tibetan *r-gun* 'vine, grape', etc. (**7.39**)[381]
- Basque *ardo* < **ardano (*ar-dano)* 'wine' ~ Tindi *žana* 'wine', Archi *čon* 'wine', etc.

---

[381] Note the same prefix (as well as same root) in Basque *ar-han* 'plum' and Tibetan *r-gun* 'grape'.

< PNC *ǯw[ə]nʔi (NCED 1104)[382]

- Basque (R) *arsto (ar-sto)* = common Basque *asto* 'donkey' ~ Ubykh *čədə*, Proto-Abkhaz **čada* 'donkey' (**3.48**)
- Basque (R) *arska (ar-ska)* = common Basque *aska* 'crib, trough' ~ Ubykh *čaq́ʷə́* 'basin, tureen', etc. ~ Burushaski (Y) *ćhiq* 'sifting tray', etc. (**3.62**)

These words are all associated with agricultural products, implements, and domestic animals. *ar-* is probably to be compared with the East Caucasian prefix **r-* 'IV-class singular'. An example of the latter in fossilized form is found in the Lezgi word *rufun (ru-fun)* 'belly' (NCED 771).[383] A fossilized prefix *r-* is also frequent in Sino-Tibetan (see below).

Basque also has a fossilized prefix in the shape *a-*, for example:

- Basque *a-hizpa* 'sister (of a woman)' ~ Bezhta *is* 'brother', *isi* 'sister', etc. ~ Burushaski *-ċo* 'brother (of a man), sister (of a woman)' (**3.37**)
- Basque *abere (a-bere)* 'domestic animal' ~ Udi *bele* 'cattle', etc. (**1.23**)
- Basque *ametz (a-metz)* 'gall oak' ~ Chechen *naž* 'oak tree' etc. ~ Burushaski (Hunza) *meṣ* ~ (Yasin) *noṣ* 'bush, shrub, sapling' (**3.68**)
- Basque *aho (a-ho)* 'mouth' ~ PNC **χwɨ-* in **χwɨm(V)ṗV* 'mouthful', etc. (**7.47**)

Cf. also *a-tso* 'old woman' (**3.21**); *a-zeri* 'fox' (**3.5**); *a-kain* 'tick' (**6.14**); *a-hur* 'hollow of the hand' (**5.7**); *a-dar (*a-rðar)* 'horn' (**4.17**); *a-huña* 'kid' (**5.8**); *a lontza* 'measure of grain' (**7.32**); *a-ztapar* 'paw, claw' (**2.13**). These words refer to persons, animals, plants, and body parts. There is no apparent counterpart to this *a-*prefix among the East Caucasian class markers. *a-* could of course represent the trace of a class lost in the East Caucasian system, or it could correspond to the West Caucasian **a-* 'possessive prefix of third person singular', as for example Abkhaz *á-la* ~ *á-bla* 'its eye' (CWC 364f).

---

[382] Nikolayev & Starostin (1991) previously reconstructed this word as **δwōnʔi*, which is even closer to the Basque word *(*-dano)*.

[383] The class system is lost in Lezgi, while it persists in some other Lezgian languages such as Tabasaran, Rutul, etc. (Catford 1977).

In addition to the prefixes already mentioned, there is another "leftover' element in Basque, -z-, that always appears *after* the other fossilized prefixes.

- Basque *bizkar (bi-z-ka-r)* 'back' ~ Caucasian: Abkhaz *azkʷa* 'back' ~ Burushaski *-sqa* 'on one's back' ~ ST: Tibetan s-*ku* 'body' ~ Na-Dene: Haida s-*ku* 'back'
- Basque *iztai (i-z-tai)* 'groin' ~ Caucasian: Adyge *śʷt:ə* 'genitals' ~ Burushaski (Y) *-ṣtiŋ* 'loins, waist' ~ PST *tə̄jH* 'bottom' > Lushai *tāi* 'lower abdomen, waist', etc. (ST II: 124)
- Basque *izter (i-z-te-r)* 'thigh' ~ Avar *ħet'é* / *ħet'* 'foot', etc. < PEC *tw̄īħV* (NCED 1007)
  ~ Burushaski *-úṭ* ~ *-úṭis* ~ *-húṭes* 'foot' ~ PST *tə̆H* > Old Chinese *tə?* 'foot, heel' (ST II: 123) ~ Na-Dene: Haida s-*t'áay*, s-*t'a-* 'foot'
- Basque *uzki (u-z-ki)* 'anus' ~ ST: Tibetan s-*kyi*-ša 'anus' ~ Na-Dene: Haida s-*k'yáaw* 'tail'; Tlingit *k'i* 'rump, buttocks'
- Basque *aztal (a-z-tal)* 'heel' ~ Na-Dene: Eyak *taλ* 'heel', Navajo *-tal* 'heel', etc.

I think this -z- is identical with the DC prefix *s- that is most abundantly attested in one Na-Dene language (Haida) and in some Sino-Tibetan languages, as shown in some comparisons of Haida and Tibetan:

Haida	s-qál	'shoulder'	Tibetan	s-gal-(pa)	'small of the back'
	s-ku	'back'		s-ku	'body'
	s-kyúu-	'on one's shoulder'		s-gu-stegs	'elbow, angle'
	s-kyáaw	'tail'		s-kyi-ša	'anus'
	s-q'ut	'armpit'		s-ked-pa	'waist'
	s-gíl	'navel'	Balti	s-kil	'center'

I find the most plausible explanation for these fossilized prefixes is that they are "stage III articles" (Greenberg 1978), that is, prefixes that once marked class distinctions and remained as phonetic segments after their morphological meaning was lost. Within Dene-Caucasian the most abundant supply of stage III articles is found in Sino-Tibetan, for example:

Tibetan *m-čhin* 'liver', *b-žin* 'face', *r-nag ~ s-nag* 'pus', *r-na-ba* 'ear', *d-gun* 'winter', *l-ga ~ s-ga* 'ginger', *s-ked-pa* 'waist', *s-b-rul* 'snake' etc.

In some Sino-Tibetan languages a vowel has developed between prefix and stem, convergent with the development in Basque (*be-/bi-*):

Garo *bi-bik* 'bowels', *bi-bal* 'flower', *bi-mik* 'sprout', *bi-tši* 'egg', etc.

In the Caucasian languages relics of stage III articles appear more sporadically, for example:

Avar *mi-ƚír* 'wing', *ma-xá* 'abomasum', *me-géž* 'beard'; Lezgi *ru-fun* 'belly'; Tsakhur *wu-xun* 'belly'; Ubykh *t-χamɔ́* 'skin, fur', *t-χʷa* 'ashes', *b-ɮa* 'eye', *b-ɓa* 'top', etc.

Trask (1995: 73-74) objects that many Basque nouns carry no "fossilized prefixes" at all, which is true. However, as we can see from the Caucasian and Sino-Tibetan examples, it is typical of stage III articles that they appear "with some nouns but not with others in a quite sporadic way that differs from language to language" (Greenberg 1978: 47). For example, Basque *hur* 'hazelnut' vs. *a-hur* 'hollow of hand'; *lur* 'earth' vs. *e-l(h)ur* 'snow'; *larri* 'sadness' vs. *be-larri* 'ear'. Cf. also Tibetan *gun* 'loss' vs. *r-gun* 'vine, grape', *d-gun* 'winter'. These examples and others suggest that some stage III articles serve to distinguish homonyms.

Many Basque nouns, when compared with Caucasian and other DC languages, have another "leftover" element at the end of words, namely final *-r*:[384]

- Basque *bel(h)ar* 'forehead' *(belha-r)* ~ PEC **b ƒ ā̄thŏ* 'edge, end' ~ Burushaski *bal* 'wall' (< ***'edge') (**1.12**)

---

[384] " A final morph *-ar* is exceedingly frequent in nouns: *adar* 'horn', *ilar* 'pea', *nigar* 'tear', [etc.] ... No one knows if this represents a single ancient morpheme" (Trask 1997: 256). In the case of *adar* 'horn' (as well as *adar* 'branch'), I consider *-r* part of the noun stem (cf. Avar *ƛ:ar,* Burushaski *-ltúr* 'horn', etc.).

- Basque *bizar* 'beard' *(biza-r)* ~ PEC **bilʒ́V* 'beard' (**1.13**)
- Basque *izter* 'thigh' *(izte-r)* ~ PEC **twīħV̄ / ħwīṭV̄* 'foot' (**2.12**)
- Basque *zamar* 'fleece' *(zama-r)* ~ PEC **čħwĕme* 'eyebrow' (**3.11**)
- Basque *hondar* 'sand, beach' *(honda-r)* ~ PEC **ʔantV* 'earth, ground' (**6.41**)
- Basque *el(h)ur* 'snow' (< **e-ɬu-r*) ~ PEC **λ̌iwV* 'snow' (**7.34**)
- Basque *aztapar* 'claw' *(aztapa-r)* ~ PEC **tw‡bi* 'finger' (**2.13**)
- Basque *k(h)edar* 'soot' *(kheda-r)* ~ PEC **ġidV* 'soot, dust' (**6.10**)
- Basque *helder, elder* 'drivel' (< **herde-r),* (G) *bilder* 'drivel' (< **bi-helder)* ~ PNC **ħăm ˅ă* 'sweat' (**4.20**)
- Basque *hamar, hama-* 'ten' ~ Proto-Lezgian **ʡ:am:* 'hand(ful), arm(ful)' < PEC **mHŏχɨ* (**7.45**)
- Basque (B) *mukur* 'trunk, base of tree' *(muku-r)* ~ PEC **mħŏqwe* 'oak-tree' (**6.5**)
- Basque *il(h)ar* 'vetch, peas, beans' *(ilha-r)* ~ PEC **hōwɬ[ā]* 'legumes' (**7.69**)
- Basque *nigar (niga-r), negar (nega-r)* 'weeping, tears' ~ PEC **nĕwqŭ* 'tears, pus' (**6.31**)
- Basque *lantzer* 'drizzle, fine and minute rain' *(lantze-r)* ~ PEC **λã̆[m]çV* 'to sift, filter' (**7.25**)
- Basque *bul(h)ar* 'chest, breast' *(bulha-r)* ~ PEC **Gwă̄ɬħē* 'udder, breast' (**6.27**)
- Basque *bizkar* 'back' *(bizka-r)* ~ Caucasian: Abkhaz *azkʷa* 'back' ~ Burushaski *-sqa* 'on one's back' ~ ST: Tibetan s-*ku* 'body' ~ Na-Dene: Haida s-*ku* 'back'

This Basque *-r* is probably cognate with the plural ending **-r* well known in Caucasian languages. Plural **-r* also remains in certain sporadic fossilized forms in Caucasian languages, plural in form but singular in meaning, for example:

- Tabasaran *marc-ar* 'hearth (NCED 308)
- Khinalug *cul-oz* 'tooth' (*-oz* < **-or*: NCED 326)

- Agul *muž-ur* 'beard' (NCED 304)
- Dargwa (Akushi, Chirag) *nerɣ* 'tear' < **neɣʷ-r* (NCED 848)

The last two examples are entirely parallel with Basque: *biza-r* 'beard'; *nega-r, niga-r* 'weeping, tear(s)' (except that Dargwa has taken the further step of metathesizing the last two consonants *(¨r > r¨)*).

APPENDIX B:
NOTE ON CONSONANT CLUSTERS

PDC *-lc'- / -rc'- / -lč'- > Basque *x > /h/ (>∅)

Some examples show that PDC intervocalic clusters of liquid + affricate (such as *-lc'- / -rc'- / -lč!-) have evolved into medial Basque /h/, probably through intermediate stages such as * -ṣ- > -x-. The following lexical comparisons emphasize the parallels between Basque and the Avar-Andian languages:

meaning	Basque	Godoberi	Andi	Avar	Proto-Caucasian	
'tongue'	*mi(n)hi	mic:i	mic':i	mac':	*mĕlc̆i	(3.18)
'cow'	behi	purc:I 'cattle'	buc'ir 'cattle'	bóc':i 'cattle'	*bℏ^rcw V	(1.16)
'grain'	bihi	buča 'millet'	beča	muč	*bŏlcwi	(1.18)

Basque /h/ is still audible in northeastern dialects (Basse Navarre, Lapurdi, Zuberoa), silent in the others (Bizkaia, Gipuzkoa, Alto Navarro). The following patterns are evident: (a) the identity of the second vowel /i/ in most of the words cited (see Bengtson 1996 for other examples); (b) the regular correspondence of internal Basque /h/ to Proto-Caucasian clusters of the type liquid + glottalized affricate, specifically -lc'-, -rc'-. -lč'-. As I have proposed in earlier papers (Bengtson 1995b, 1999b), the Proto-Caucasian clusters most likely represent the more archaic stage, and Basque /h/ (in these words) can be derived from the clusters by the following hypothetical sequence:

*-lc'- / -rc'- / -lč'- > * -lṣ- / -rṣ- > * -ṣṣ- > * -ṣ- > -x- > -h-

The change of -ṣ- > -x- is well known, as for example Sanskrit pṛṣ- 'to sprinkle', snuṣā́ 'daughter-in-law', corresponding to Russian pórox 'gunpowder', snoxá 'daughter-in-law', respectively. In the case of the Basque word for 'tongue', we can postulate the following sequence:

*mĕlc'ĭ > *milṣi > *miṣṣi > *miṣi > *mixi > mihi (> W. Basque mii > mi)

The stage *mixi is not merely hypothetical, but actually attested in archaic dialectal forms such as Baïgorry [mihçja] 'the tongue' (= literary

195

mihia), recorded by Nicole Moutard (1975). The fricative **[ç]** is the fronted allophone of the **[x]** heard in words such as **[axhwa]** 'the mouth' (= lit. *ahoa*), **[oxhja]** 'the bed' (= lit. *ohea*), etc. (*ibid.,* and Bengtson 1999b).

APPENDIX C:
KEY TO PHONETIC CHARACTERS

ã ẽ ĩ õ ũ	nasal vowels
c: k: ƛ: p: s: t:, etc.	tense obstruents
c' k' ƛ' p' t', etc.	glottalized obstruents (NCED ç̣ ḳ ƛ̣ ṗ ṭ , etc.)
ć ć' ʒ́	hissing-hushing affricates (NCED c̀ c̀̓ ʒ̀)
č č' ǯ	hushing affricates (NCED č č̓ ǯ)
ċ	voiced dental fricative: e.g., Basque *adar* [aðar̄] 'horn', *erdi* [er̄ði] 'half, middle'
G	voiced uvular stop
γ	voiced velar fricative (Caucasian, Na-Dene); voiced uvular fricative (Burushaski)
γ̣	voiced uvular fricative (NCED ʁ)
ħ	voiceless emphatic laryngeal fricative
ɦ	voiced laryngeal fricative
ɬ	lateral resonant or glide (in PNC and PST reconstructions)
ɬ̣	voiceless lateral fricative (NCED λ)
L	voiced lateral fricative in NCED (= ɮ)
ə̄	voiced lateral affricate (NCED)
λ	voiceless lateral fricative in NCED (= ɬ̣)
ƛ	voiceless lateral affricate
ƛ́	palatalized voiceless lateral affricate
ƛ'	glottalized voiceless lateral affricate (NCED λ̣)
ƛ́'	palatalized glottalized lateral affricate
ʎ	palatalized lateral resonant
ɮ	voiced lateral fricative (NCED L)
ŕ	palatalized rhotic resonant
r̄	rhotic trill (= Basque *rr*)

197

ʁ	voiced uvular fricative (= Burushaski γ)
ś	voiceless hissing-hushing fricative
š	voiceless hushing fricative
ṣ	voiceless retroflex fricative (Burushaski)
ṭ	voiceless retroflex stop (Burushaski)
u̯	labial glide (in Caucasian reconstructions)
x	voiceless uvular fricative (Burushaski);
x	voiceless velar fricative (Caucasian, Na-Dene)
χ	voiceless uvular fricative (= Burushaski x)
χ̣	pharyngealized voiceless uvular fricative (NCED χI)
y̭	retroflex velarized spirant (Burushaski)
ʒ	voiced hissing affricate (= $\underline{dz}$)
ʒ́	voiced hissing-hushing affricate (= $\underline{dź}$) (= Burushaski j)
ǯ	voiced hushing affricate (= $\underline{dž}$)
ʔ	glottal stop
ʔ̣	glottalized emphatic laryngeal stop (Caucasian)
ʕ	voiced emphatic laryngeal fricative

APPENDIX D:
INDEX OF BASQUE WORDS CITED

Words are generally cited in their common Basque (*euskara batua*) form, following Aulestia & White (1992). The glosses are minimal: see the respective etymologies for fuller definitions of the Basque words. Some dialectal forms, especially Bizkaian and Zuberoan, are also cited with a cross-reference to the common Basque form (*e.g., aizta* [Bizkaian] see *ahizpa*). Phonemic /h/ that is pronounced in northern Basque dialects but not found in standard Basque spelling is shown as *(h)*, e.g., *k(h)edar* 'soot', *il(h)e* 'hair'.

a-, -a *see* ha-
abere 'domestic animal(s), cattle' **1.24, 8.69.a, 9.46**
adar 'branch' **12.4**
adar 'horn' **4.17, 8.36**
agor 'dry' **6.23, 8.33**
agure 'old man' **6.9, 8.68**
ahari 'ram' **6.44, 7.49, 8.69.b**
ahizpa 'sister (of a woman)' **3.37, 9.66**
aho 'mouth' **7.47, 9.82**
ahuntz '(female) goat' **5.8.a**
ahuña, ahuñe 'kid' **5.8.a, 9.91**
ahur 'palm, hollow (of hand)' **5.7, 9.99**
aizta *see* ahizpa
akain 'large tick' **6.14**
al(h)a 'grazing', al(h)a-tu 'to feed, graze' **6.47, 8.85**
al(h)abaso 'granddaughter' **7.24**
ale 'seed' **7.32, 9.80**
al(h)o *see* ol(h)o
alontza 'mixture of grain' **7.32, 9.80**
al(h)or 'field (destined for sowing)' **7.32, 9.80**
ametz 'gall oak' **3.68**
angio 'pasture' **6.7**
antzigar 'hard frost' **3.35, 8.104**
apa 'kiss' **1.10**
apal 'shelf' **1.6, 8.60, 9.11**
apo 'hoof' **1.9**
ar 'male' **6.36**
ardai 'tinder' **4.19, 6.40, 9.29, 13.4**
ardatz 'axle, spindle' **4.18.c, 6.50**
ardo 'wine' **Appendix A**

argi 'light' **6.35**
ar(h)an 'plum, sloe' **7.39, 8.25**
ar(h)e 'harrow, rake' **7.63, 7.68, 8.50, 9.19**
aska 'manger, crib' **3.62**
aski 'enough' **3.64**
asko 'much, many' **3.64**
asto 'donkey' **3.48**
atso 'old woman' **3.21, 9.69**
atzapar *see* aztapar
atze 'tree' **3.71**
aundi *see* handi
azal 'bark, skin' **3.38**
azaro 'November' **3.7, 8.66**
azegari *see* azeri
azeri 'fox' **3.5, 7.94, 8.69.c**
azkon(ar), hazkz *see* hartz
aztal 'heel' **Appendix A**
aztapar 'paw, claw' **2.14**

bahe 'sieve' **7.5, 8.94, 13.2**
barda, bart 'last night' **4.15.c**
bardin 'the same, even' **4.15.b**
baso 'forest, desert' **3.3.a, 8.93**
be- / bi- (fossilized prefix) **8.97**
begi 'eye' **12.2**
be(h)arri *see* belarri
behatz 'toe, thumb' **3.66, 5.1, 9.3**
behazun 'bile' **3.6, 5.35**
behe 'bottom, floor', behean 'below' **8.98**
behi 'cow' **1.16, 3.18, 9.43**
behor 'mare' **7.4**
bek(h)o 'forehead' **1.17, 5.15, 9.30**
bela, bele 'crow, raven' **6.26, 8.81**
belarri 'ear' **8.55, 9.22**
belatz *see* bela
bel(h)ar 'forehead' **1.13, 7.79, 8.87, 13.4**
bel(h)ar 'grass, hay' **7.40, 8.89, 8.99, 9.32**
bel(h)aun 'knee' *see* chapter **11**
berdin *see* bardin
bero 'hot' **1.19, 8.64**
beso 'arm' **7.22, 8.95, 9.45**
bet(h)e 'full' **1.27**

bi, biga 'two' **12.1**
bi- *see* be-
bigar *see* bihar
bihar 'tomorrow' **1.12, 5.6**
bihi 'grain, seed' **1.18**
bil(-du) 'gather, collect, unite' **4.27**
bilder *see* elder
bil(h)o 'hair, mane' **1.8, 8.84**
biribil 'round' **5.26**
birika 'lung' **5.17, 8.47**
bizar 'beard' **1.14, 3.73, 9.48**
bizi 'to live; alive; life' **7.13, 9.51**
bizkar 'back' **Appendix A**
borobil *see* biribil
bortz *see* bost
bost 'five' **1.15, 3.9**
budar *see* bul(h)ar
bul(h)ar 'breast, chest' **6.27, 7.88, 8.91, 9.102**
burdi *see* gurdi
burkhi *see* urki

edur *see* el(h)ur
egarri 'thirst' **6.23, 8.33**
egin 'to do, make' **6.33**
egun 'day' **6.32**
egur 'firewood' **5.24.a, 8.32**
eho 'to grind' **7.51**
eho 'to beat' **7.52, 8.45**
eho, ehun 'to weave' **5.32, 7.53, 8.44**
eihera 'mill' **7.51**
eio *see* eho
ek(h)arri 'to bring' **6.4**
eke *see* k(h)e
ek(h)ei *see* gai
elder, erde 'drool, drivel' **4.20, 7.72**
el(h)e 'speech, story, word' **8.86, 9.34**
el(h)ur 'snow' **7.34, 9.104, 13.7**
emazte 'wife' **3.40**
entzun 'hear' **3.15**
eperdi, epurdi *see* ip(h)urdi
erbi 'hare' **5.27, 8.27**
erde *see* elder

erdera, erdara 'foreign language' **4.23, 8.70**
erdi 'half, middle' **4.18.a, 9.33**
erdoil 'rust' **4.16, 9.77**
erdu 'come ye!' **4.15.a**
ergi 'bull calf' **7.41**
er(h)i 'finger' **5.37, 8.50.c**
erori 'to fall' *see* chapter **11**
erreka 'creek, brook' **6.18, 8.26**
erro, herro 'root, teat, ray' **7.37**
esan 'to say' **3.3.b**
esku 'hand' **3.41, 5.25**
esne 'milk' **7.23**
estu 'narrow, cramped' **2.26, 3.63**
et(h)en 'to break, cut' **2.10**
et(h)orri 'to come' **2.9**
etzan 'to lie down, rest, put down' **3.14**
euli 'fly' **8.77**
eutsi 'to take, seize' **3.51**
ez 'not' **9.40**
ezagutu 'to know' **3.13, 7.59**

fuiñ *see* (h)un, hün

gai 'material, subject' **6.30**
gal- 'to lose' **5.21, 8.56**
garagar *see* gari
gar(h)i 'thin' **6.29, 7.87, 8.49, 9.16**
gari 'wheat' **6.21, 8.71, 13.5**
garkola, garkhora 'nape' **6.2, 8.83, 9.70**
gau 'night' **7.56, 9.18**
gedar *see* k(h)edar
giltz, giltza 'key' **6.22**
gitxi *see* guti
gizon 'man' **12.6**
gogor 'hard', gor 'deaf' **6.19, 8.35, 9.78**
gordin *see* gorri
gor(h)i *see* gurin
gorri 'red' **6.25**
gorringo *see* gorri
gose 'hunger, hungry' **5.22, 7.20, 9.36**
gune 'place, space' **6.24, 9.96**
guraso 'parent' **7.24**

gurdi 'wagon' **5.23**
gurin, gur(h)i, gor(h)i 'butter, fat' **7.57, 7.83, 8.75, 9.94, 13.1**
gurpil 'wheel' **5.23**
guti, gutxi 'few, little' **2.10**

ha- article, demonstrative **9.1**
habe 'pillar, beam' **1.25, 7.66**
haga 'long pole, rod' **5.20, 7.65, 9.20**
haitz 'rock, stone' **3.17, 7.71, 13.4**
haize 'wind' **6.49**
hamar 'ten' **7.45, 8.12**
handi 'big, great' **5.2, 9.13**
har 'worm' **7.70, 8.34, 9.17**
haran 'valley' **6.39, 8.46, 13.4**
hardo *see* ardai
hari 'thread, string, wire' **7.43, 8.72, 9.12, 13.2**
harri 'stone, rock' **7.44, 8.29, 9.25**
har-tu 'to take, receive' **5.4, 9.21**
hartz 'bear' **3.65, 7.46**
hatz 'finger' **3.66, 5.1, 9.3**
hauts 'ashes, powder' **3.44, 8.103**
hauzo 'neighbor' **3.61, 7.76, 13.4**
hazi 'to grow; seed' **3.72**
hega- 'to fly' **7.61, 7.82**
hegi 'edge, ridge' **7.93, 8.40, 9.44**
helder, herde *see* elder, erde
herri 'town, people, nation' **6.46, 8.28, 9.42**
herro *see* erro
hezur 'bone' **7.15, 9.90**
hi 'thou' **12.3**
hil 'die; dead; death' **4.26, 9.47**
hiri 'village, city' **5.3, 9.60**
hitz 'word' **3.8, 9.53**
hobe 'better' **7.54, 7.84**
hobi 'grave' **7.1, 8.102**
hobi 'gum(s)' **6.28, 7.73, 8.18, 9.73**
hodei 'cloud, thunder' **2.22, 7.77**
hogei 'twenty' **6.20**
hondar *see* ondar
hor, ho *see* or
hortz 'tooth' **3.74, 5.5**
hosin *see* osin

hotz 'cold' **3.67, 7.78, 9.84**
(h)un, hün 'marrow, pith, brain' **7.64, 9.88**
hunki 'touch, feel' **7.2**
hun *see* on
huñ *see* oin
hur *see* ur
huts 'empty; nought, fault' **3.23.a, 7.80**
hutsal 'trifling' **3.23.b, 8.59, 7.81**

i(h)az 'last year' **7.18.b**
ibai 'river' **7.55, 8.19, 8.105**
idar *see* il(h)ar
idor 'dry' **4.24.b**
idulki 'block of wood' **2.24, 9.103**
ihintz 'dew' **3.16, 7.35, 9.64**
ik(h)usi 'to see' **6.12, 8.43**
il(h)ar 'pea(s)' **7.69, 8.88**
il(h)argi *see* argi
il(h)e 'hair, wool, fur' **6.43, 7.62, 8.92**
il(h)inti, ilindi 'firebrand' **7.33, 9.61**
imiñi *see* ipini
intzigar 'frost' **3.35**
ip(h)urdi, iperdi 'buttocks' **1.5, 2.15, 8.37**
ipini 'to put, place' **9.49**
irten *see* urten
it(h)ain 'tick' **2.8, 8.24**
itoi 'drop' **2.1**
itsu 'blind' **3.4**
itzuli 'to turn' **3.10, 8.82, 9.57**
izan 'to be; being' **7.12**
izar 'star' **3.28, 9.6**
izardi *see* izerdi
izeba 'aunt' **3.39**
izen 'name' **7.14**
izerdi 'sweat, sap' **3.59, 4.21**
izter 'thigh' **2.13**
izu 'fright, horror' **3.60, 7.75**

jakin 'to know' **6.15**
jarri 'to sit; set' **8.31.b, 9.23**
jaugin 'to come' **6.34**
jin *see* jaugin

joan 'to go' **6.42**

kaiku 'wooden bowl' **6.3**
kain 'fog, storm clouds' **5.11**
k(h)ako 'hook' **5.9**
kankano 'fruit-stone, kernel' **5.10**
k(h)arats 'bitter, sour' **6.9, 8.65.a**
k(h)e 'smoke' **5.13, 5.36**
k(h)edar 'soot' **2.21, 6.10**
k(h)en-du 'to take away, remove, leave' **6.1**
k(h)ino 'bad odor, bad taste' **5.13, 9.63**
kirats *see* k(h)arats
koko 'bug', kokoso 'flea' **5.12**
kokots, kokotz 'chin' **3.26, 6.11**

lahar 'bramble' **4.11, 6.48**
lai 'two-pronged fork' **4.7**
laino 'fog, mist' **4.3.a, 9.28**
lamika-tu 'to lick' **8.13, 8.53, 9.9**
lanbro 'fog, mist' **4.3.b**
lantzer, lantzurda 'drizzle' **7.25**
lape 'shelter' **1.11, 4.8, 9.27**
larrain 'threshing floor' **4.13.c**
larre 'meadow, pasture' **4.13.b**
larri 'worried, serious', etc. **4.13.a, 8.31.a, 9.26**
larru 'skin, leather' **4.12**
lasto 'straw, hay' **3.49, 4.5, 9.8**
lau, laur 'four' **12.5**
laz 'beam, rafter' **3.42, 4.9**
legar 'pebble, gravel' **4.2.c**
leher, ler 'pine' **7.28, 7.85**
lehia 'diligence, laboriousness', etc. **4.14.a**
leka 'bean pod, husk' **5.18, 8.51, 9.31**
lema 'rudder' **4.10, 8.16, 9.41**
lerde 'drivel, drool' **2.25, 7.27, 8.38**
lerra 'slip, slide' **4.2.b**
lerro 'line, file, row' **4.6.b**
limuri 'slippery; humid' **4.2.a, 8.15**
lirain 'slender, svelte' **4.6.a, 9.65**
lirdi *see* lerde
lizun 'mold, mildew' **4.1, 9.56**
lo 'to sleep' **4.2.d**

loki, lokun 'temple (of head)' **4.4, 8.42**
lorratz 'track, footprint' **7.26**
lotu 'to tie' **2.12, 8.54**
lurrin 'steam, odor' **7.29, 9.98**
lur 'earth, land, soil' **4.14.b, 8.52**
luze 'long' **7.11, 7.30**

magal 'lap, breast' **1.21, 8.58**
maket *see* makila
mak(h)ila 'stick, baton' **1.20**
mardo 'luxuriant, vigorous; soft, smooth' **4.24.a, 8.8**
mardul 'robust, healthy, strong' **4.24.a, 8.8**
mendi 'mountain' **1.28**
mihi 'tongue' **3.18, 8.4**
miko 'a little bit' **5.14, 8.5, 9.54**
mintz *see* p(h)intz(a)
mok(h)o 'beak' **8.9**
muga 'limit, border' **6.8, 8.3, 8.41**
muin, muñ 'pith, marrow, brain' **8.7**
muk(h)ur 'tree trunk' **6.5, 8.1**
mul(h)o 'heap, mound' **8.6, 8.90, 9.86**
musu 'kiss, face; nose' **3.50, 8.2**

nahi 'will, wish' **7.67, 8.21, 13.3**
naka, nakaitz 'mockery, disgust' **5.29**
negar, nigar 'weeping, tears' **6.31, 8.22, 9.35**
negu 'winter' **7.58, 8.20**
neke 'pain, fatigue' **5.31**
ni 'I' **5.28, 9.68**
nini 'child, doll, pupil' **5.30**

odol 'blood' **2.23**
ohe 'bed' **7.48.a, 13.2**
oi *see* ohe, hobi
oihal 'cloth' **4.25, 7.50**
oihan 'forest' **7.3**
oin, oñ 'foot' **6.45**
okotz *see* kokots
ol(h)o 'oats' **7.31, 9.83**
on 'good' **5.8.b**
ondar 'sand, beach' **2.4, 6.41**
ondiko 'misery, misfortune' **6.37**

ontzi 'vessel' **1.22, 3.34, 9.71**
or 'dog' **7.42, 9.76**
orde-zü (Z) 'go!' **4.15.a**
oreitz 'colostrum' **3.75**
orri 'leaf' **7.48.b**
osaba *see* al(h)aba-so
osin 'well, depth' **3.2, 9.67**
oski 'shoe' **6.16**
oso 'whole, complete' **3.24, 9.68**
otso 'wolf' **1.23, 3.22, 9.75**

pinpilin, pinpirin 'butterfly' **1.2**
p(h)intz(a) 'membrane' **1.1**
punpu(i)l(l)a 'tear, blister, bubble' **1.4, 8.79, 9.87**
puspulu 'bubble' **1.3, 7.21**
puxika 'bladder' **1.3, 7.21**

sabel 'belly' **1.26, 3.47, 9.7**
sagu 'mouse' **3.1.a, 5.24.b, 8.39, 9.10**
sare, sale 'net(-work)' **3.45, 8.67, 9.2, 9.38**
sits 'moth' **7.19**
soin 'shoulder', etc. **3.20.b, 5.33**
solo *see* sor(h)o
sor- 'body' **3.46, 9.74**
sor-balda 'shoulder' **8.96**
sor(h)o 'field, meadow' **3.44, 7.89, 8.76**
su 'fire' **3.20.a**
sustar, sustrai 'root' **3.1.b**

tako 'wedge, block' **2.19**
takoin 'heel (of shoe)' **2.16, 9.14**
tanga, tanka 'drop' **2.7**
-tilla 'little' (dim. suffix) **2.4**
t(h)ini 'summit, top' **2.3, 8.23**
tinka 'a little' **2.7**
tipi 'little, small' **2.5. 9.55**
toki 'place' **2.6.a, 5.16**
toska 'fine clay' **2.2, 3.25**
t(h)u 'to spit' **2.1**
tuka *see* t(h)u
tuntun 'Basque drum' **2.18, 9.97**
tupin(a) 'pot, kettle', etc. **1.7, 2.6.b**

tutu 'tube, pipe' **2.17, 9.101**

txahal 'calf' **3.54, 7.90, 8.57**
txanket, txanku, txainku 'lame' **3.57**
txeme 'half-span' **3.58, 7.91, 8.14**
txiki 'little' **3.52**
tximitxa 'bedbug' **3.53, 8.17, 9.59**
txingurri *see* zinaurri
txonta 'chaffinch' **3.56.b**
txori 'bird' **3.56.a, 8.73, 9.81**
txorru 'root of hair' **3.55, 8.30, 9.79**

udagara 'otter' **2.20, 8.48, 9.5**
ugabere, ugadara, ugadera *see* udagara
ugaldu *see* ugari
ugari 'abundant' **7.60, 8.74**
uhin 'wave' **7.36**
uk(h)ondo 'elbow' **6.13**
ule *see* il(h)e
uli, üli, ülü *see* euli
un *see* (h)un
une *see* gune
untzi *see* ontzi
ur 'water' **7.74, 8.61, 9.92**
urdail 'stomach, abomasum, womb' **4.22**
urde '(male) pig' **8.100**
uri *see* hiri
urin *see* gurin
urki 'birch tree' **6.6, 8.101**
urten 'go out, leave' **4.18.b**
uzen *see* izen
uzki 'anus' **Appendix A**

xahal *see* txahal
xanku *see* txanku
xe(hu)me *see* txeme
xori *see* txori

-z instrumental suffix **7.16**
zahar 'old' **7.7, 7.86, 9.24**
zain, zañ 'nerve, blood vessel, tendon' **7.6**
zamar 'fleece' **3.11, 8.11**

ze 'not' **9.40**
zeden 'moth, weevil' **7.8**
zel(h)ai 'meadow, plain' **3.31, 8.78, 9.39**
zein 'which' **7.10**
zer 'what' **7.10**
ziho 'fat, tallow' **3.12, 7.38**
zik(h)iro 'castrated ram' **3.29, 9.52**
zilaga 'stake, post' **3.69.b**
zil(h)o *see* zul(h)o
zimitz, zimintza 'bedbug' **3.32, 9.58**
zinaurri 'ant' **3.30**
zintzur, züntzür 'throat' **3.36**
zirin 'diarrhea, bird excrement' **7.18.a, 8.65.b**
zoli *see* zori
zori 'luck' **3.33, 8.63, 9.72**
zu 'you' **9.85**
zuhaitz 'tree' **3.71**
zul(h)o 'hole, burrow' **7.17, 8.80, 9.100, 13.6**
zumar 'elm' **3.69.a, 7.92, 8.11, 9.84**
zur, zul 'wood, timber, lumber' **3.70, 8.62, 9.89**
zuri 'white' **8.50.b**
zurzulo, zurzuil 'nape' **3.36, 9.95**
zuzen 'straight, right' **3.27, 5.34, 9.93**
zuzun 'poplar, aspen' **7.9**

ON THE POSITION OF HAIDA

When Edward Sapir (1915) first proposed the Na-Dene family of languages, it was thought to consist of three linguistic units: (a) the Haida language, (b) the Tlingit language, and (c) the Athabaskan family (Tanana, Carrier, Sarsi, Mattole, Hupa, Navajo, etc.). At that time the Eyak language was little known, but it eventually became clear that it belonged to Na-Dene and was close to Athabaskan. The following structure of the Na-Dene family became generally accepted:

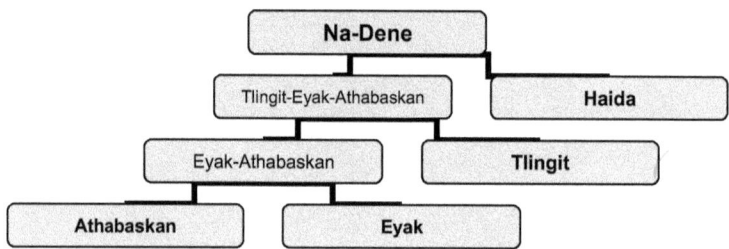

It was thought that Haida was the most divergent of the languages, and thus had split off first from the rest of the family. Then Tlingit split off, then Eyak, leaving the core Athabaskan family.

Even from the beginning some experts were unwilling to accept the Na-Dene family. For example, Pliny Earle Goddard could not even accept the relatedness of Tlingit and Athabaskan (let alone Haida), and published an article highlighting the differences between the languages. Later Robert Levine (1979) published an article purporting to demolish Sapir's evidence for connecting Haida to the rest of Na-Dene. Many experts concurred with Levine, excluding Haida from Na-Dene, while still accepting the original unity of Tlingit-Eyak-Athabaskan.

Meanwhile, Jürgen Pinnow (1966, 1985, et alia) continued to amass evidence for a Na-Dene family that still included Haida, correcting and adding to Sapir's evidence. As part of his book *Language in the Americas* Greenberg (1987c) published an article that critically examined Levine's methods and conclusions, arguing that many of Levine's criticisms were invalid, and even if the criticism were accepted, much of Sapir's evidence remained intact.

Based on the work of Sapir, Pinnow and Greenberg, I accept Haida as a branch of Na-Dene. Recently an anthropologist colleague asked me if I thought Haida might be a branch of Dene-Caucasian, but not part of Na-

Dene. I thought it was a stimulating question. If true, the classification of Dene-Caucasian could be as follows:

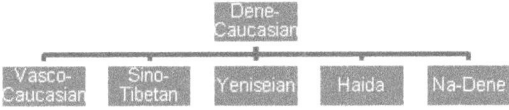

It is true that Haida has a fair number of words that are shared with other branches of Dene-Caucasian, but not with Tlingit-Eyak-Athabaskan, for example:

Haida ɢut 'buttock, rump': cf. Burushaski (Nagir) giṭ 'After, Vulva' ~ (H) gik (< *git-kV)

Haida skuts (s-kuts) 'bone': cf. Old Chinese *kūt 'bone'; Caucasian (PEC) *kŏc'a 'a kind of bone' > Hunzib k'oc'u 'back of the head', etc.

Haida hluu = [ɬuˑ] 'body': cf. Tibetan lus 'body', lhu 'portion of the body of an animal', etc. < PST *l˅(w) 'body, side of body'

Haida ɬɢaˑ ~ ɬχaˑ 'stone': cf. PST *T-ləŋ / *T-lək 'stone' > Lushai luŋ 'stone, rock', etc.; Caucasian (PEC) *ƛănχwV 'ruins, cobble-stones'

Haida xil àa 'to be dry', xíl-gal 'to become dry': cf. PST *χial 'dry'

Haida ƛú 'canoe', ƛú- 'by canoe': cf. PST *T-lij 'boat' > Burmese hlij 'boat', etc.

Haida ƛaas 'branch': cf. PEC *˅VćV 'log, pole' > Akhwakh ˅:eća 'log', etc.; Basque (Lapurdi) laz 'beam, rafter'

In addition to the lexical peculiarities, Haida also naturally has grammatical differences from the rest of Na-Dene. One of these is the prefix *s-* on nouns which is not found in other Na-Dene languages but is frequent in Sino-Tibetan languages, notably in Tibetan and Old Chinese:

- Haida *s-qál* 'shoulder': cf. Tibetan *s-gal*-pa 'small of the back'
- Haida *s-ku* 'back': cf. Tibetan *s-ku* 'body'
- Haida *s-kyáaw* 'tail': cf. Tibetan *s-kyi*-ša 'anus'
- Haida *s-q'ut* 'armpit': cf. Tibetan *s-ked*-pa 'waist'
- Haida *s-kyúu-* 'on one's shoulder': cf. Tibetan *s-gu*-stegs 'elbow, angle'
- Haida *s-gíl* 'navel': cf. Balti[385] *s-kil* 'center'

Recently John Enrico (2004) has restated the case for a Na-Dene family that includes Haida, incorporating new material he has uncovered in his extensive research on the language.

---

[385] Balti is a Tibetic (Bodic) language spoken in northeastern Pakistan, adjoining the homeland of Burushaski speakers.

LATERAL AFFRICATES IN NA-DENE

The precise reconstruction of Proto-Na-Dene phonology is yet to be fully demonstrated. That Haida belongs to this family is no longer widely accepted among Na-Dene specialists, though most agree with the genetic unity of Tlingit-Eyak-Athabaskan. Mainly on the basis of Jürgen Pinnow's work I accept the larger Na-Dene family, including Haida. And whatever details of Na-Dene phonology eventually become established, it is already quite clear that Proto-Na-Dene must have had lateral affricates, and probably the same ones as are found in Proto-Caucasian: voiced or lenis *λ, voiceless or fortis *ƛ, and glottalized *ƛ'.

Nikolayev (1991) made several Caucasian-Na-Dene comparisons involving the lateral affricates. The following seem to be valid, or at least promising, and have been incorporated into this chapter. (Here the Caucasian reconstructions have been modified to conform with NCED; some Na-Dene reconstructions have also been modified.):

Na-Dene	Caucasian	(other DC)	(general gloss)
Eyak ƛ'aʔ 'to beat, cut'	PEC *=Vƛ'Vw 'to beat, hit'	PST *T-lŏk 'to strike, kick'; Bur *-lta-n- 'to pound'	BEAT
Eyak de·ł 'backbone'	PNC *fireƛ'wĕ 'bone'	PST *rāk / *rāŋ 'bone'; PY *ʔuʎ-a₃ 'rib'	BONE
PEA *ƛ'a·h 'bottom, ground, buttocks'	PNC *Hƛ'ŏnŭ 'bottom'	PST *[lj]ɔŋ 'lower, down'; Bur táno 'rectum'	BOTTOM
PEA *q'ał 'fork'	PEC *k'wənƛ'V 'pitchfork'	PST *k(h)āk 'fork'	FORK
PND *ƛ'uʔχʷ 'grass'	PEC *ʔwēƛ'V 'a kind of grass, herb'	PST *lūH 'weed'; Bsq *fiařdo 'tinder'	GRASS
PEA *łaʔ 'hand'	PNC *Hluƛ'E 'arm' (or) PEC *HłuλV̄ 'sleeve, wing'	PST *lăk 'hand, arm' (or) PST *T-lŭ(H) ~ *T-lŭk 'hand, arm, wing'	HAND₁, HAND₂
Eyak χaʔł 'handle, mollusc shell'	PEC *ʕülƛ'wɨ 'handle'	PY *ʔuʎ- 'handle'	HANDLE
PEA *λu·nʔ 'mouse, squirrel'	PNC *λărV	PST [*T-laj] 'squirrel, rabbit'; Bur *tur- 'marmot'	RODENT
PEA *weł 'sleep'	PEC *nhewƛ'ŭ ~ *mhewƛ'ŭ	PST *miał 'sleep'	SLEEP
PEA *ƛe·ʔχ 'wet; to swim'	PEC *ƛHwemV	PST *li(a)m 'to soak'; Bur *tam 'bathe, swim, wash'	WET₁

215

Here we can already see hints of phonological regularity: in initial position Na-Dene *ƛ = Caucasian *ƛ (RODENT), Na-Dene *ƛ̃ = Caucasian *ƛ̃ (WET₁), and Na-Dene *ƛ̃' = Caucasian *ƛ̃' (BEAT, BOTTOM, GRASS), while in Na-Dene final position all lateral affricates tend to resolve into the voiceless lateral fricative *ɬ (see BONE, FORK, HANDLE, SLEEP; Eyak *xulʔƛ̃'* is possibly the result of recent metathesis). For HAND, see the table near the end of this Appendix

Nikolayev's other comparisons involving lateral affricates are, in my opinion, untenable for various reasons, including changes in Caucasian reconstruction since the early 1980s (when his paper was written). To supplement Nikolayev's comparisons, I (sometimes in collaboration with Blažek) have added the following etymologies involving Na-Dene and Caucasian (and/or Sino-Tibetan) lateral affricates:

Na-Dene	Caucasian	(other DC)	(general gloss)
Haida =ƛ̃'o=Ga (completeness of action)	PNC *=Vnƛ̃'V 'all'	PST *T-lă-ŋ 'all, everything'; PY *biʔl - 'all'; Bsq *bil 'to gather'	ALL
Eyak ƛ̃'əǯ ~ ƛ̃'iǯ 'buttocks'	PEC *ƛ̃'i 'below, down'	Bur –lji 'behind'	BELOW
Haida ƛ̃'íí 'to sew'; PA *-ƛ̃'u- 'to bind'	PEC *ƛ̃üɦV 'seam'	Bur *-ltur- 'unravel, undo a seam'	BIND
Haida ƛamat 'cross-pieces in canoe'	PEC *ƛ̃'VɦVmV 'shelf' (or) PEC *ƛ̃'əmʔV 'roof'	PST *T-lăŋH 'frame, grating' (or) PST *T-lam 'a kind of stick'	BOARD
Haida ƛúu 'canoe', ƛúu- 'by canoe'		PST *T-lij 'boat'	BOAT
Tlingit ƛ̃'ùq 'scabs, sores'	PEC *ƛ̃'wĕ[n]χV 'pus, snot'	PST *liŋ (~ *laiŋ) 'pus, abscess'; Bsq *lega- 'ulcer'	BODY FLUID₁
Navajo ƛ̃'iž 'gall, bile'	PEC *ƛ̃ămVč̣'V 'saliva, pus'	Bsq *lić 'saliva'	BODY FLUID₂
Haida ƛ̃'an 'saliva'	PNC *ɦămƛ̃'ă 'sweat'	Bsq *ɦeřdc 'drivel'	BODY FLUID₃
Haida ƛ̃'ánuu 'female breast'	PNC *Hl[a]ƛ̃'V̄ 'breast, back'	Bur *-ltáltar 'woman's breast', etc.	BREAST
Haida ƛuuʔúŋ 'to crawl'	PEC *ʔVƛ̃V(r) 'crawl, glide'	Bsq *leřa 'to slip, slide'	CRAWL
Haida ƛ̃'a-dáa 'to kill (several)'	PNC *=iwƛ̃'E 'to die, kill'	Old Chinese *ƛij 'corpse'; Bsq *hil 'die, dead, death'; Bur *-l- 'hit, kill', etc.	DIE

216

Na-Dene	Caucasian	(other DC)	(general gloss)
Tlingit λ'éχ'kw 'soil'; Haida λak 'land, place'		PST *T-l[ia]k 'iron'; Bur *tik 'earth, ground, rust'; Bsq *leku 'place'	EARTH₁
Navajo λ'áá 'rim, edge'	PEC *λ'ānpV 'lip'	PST *T-lĕp 'border, side'; Bsq *laba- 'edge, coast'	EDGE/LIP
PA *λ'əγəš(ʷ) 'eel, leech, snake'	PEC *λ'ećV ~ *ćeλ'V 'fish; lizard'		EEL
Haida -λ'aʔaa, -λ'aa 'arriving'	PEC *=VmλʹV 'to go, come'	PST *T-lā(H) 'to come'; Bur *-ltá- 'to follow'; Bsq *ür̃ten 'go out'	GO
Navajo λò 'to laugh'	PNC *=ŏλE 'to laugh'	PST *T=lĕw 'to play, joke'	LAUGH
Mattole λ'eheʔ 'left-handed'	PEC *ʔV̄nλV 'left (hand)'		LEFT
Navajo λ'èh 'crotch'	PEC *λ'wVnʔV 'groin, part of leg'	PST *lVŋ 'shin, ankle'; Bur *-ltén 'bone'	LEG
Haida λ'uu 'to sit' (pl.)	PNC *=äλEw 'to lie, put; lead'	PST *T-ləj 'to tarry'	LIE
Haida λ'akúl 'liver' (and/or) Tlingit λ'él 'milt'	PEC *Hläλ'V ~ *Hλ'älV 'liver'	Bur *tal 'stomach, belly'	LIVER
Haida λaas 'branch'	PEC *λ'VćV 'log, pole'	Bsq *las 'beam, rafter'	LOG
Haida λáál 'husband'	PNC *λĭwlE ~ *līwλE 'man, male'	PST *līk 'testicle, glans penis'; Bur *dul-as 'boy'	MAN
Sarsi -λ'ú·, -λ'ù· 'to be moldy'	PEC *λwĕɬʔĕ 'mold'	PST *tŏɬ (*T-rĭt) 'dust'; PY *juʔl 'sludge'; Bsq *er̃doil 'rust'	MOLD
Sarsi -λ'i·z '(be) swampy'	PEC *λwilc̣'wV 'dirt, bog, marsh'	Bsq *lisun 'moldy, musty, dirty'	MUD₁
Tlingit quλ'kʷ 'mud'		PST *T-lō(k) 'mud, marsh'; Bur *toq 'mud'	MUD₂
Navajo λ'ééʔ 'night'	PNC *ʔlēλă 'night'	PST *rjăk 'day/night'	NIGHT₁
Haida s-λo 'to put inside, arrange'	PEC *=iλV 'to put'	PST *T-luaH 'to do, make'	PUT
Tlingit xɪλa ~ xɪλa 'herring rake'	PEC *λVχwV ~ *λ'VχwV 'rake'	Bsq *la(H)ia 'two-pronged fork'	RAKE
Sarsi -λá- 'to run', etc.	PEC *=iλwVn (or) PEC *ʔīλ'V 'to run, leap'	PST *T-lăj(H) 'to run, gallop'	RUN

Na-Dene	Caucasian	(other DC)	(general gloss)
Haida λúu 'the same'; Sarsi -λu 'to seem'	PEC *=ăx̣wVn 'to resemble, similar'	PST *T-lōm 'accompany, assist'; Bur *ltú-r/l 'same, imitate', etc.	SAME
Navajo -ƛé, -ƛèèʔ 'stockings'	PEC *=ōmλ̣V 'to put on (trousers, shoes)'	Bur *-ltá- 'to put on (shoes, stockings)'	SHOE
Chipewyan -ƛ'í 'to lean'		PST *T-lăj 'slant, be awry'	SLANT
Tlingit ƛ'áxč' 'dead branches'	PEC *ƛ̣'ĥwāχV 'stick, chip'	PST *T-lāk 'stick, stake'; Bur *taγ 'branch, shoot'	STICK
Haida s-λáan 'intestines'	PEC *=īraλ̣V 'stomach, rennet, abomasum'	PST *T-lŏw 'belly, stomach'; Bsq *ur̄dail 'stomach'; Bur *-úl 'abdomen, bowels'	STOMACH
Navajo ƛ'ééɬ 'flint and steel'	PEC *ƛ'ăɬū 'stone'	Bur *tali 'slope, steep ascent'	STONE$_1$
PA *-ləŋ, -lən 'steep'		PST *T=lāiŋ 'straight'	STRAIGHT
Navajo ƛ'àh 'temples'	PEC *ƛ'arq'w ĕ 'forehead; cap'	PST *T-lĕkʷ (*ƛuak) 'back, nape'; Bsq *lokV 'temple'	TEMPLE
Haida ƛ'a- 'thin, flat object'	PNC *=iƛ'ĭlV 'thin'	PST *rial 'thin, watery'; Bsq *lirain 'svelte, lithe'; Bur *tharén- 'narrow, tight'	THIN$_1$
Haida (A) ƛaʔáa 'a long time'	PNC *ƛăjV 'time, day'	PST *ləH 'year, season'; Bur *jult '(right) time'; Bsq *or̄du 'hour, time'	TIME
Haida (A) ƛaɬ-q'án 'to tangle'	PEC *ƛwīri 'wheel'	PST *r[ua]ɬ 'round, roll, wheel'; Bur *-ltál- 'to turn, wind'	TURN
PND *λaNH 'to drink, flow, wash'	PEC *=Vƛ'Vn 'to wash, pour; weep'	PST *T-lāŋ 'to wash, clean'; Bur *-hált- 'to wash'	WASH
Navajo ƛ'éžìì 'horsefly'	Avar ƛ':ož 'wasp'	Bsq *los- / *leis- / *liSt- 'stinging insect'	WASP
Haida ƛ'ak-dáa 'to soak'		PST *T-lă(k) 'to boil, cook'; Bur *-ltaγá- 'cleanse, smear'	WET$_2$
Haida ƛ'ad- 'too wide'	PEC *ĥwVnƛ'V 'wide, spacious'	PST *T-lăj 'wide, expand' (or) *T-loŋ 'wide, spacious'; Bsq *or̄do- 'level, plain'	WIDE

Altogether more than 50 etymologies connect Na-Dene lateral affricates with lateral affricates in other Dene-Caucasian languages. Between Caucasian and Na-Dene, the proto-languages preserving all three original lateral affricates, the most common correspondence is *ƛ' = *ƛ', which holds for 19 comparisons (ALL, BEAT, BODY FLUID$_1$, BODY FLUID$_3$, BOTTOM, BREAST, DIE, EDGE/LIP, EEL, GO, GRASS, LEG, LIVER, STICK, STONE$_1$, TEMPLE, THIN$_1$, WASP, WIDE). The correspondence of *ƛ = *ƛ is found in five comparisons (CRAWL, RUN, TIME, TURN, WET$_1$), and the correspondence of *λ = *λ is found in three (PUT, RODENT, STOMACH). These are all "trivial correspondences," the equation of like with like.

There are some counter-examples in which the Na-Dene lateral affricate is not the same as the Caucasian, for example: ND *λ = Cauc. *ƛ (LAUGH, SAME); ND *λ = Cauc. *ƛ' (WASH); ND *ƛ' = Cauc. *λ (BIND); ND *ƛ = Cauc. *λ (MAN, SHOE); ND *ƛ' = Cauc. *ƛ (BODY FLUID$_2$, LEFT, LIE, MOLD, MUD$_1$, NIGHT); and ND *ƛ = Cauc. *ƛ' (BOARD, LOG). One will note, however, that the number of like-to-like correspondences (28 in the preceding paragraph) is roughly twice as many as the seemingly "irregular" matches listed in this paragraph (14).

In several other cases (BOAT, EARTH$_1$, MUD$_2$, RAKE, SLANT, STRAIGHT, WET$_2$) the evidence is ambiguous (*e.g.,* cognates are restricted to Sino-Tibetan, where all lateral affricates merged; or the Caucasian reconstruction is uncertain), and we cannot yet determine whether the correspondences are regular or not.

Possibly some of the "irregular" cases will eventually be explained by a number of secondary developments. For example, in the comparison of Na-Dene (Navajo) ƛ'ééʔ 'night' with Caucasian (PNC) *ʔlēƛ̃ã 'night' it is possible that the glottalization either was added in Na-Dene (by assimilation with the following glottal stop) or was lost in Caucasian (by dissimilation) — we may never know which was original. (See Starostin [2002a] for a clear exposition of the seeming "irregularities" that develop in the later stages of obviously related languages.) Nevertheless, we may for the moment conclude, as Nikolayev did, that the regular correspondences between Na-Dene and Caucasian are "like with like", that is: *ƛ' = *ƛ', *ƛ = *ƛ, and *λ = *λ. Again, some of the counter-examples may of course simply turn out to be false cognates.

Another phonological pattern may be in evidence. Where PDC had words containing two different laterals and a laryngeal, Na-Dene has simplified the words by eliminating one of the laterals. See:

Proto-Dene-Caucasian	Na-Dene	(general gloss)
PDC *HɫuλV̄ >	PND *laʔ > PA *laʔ 'hand'	HAND$_1$
PDC *Hlúƛ'V / *ƛ'úlHV >	PND *ƛ'/'[a]H > Haida s-ƛáa-, s-ƛa- 'hand'	HAND$_2$
PDC *ƛwVɫʔV >	PND *ƛ'[u]ʔV > Sarsi -ƛ'ú·, -ƛ'ù· 'to be moldy'	MOLD
PDC *ʔlēƛă >	PND *ƛ'eʔ > Navajo ƛ'ééʔ 'night', etc.	NIGHT$_1$

REFERENCES

Aulestia, Gorka, and Linda White, eds. 1992. *Basque-English English-Basque Dictionary.* Reno, Las Vegas, London: University of Nevada Press.
Azkue, R.M. de. 1905-1905. *Diccionario vasco-español-francés.* Bilbao.
Bashir, Elena. 2000. "A Thematic Survey of Burushaski Research." *History of Language.* 6.1: 1-14.
Benedict, Paul K. 1966. "Austro-Thai." *Behavior Science Notes* 1: 227-261.
--- 1975. *Austro-Thai: Language and Culture with a Glossary of Roots.* New Haven: HRAF Press.
--- 1990. *Japanese/Austro-Tai.* Ann Arbor: Karoma.
Bengtson, John D. 1989. "On the Fallacy of 'Diminishing Returns' in Long-Range Lexical Comparison." In Shevoroshkin (1989): 37-40.
--- 1992a. "A Case for the Austric Affiliation of Ainu." In Shevoroshkin (1992), p. 364. [One-page abstract derived from unpublished notes.]
--- 1992b. "Global Etymologies and Linguistic Prehistory." In Shevoroshkin (1992): 480-495.
--- 1994a. "Edward Sapir and the 'Sino-Dene' Hypothesis." *Anthropological Science* 102: 207-230.
--- 1994b. "On the Genetic Classification of Basque." *Mother Tongue* (Newsletter) 22: 31-36.
--- 1995a. "Is Basque Isolated? (ad Trask [1994-95])." *Dhumbadji!* 2.2: 33-44.
--- 1995b. "Basque: An orphan forever? A response to Trask." *Mother Tongue* 1: 84-103.
--- 1996a. "Correspondences of Basque and Caucasic Final Vowels: -i/-e, -u/-o." *Fontes Linguae Vasconum* 71: 7-15.
--- 1996b. "Nihali and Ainu." *Mother Tongue* (Journal) 2: 51-55.
--- 1997a. "Some Comments on Ilia Peiros" "Nihali and Austroasiatic"." *Mother Tongue* (Journal) 3: 47-50.
--- 1997b. "The Riddle of Sumerian: A Dene-Caucasic Language?" *Mother Tongue* 3: 63-74.
--- 1997c. "Ein Vergleich von Buruschaski und Nordkaukasisch." *Georgica* 20: 88-94.
--- 1997d. "Basque and the Other Dene-Caucasic Languages." In *The Twenty-Third LACUS Forum,* ed. by A.K. Melby, pp. 137-148. Chapel Hill, NC: LACUS.
--- 1997e. "Long Ranger Extraordinaire: Sergei A. Starostin." *Mother Tongue* 3: 99-102.
--- 1998a. Review of Patrie (1982). *Mother Tongue* (Journal) 4: 111-113.

--- 1998b. "Dene-Caucasian 'Navel': some proposed etymologies." *Dhumbadji!* 4.1: 86-90.
--- 1998c. "Caucasian and Sino-Tibetan: A Hypothesis of S.A. Starostin." *General Linguistics* 36.1/2: 33-49.
--- 1998d. "Some Yeniseian Isoglosses." *Mother Tongue* (Journal) 4: 27-32.
--- 1999a. "Wider Genetic Affiliations of the Chinese Language." *Journal of Chinese Linguistics* 27.1: 1-12.
--- 1999b. "'Eye, Ear, Tongue' in Basque and East Caucasian." In *From Neanderthal to Easter Island (Tribute to W.W. Schuhmacher)*, ed. by N.A. Kirk and P.J. Sidwell, pp. 3-10. Melbourne: Association for the History of Language.
--- 1999c. "A Comparison of Basque and (North) Caucasian Basic Vocabulary." *Mother Tongue* 5: 40-57.
--- 1999c. Review of Trask (1997). *Romance Philology* 52: 219-224.
--- 2000. Review of I. Čašule, *Basic Burushaski Etymologies: The Indo-European and Paleo- Balkanic Affinities of Burushaski.* In *History of Language* 6 (1): 22-26.
--- 2001a. "Roger Williams Wescott 1925-2000." *Mother Tongue* (Journal) 6: 3.
--- 2001b. Review of J.H. Greenberg, *Indo-European and Its Closest Relatives. Mother Tongue* (Journal) 6:131-135.
--- 2001c. Review of B. Heine & D. Nurse (Ed.), *African Languages: An Introduction. Mother Tongue* (Journal) 6: 137-143.
--- 2001d. Review of V. Blažek, *Numerals: Comparative-Etymological Analyses of Numeral Systems and Their Implications. Mother Tongue* (Journal) 6: 182-183.
--- 2001e. Review of H. Berger, *Die Burushaski-Sprache von Hunza und Nager. Mother Tongue* (Journal) 6: 184-187.
--- 2002a. "The Dene-Caucasian Noun Prefix *s-." In *The Linguist's Linguist: A Collection of Papers in Honour of Alexis Manaster Ramer*, ed. by F. Cavoto, vol. 1, pp. 53-57. Munich: LINCOM EUROPA.
--- 2002b. "Dene-Caucasian *X(w)owHV 'mouth ~ tooth." In *Languages and their Speakers in Ancient Eurasia*, ed. by V. Shevoroshkin & P. Sidwell, pp. 51-53. Canberra: Association for the History of Language.
--- 2003. "Notes on Basque Comparative Phonology." *Mother Tongue* 8: 21-39.
--- 2005. "Some features of Dene-Caucasian phonology (with special reference to Basque)." *Cahiers de l'Institut de Linguistique de Louvain (CILL)* 30.4: 33-54.

--- 2006. "A Multilateral Look at Greater Austric." *Mother Tongue* (Journal) 11: 219-258. Bengtson, John D., and Václav Blažek. 1995. [See Blažek & Bengtson (1995).]
--- 2000. "Lexical Parallels Between Ainu and Austric and Their Implications." *Archiv Orientální* 68: 237-258.
--- 2005. "Sergei Anatolyevich Starostin. (1953-2005)." *Journal of Indo-European Studies* 33.3/4: 307-314. Bengtson, John D., and Merritt Ruhlen. 1994. "Global Etymologies." In Ruhlen (1994), pp. 277-336.
Berger, Hermann. 1956. "Mittelmeerische Kulturpflanzennamen aus dem Burušaski." *Münchener Studien zur Sprachwissenschaft* 9: 4-33.
--- 1959. "Die Burušaski-Lehnwörter in der Zigeunersprache." *Indo-Iranian Journal* 3.1: 17-43.
--- 1974. *Das Yasin-Burushaski (Werchikwar).* (= Neuindische Studien herausgegeben von Hermann Berger, Lothar Lutze und Günther Sontheimer, Band 3.) Wiesbaden: Otto Harrassowitz.
--- 1998. *Die Burushaski-Sprache von Hunza und Nager.* (= Neuindische Studien herausgegeben von Hermann Berger, Heidrun Brückner und Lothar Lutze, Band 13.) Wiesbaden: Harrassowitz Verlag.
Blažek, Václav. 1989. "Materials for Global Etymologies." In Shevoroshkin (1989a): 37-40.
--- 1995. "Towards the Position of Basque: a reply to Trask's critique of the Dene-Caucasian hypothesis." *Mother Tongue* (Journal) 1: 104-110.
--- 1997. "Review of Ruhlen's *A Guide to the World's Languages* (1987)." *Mother Tongue* 3: 159-183.
Blažek, Václav, and John D. Bengtson. 1995. "Lexica Dene-Caucasica." *Central Asiatic Journal* 39.1: 11-50, 39.2: 161-164. {LDC}
Blechsteiner, Robert. 1930. "Die Werschikisch-Burischkische Sprache Impamir-Gebiet und Ihre Stellung zu den japhetitensprachen des kaukasus." *Weiner Beiträge Zu Kunde des Morgenlandes* 1: 289-331.
Bouda, Karl. 1954. "Burushaski Etymologien." *Orbis* 3.2: 228-230.
Catford, J.C. 1977. "Mountain of Tongues: The Languages of the Caucasus." *Annual Review of Anthropology* 6: 283-314.
Chirikba, Viacheslav A. 1996. *Common West Caucasian.* Leiden: Research School CNWS.
Diakonoff, I.M., and S.A. Starostin. 1986. *Hurro-Urartian As an Eastern Caucasian Language.* Munich: Kitzinger.
Diffloth, Gérard. 1990. "What Happened to Austric?" *Mon-Khmer Studies* 16-17: 1-9.
--- 1994. "The lexical evidence for Austric, so far." *Oceanic Linguistics* 33.2: 309-321.
Dolgopolsky, A(h)aron B. 1996. "Nihali and Nostratic." *Mother Tongue* (Journal) 2: 61-66.

van Driem, George. 1999. "Four Austric Theories." *Mother Tongue* (Journal) 5: 23-27.
--- 2001. *Languages of the Himalayas: An Ethnolinguistic Handbook of the Greater Himalayan Region.* 2 vols. Leiden: Brill.
Embleton, Sheila M. 1986. *Statistics in Historical Linguistics.* (Quantitative Linguistics vol. 30.) Bochum: Brockmeyer.
Enrico, John. 2004. "Toward Proto-Na-Dene." *Anthropological Linguistics* 46.3: 229-302.
Fleming, Harold C. 1987. "Toward a Definitive Classification of the World's Languages" (Review of Ruhlen 1987). *Diachronica* 4.1/2: 159-223.
--- 1996a. "Nihali Lexicon: Supplement I. Words Collected by Bhattacharya and Konow." *Mother Tongue* (Journal) 2: 41-45.
--- 1996b. "Looking to the West and North: Nihali and Kusunda Find Links." *Mother Tongue* (Journal) 2: 67-74.
--- 2001. "Joseph Harold Greenberg: A Tribute and an Appraisal." *Mother Tongue* (Journal) 2: 9-27.
--- 2006. *Ongota: A Decisive Language in African Prehistory*. Wiesbaden: Harrassowitz.
Gjerdman, Olof. 1926. "Word-parallels between Ainu and other languages." *Le Monde Oriental* 20: 29-84.
Goddard, P.E. 1920. "Has Tlingit a Genetic Relation to Athapaskan?" *InternationalJournal of American Linguistics* 1: 266-279.
Greenberg, Joseph H. 1978. "How Does a Language Acquire Gender Markers?" In *Universals of Human Language,* ed. by J.H. Greenberg. Stanford: Stanford University Press.
--- 1987a. *Language in the Americas.* Stanford, CA: Stanford University Press.
--- 1987b. "A Generalization of Glottochronology to *n* Languages." In Greenberg (1987a), pp. 341-344.
--- 1987c. "The Na-Dene Problem." In Greenberg (1987a), pp. 321-330.
Hayes, La Vaughn H. 1992. "On the Track of Austric, Part I: Introduction." *Mon-Khmer Studies* 21:143-77.
--- 1996. *Comments on entries in "Lexical Parallels between Ainu and Austric"*. Ms.
--- 1997. "On the Track of Austric, Part II: Consonant Mutation in Early Austroasiatic." *Mon-Khmer Studies* 27:13-41.
--- 1999. "On the Track of Austric, Part III: Basic Vocabulary Correspondence." *Mon-Khmer Studies* 29:1-34.
--- 2000. The Austric Denti-alveolar Sibilants. *Mother Tongue* (Journal) 5: 3-14.

--- 2001. On the Origin of Affricates in Austric. *Mother Tongue* (Journal) 6: 95-117.
--- nd. "Austric Glossary."
[http://home.att.net/~lvhayes/Langling/langpg3.htm]
Hualde, José Ignacio. 1991. *Basque Phonology.* London/New York: Routledge.
Itabashi, Yoshizo. 1998. "Some Morphological Parallels between Ainu and Austronesian." Mother Tongue (Journal) 4: 40-95.
Jacobsen, William H., Jr. 1995. "Comment on R.L. Trask's 'Basque and Dene-Caucasian: A Critique from the Basque Side.'" *Mother Tongue* (Journal) 1: 120-142.
Kosaka, Ryuichi. 2002. "On the affiliation of Miao-Yao and Kadai: Can we posit the Miao-Dai family." *Mon-Khmer Studies* 32: 71-100.
Kuiper, F.B.J. 1948. "Munda and Indonesian." In *Orientalia Neerlandica. A Volume of Oriental Studies,* pp. 372-401. Leiden: Sijthoff's.
--- 1962. "Nahali: A Comparative Study." In *Mededelingen der Koninklijke Nederlandse Akademie van Wetenschappen, Afd. Letterkunde, (Nieuwe Reeks)* 25.5: 239-352.
--- 1966. "The Sources of the Nahali Vocabulary." In Zide (1966): 57-81.
Larrasquet, J. 1939. *Le Basque de la Basse-Soule orientale.* Paris.
Levine, Robert D. 1979. "Haida and Na-Dene: A New Look at the Evidence." *International Journal of American Linguistics* 45: 157-170.
Matisoff, James A. 1990. "On megalocomparison." *Language* 66.1: 106-120.
Meyer-Lübke, Wilhelm. 1935. *Romanisches etymologisches Wörterbuch.* 3rd. Ed. Heidelberg: Carl Winter.
Michelena, Luis. 1961. *Fonética Histórica Vasca.* San Sebastián: Diputación de Guipúzcoa.
Moutard, Nicole. 1975. "Étude phonologique sur les dialects basques, I." *Fontes Linguae Vasconum* 19: 5-42.
Mundlay, Asha. 1996a. "Who are the Nihals? What Do They Speak." *Mother Tongue* (Journal) 2: 5-9.
--- 1996b. "Cognates in the Nihali Lexicon." *Mother Tongue* (Journal) 2: 11-16.
--- 1996c. "Nihali Lexicon." *Mother Tongue* (Journal) 2: 17-40.
Nikolayev, Sergei L., and Sergei A. Starostin. 1994. *A North Caucasian Etymological Dictionary.* Moscow: Asterisk Press. {NCED}
Norquest, Peter. 1998. "The Contact and Genetic Relationships of Ainu." *Mother Tongue* (Journal) 4: 96-110.

Patrie, James. 1982. *The Genetic Relationship of the Ainu Language.* Honolulu: The University Press of Hawaii.

Peiros, Ilia. 1992. "The Austric Macrofamily: some considerations." In Shevoroshkin (1992), pp. 354-363.

--- 1997. "Macro Families: Can a Mistake Be Detected?" In *Indo-European, Nostratic, and Beyond: Festschrift for Vitalij V. Shevoroshkin,* ed. by Irén Hegedűs, et al., pp. 265-292. Washington, D.C.: Institute for the Study of Man. (JIES Monograph No. 22.)

Peiros, Ilia, and Sergei A. Starostin. 1996. *A Comparative Vocabulary of Five Sino-Tibetan Languages.* 6 fascicles. Melbourne: University of Melbourne, Departmentof Linguistics. {ST}

Pinnow, H-J. 1966. *Grundzüge einer historischen Lautlehre des Tlingit.* Wiesbaden: Harrassowitz.

--- 1985. *Das Haida als Na-Dene Sprache.* (Abhandlungen der völkerkundlichen Arbeitsgemeinschaft, Hefte 43-46.) Nortorf, Germany: Völkerkundliche Arbeitsgemeinschaft.

--- 2006a. *Die Na-Dene-Sprachen im Lichte der Greenberg-Klassifikation. / The Na-Déné Languages in Light of Greenberg's Classification.* Zweite erweiterte Auflage / Second revised edition. Bredstedt: Druckerei Lempfert.

--- 2006b. *Sprachhistorische Untersuchung zur Stellung des Haida als Na-Dene-Sprache.* (Unveränderte Neuausgabe aus INDIANA 10, Gedenkschrift Gerdt Kutscher. Teil 2. Berlin 1985. Mit einem Anhang = Die Na-Dene-Sprachen imVerhältnis zum Tibeto-Chinesischen.) Bredstedt: Druckerei Lempfert.

Reid, Lawrence A. 1994. "Morphological evidence for Austric." *Oceanic Linguistics* 33.2: 323-344.

Ruhlen, Merritt. 1987. *A Guide to the World's Languages: Volume 1: Classification.* Stanford University Press.

--- 1994a. *On the Origin of Languages: Studies in Linguistic Taxonomy.* Stanford University Press.

--- 1994b. *The Origin of Language: Tracing the Evolution of the Mother Tongue.* New York: John Wiley & Sons, Inc.

--- 1995. "Comments on R.L. Trask's Critique: Is Basque an Isolate?" *Mother Tongue* (Journal) 1: 149-156.

--- 1998. "The Origin of the Na-Dene." *Proceedings of the National Academy of Sciences* 95: 13994-13996.

--- 2005. "Taxonomy, Typology and Historical Linguistics." In *Language Acquisition, Change and Emergence: Essays in Evolutionary Linguistics,* ed. by J.W. Minett & W. S-Y. Wang, pp. 341-368. City University of Hong Kong Press.

Sapir, Edward. 1915. "The Na-Dene Languages: A Preliminary Report." *American Anthropologist* 17: 188-194.
Schmidt, W. 1906. *Die Mon-Khmer-Völker, ein Bindeglied zwischen Völkern Zentralasiens und Austronesiens.* Braunschweig.
Schuhmacher, W.W. 1994. "Lexical Parallels between Ainu and Austroasiatic." *Archív orientální* 62: 415-16.
Shafer, Robert. 1940. "Nahālī. A linguistic study in paleoethnography." *Harvard Journal of Asiatic Studies* 5: 346-71.
Shevoroshkin, Vitaly. 1989a. (Ed.) *Reconstructing Languages and Cultures.* (Bochum Publications in Evolutionary Cultural Semiotics, vol. 20.) Bochum: Brockmeyer.
--- 1989b. (Ed.) *Explorations in Language Macrofamilies.* (Bochum Publications in Evolutionary Cultural Semiotics, vol. 23.) Bochum: Brockmeyer.
--- 1989c. "Methods in Interphyletic Comparisons." Ural-Altaische Jahrbücher 61: 1-26.
--- 1991. (Ed.) *Dene-Sino-Caucasian Languages.* (Bochum Publications in Evolutionary Cultural Semiotics, vol. 32.)Bochum: Brockmeyer.
--- 1992. (Ed.) *Nostratic, Dene-Caucasian, Austric and Amerind.* (Bochum Publications in Evolutionary Cultural Semiotics, vol. 33.) Bochum: Brockmayer.
--- 1995. "On Basque and Other Sino-Caucasian (Dene-Caucasian) Languages." *Mother Tongue* (Journal) 1: 157-158.
Shorto, Harry L. 1976. "In Defense of Austric." *Computational Analyses of Asian and African Languages* 6:95-104.
Sidwell, Paul. 1998. "The External Relations of Ainu: Problems and Prospects." *Mother Tongue* (Journal) 4: 33-39.
Schweitzer, M. H., J.L. Wittmeyer, J.R. Horner, J.K. Toporski. 2005. "Soft-Tissue Vessels and Cellular Preservation in *Tyrannosaurus rex*." *Science* 307: 1952-1955.
Starostin, Sergei A. 1982. Праенисейская рсконструкция и внешние связи енисейских языков. [Proto-Yeniseian reconstruction and external relations of the Yeniseian languages.] In *Кетский Сборник (Studia Ketica),* pp. 144-237. Leningrad: Nauka.
--- 1984. Гипотеза о генетических связях синотибетских языков с енисейскими и севернокавказскими языками. In *Лингвистическая реконструкция и древнейшая история Востока,* часть 4, pp. 19-38. Moscow: Akademija Nauk, Institut Vostokovedenija. [see Starostin 1991]
--- 1989. "Nostratic and Sino-Caucasian." In Shevoroshkin (1989b): 42-66.

--- 1991. "On the Hypothesis of a Genetic Connection Between the Sino-Tibetan Languages and the Yeniseian and North Caucasian Languages." In Shevoroshkin 1991: 12-41. [Translation of Starostin 1984]
--- 1995. Сравнительный словарь енисейских языков. [Comparative dictionary of the Yeniseian languages.] In *Кетский Сборник (Studia Ketica)*, ed. by S.A. Starostin, pp. 176-315. Moscow: Shkola Jazyki Russkoj Kul'tury. {SSEJ}
--- 1996. "Comments on the Basque-Dene-Caucasian Comparisons." *Mother Tongue* 2: 101-109.
--- 2000. "Genesis of the Long Vowels in Sino-Tibetan." In *Проблемы изучения дальнего родства языков на рубеже третьего тысячелетия. Доклады и тезисы международной конференции.* [Problems in the study of distant relations of languages, on the verge of the Third Millennium. Abstracts and documents from the International Conference.] pp. 224-231. Moscow: Russian State University of the Humanities.
--- 2002a. "A response to Alexander Vovin's criticism of the Sino-Caucasian theory." *Journal of Chinese Linguistics* 30.1: 142-153.
--- 2002b. "North Caucasian Morphology." (ms.)
--- 2005a. "Sino-Caucasian Phonology." (ms.)
    [http://starling.rinet.ru/Texts/scc.pdf]
--- 2005b. "Sino-Caucasian Glossary." (ms.)
    [http://starling.rinet.ru/Texts/glossary.pdf]
Starostin, Sergei A., and Merritt Ruhlen. 1994. "Proto-Yeniseian Reconstructions, with Extra-Yeniseian Comparisons." In Ruhlen (1994a), pp. 70-92. Stanford: Stanford University Press. [Partial translation of Starostin 1982, with additional comparisons by Ruhlen.]
Trask, R.L. 1994-95. "Basque: The Search for Relatives (Part 1)." *Dhumbadji!* 2.1: 3-54.
--- 1995. "Basque and Dene-Caucasian: A Critique from the Basque Side." *Mother Tongue* 1: 3-82.
--- 1997. *The History of Basque.* London: Routledge.
--- 1999. "Why should a language have any relatives?" In *Nostratic: Examining a Linguistic Macrofamily,* ed. by C. Renfrew & D. Nettle, pp. 157-176. Cambridge, UK: McDonald Institute for Archaeological Research.
Uhlenbeck, C.C. 1927. "Die mit *b-* anlautenden Körperteilnamen des Baskischen." In *Festschrift Meinhof,* pp. 351-357. Hamburg.
Vovin, Alexander V. 1992. "The Origins of the Ainu Language." In *Pan-Asiatic Linguistics: Proceedings of the Third International Symposium on Language and Linguistics,* vol. 2, 673-685.

--- 1993. *A Reconstruction of Proto-Ainu.* Leiden: E.J.Brill.
--- 1997. "The Comparative Method and Ventures Beyond Sino-Tibetan." *Journal of Chinese Linguistics* 25.2: 308-336.
--- 2002. "Building a 'Bum-pa for Sino-Caucasian." *Journal of Chinese Linguistics* 30.1: 154-171.
Wescott, Roger W. 1995. "A Comment on 'Basque and Dene-Caucasian: A Critique from the Basque Side' by R.L. Trask." *Mother Tongue* (Journal) 1: 163-164.
Yeoman, Barry. 2006. "Schweitzer's Dangerous Discovery." *Discover* April 2006: 37-41, 77.
Zide, Norman H. (Ed.) 1966. *Studies in Comparative Austroasiatic Linguistics.* The Hague: Mouton.
--- 1996. "On Nihali." *Mother Tongue* (Journal) 2: 93-100.

www.ingramcontent.com/pod-product-compliance
Lightning Source LLC
Chambersburg PA
CBHW050141170426
43197CB00011B/1925